New Directions in Sociological Theory

New Directions in Sociological Theory

Disputes, Discourses and Orientations

Ajit Kumar Pandey
Smita Verma

RAWAT PUBLICATIONS
Jaipur • New Delhi • Bangalore • Hyderabad • Guwahati

ISBN 81-316-0367-9

Published by
Prem Rawat for **Rawat Publications**
Satyam Apts, Sector 3, Jawahar Nagar, Jaipur 302 004 (India)
Phone: 0141 265 1748/7006 Fax: 0141 265 1748
E-mail: info@rawatbooks.com
Website: www.rawatbooks.com

New Delhi Office
4858/24, Ansari Road, Daryaganj, New Delhi 110 002
Phone: 011 2326 3290

Also at *Bangalore, Hyderabad* and *Guwahati*

Typeset by Rawat Computers, Jaipur
Printed at Chaman Enterprises, New Delhi

For

My Brother Ashok

Contents

	Foreword	ix
	Preface and Acknowledgment	xiii
1	Methodology in Social Sciences: Mapping the Course of Development	1
2	Sociology of Knowledge: A Perspective for Evaluating Positivistic Method	36
3	Appraising Positivism: Phenomenology and Ethnomethodology	94
4	Positioning the Positivistic Dispute in Frankfurt Tradition	130
5	Structural Approach and the Ideology of Positivism	158
6	Postmodernism: New Conversions in Theory and Research Methodology	177
7	Towards a New Direction: Methodology and Research	246
	Index	271

Foreword

I am happy to write Foreword for the book jointly authored by Prof. Ajit Kumar Pandey and Dr. Smita Verma on Sociological Theory. A given sociological theory has two dimensions: one, it has power to provide a new paradigm to the world of knowledge by way of ideas, concepts and frameworks; and second, it emanates from a given crisis situation, namely, war, crimes, catastrophes, etc. The founding fathers of sociology, for example, Karl Marx, Max Weber and Emile Durkheim, formulated their theories based on specific conditions that prevailed in England, Germany and France, respectively. These three giant masters provided explanations, and also implicitly solutions, of the crises caused by faulty industrialization, incongruence between society and politics, and individualism and society.

The book by Prof. Pandey and Dr. Verma brings out the debates in contemporary sociological theory. They provide a comprehensive view of the strands relating to sociology of knowledge, Frankfurt School, structuralism, ethnomethodology, postmodernism and culturology. The book also brings out limitations of the Frankfurt School and critical theory. It is an excellent critique of positivism. At the same time, it focuses on the construction of theory and its intent. The authors, after having a logical appraisal of different schools of thought, have arrived at the conclusion that sociology of knowledge and phenomenology can provide relevant pathways for useful research.

According to the authors, sociological theory must be seen as a series of perspectives that reflects both the society and the individual in terms of their experiential inputs. In their analyses, the authors have systematically constructed the history of sociological thought from the 19th century onwards, though not in fact, sequentially, but in terms of what they call "disputes, discourses and orientations", which have remained at times isolated, and at times have mingled with each other. One significant point made by the authors refers to a lack of ethos of Science in theoretical formulations.

Emphasis on mechanics and systematics of empiricism has resulted into a distorted and pseudo-scientific character of sociological theory. The authors are not happy with the so-called mainstream empirical sociology. They have shown their concern for the age-old questions like: Knowledge for whom? Knowledge for what? And whose knowledge?

Thus, Prof. Pandey and Dr. Verma deal with the limitations of various approaches in sociological theorization as they do not touch upon many aspects of sociology, such as change, conflict and distribution of power. Sociological theorization has become subservient to the mechanics of its formulation, than with the substantive issues. In their analysis, the authors have reflected on the limitations, not only of theory building, but also on the very meaning and understanding of empirical research. The bearing of one upon the other is also missing as observed by Prof. Pandey and Dr. Verma. No methodology can be independent of the theme/topic of research, and a new theory cannot be simply imaginative/speculative. A theory must necessarily prove itself as a guide for understanding of social reality. It needs to stress upon corroboration/revision/modification/rejection of the existing theoretical formulations. A given new theory must prove itself different from the existing one as an alternative, as an addition or as a completely new formulation.

There is a tendency among the social scientists to take clues from a given specific social condition, and to generalize about the entire array of social diversities and complexes. On the other hand, there is also a tendency to apply general grand philosophical formulations to given concrete situations. In both cases, there is the risk of reification. Prof. Pandey and Dr. Verma are making a plea in the book for relevant theorization, which would be relevant and useful as a new paradigm and a guide for exploring new facts and new facets of social life. This cannot be simply a philosophical exercise. Social conditioning of sociological theory cannot be underrated. The founding fathers of sociology had grounded their theoretical formulations in given specific social conditions. This needs to be done continuously drawing from these giants.

The book by Prof. Pandey and Dr. Verma is a significant departure from conventional works on sociological theory. It is an admirable effort, and I am sure, both students and teachers will find this book as a useful guide in the advancement of ideas and criticism.

K.L. Sharma
Vice Chancellor
Jaipur National University, Jaipur

Preface and Acknowledgements

The emphasis of the book is upon the methodology used in contemporary research and how this reflects movements throughout the sociological spectrum. Sociologists eminent in their own fields look at current sociological paradigms in the light of concern for the increasing world shortage of resources. How can sociology adapt its theories to cope with this new situation? Social scientists debate the approach which develops from the positivist tradition with its emphasis on causality. The five perspectives, discussed in different chapters of the book, obviously contain several points of disagreement with positivism. A consideration of some of the criticisms and the logical consequences involved in adopting these approaches would seem to be in order.

A logical consequence of adopting the sociology of knowledge perspective is relativism in the basic criteria that constitute the elements of a meta-theory for science. Thus, criteria for truth, verifiability, validity and so on will vary according to the paradigm to which the community subscribes. Under these conditions, communication between scientists from different paradigms is difficult and it becomes meaningless to talk of empirically testing to find which paradigm has the better theory and method.

Popper, of course, has come out strongly against what he has dubbed 'The Myth of Framework'—Kuhn's insistence that scientists from different paradigms have considerable difficulty in communicating. For Popper, such suggestions are a threat to the scientific enterprise in that they can set a dangerous self-fulfilling prophesy in motion.

Ethnomethodologists have been drawn to some aspects of Kuhn's approach in their criticism of positivist sociology. They, like Kuhn, believe that what positivists see is dicted by the particular theoretical approach they take to the data. In this sense, positivists are prone to distort the phenomena with the presuppositions they bring to the research activity. The ethnomethodologists seem to be suggesting that it is possible to describe social behaviour in pre-theoretic 'observation' language (this is a departure from Kuhn, of course). Their long range research procedure appears to entail the accumulation of accurate description in simple 'observation', language, of everyday activities. Theories will then be built up from this empirical base by carefully developing unambiguous correspondence rules between the theoretical and observational languages. But, the ethnomethodologists come up against difficulties when they attempt to combine sociology of knowledge with their conception of the way that science is done.

In assuming that there is a world accessible empirically to observational categories, and that it is capable of being thus described accurately, the ethnomethodologists remain with in the empiricist problematic. In emphasizing the crucial role played in the scientific process by the background experiences and knowledge of individual scientist, they would seem to be insisting that the current practice of positivist sociology constitutes a rampant that goes far beyond that of Kuhn (whether or not the ethnomethodologist can surmount this problem remains an intriguing question).

Such an approach to the 'social' raises the ire of sociologists of Marxist learnings, since it remains as does positivist method at the superficial level of the '*IS*'. Not only that, but what is worse, from a Marxist viewpoint—it de-emphasizes objective structural conditions, concentrating as it does on the way that society is constructed out of what its members do.

The Frankfurt School is emphatically impatient with the fundamental irrelevance of much of positivist sociology. Its members have a Marxist vision of a better society and define the task of the social sciences as that of working towards the production of this state. In its recent form, their viewpoint can be seen as a return to an emancipatory self-reflective Marxism, which reaches back to revive phenomenological threads perceived as present in the 'Marx of the 1844 Manuscripts'.

This delving back into the supposedly more philosophical and humanistic early Marx has led to charges of 'political and practical impotence' being levelled at the Frankfurt School.

Therborn's (1970) critique is one of the more sophisticated along these lines. In Therborn's view, the return to Marx's 'Hegel era', constituting as it does a return to 'armchair philosophy', effectively ensures that criticism remains at the level of theory. In this view, such a Marxism can have no effect on the objective conditions that prevails in society.

In counteracting such criticism, there are scholars who demonstrate that the Frankfurt School's return to the more philosophical aspects of Marx was aimed specifically at developing a self-reflectiveness, especially among social scientists, which could overcome false consciousness and lead the way out of the closed universe of reified relationships. This was seen as a preliminary first step in the restructuring of society. The Frankfurt theorists are, of course, seemingly open to the standard positivist charge that they are indulging in ideology and polemics and not in science. Whether or not they are open to these charges must remain a rhetorical question, begging as it does the basic definitional differences on the notion of what is to constitute theory.

Althusserian 'Marxist structuralism' is a relative newcomer to the field (at least in sociology). There are strong voices against the thesis of an epistemological break in Marx. Others have suggested that Althusser has read too much into *Capital* that in fact it is an unjustified extension of the net to claim that a meta-theory for science underlines this work.

Althusserianism is under fire on a number of fronts. Probably, the most devastating criticism yet to hand is that of Glucksmann. The main thrust of Glucksmann's attack is that Althusser has overgeneralized. He argues too, that Balibar and Althusser display in fact, a conceptual empiricism—by raising to the power of universal, each concept found in *Capital*.

Althusser is also vulnerable at precisely the point at which he seeks to escape empiricism. That is, he separates the process of thought ('knowledge effect') from the order of reality 'society effect' specifically to avoid either the empirical practice of reducing all thought to essence of the real or the Hegelian reduction of the real to thought. But, he is still left with the problem of indicating the interface between the conceptual and non-conceptual or 'the society effect' could never be known as a 'knowledge effect'.

We recall that Althusser argues that theory concerns the real object, yet it appears that he makes no allowance for mediation between concepts and the real object. In an effort to get out of this dilemma, Althusser seems to resort to kind of Kantian transcendental epistemology.

Since late 1980s with the demise of Marxist thought, social theory looked to be in decline. For, while the collapse of the Marxist orthodoxy loosened the traditional binding of the 'social' with the theory of production or class, few alternative conceptions of 'social' (either new or re-invented from the writings of Durkheim, Weber or Simmel) immediately came to the fore. This, in part, was due to the emergence of new postmodern approaches that privileged aesthetic, language and singularity over the analysis of social institution and social structures, and in their more extreme and polemical form declared the social too be dead, to quote Baudrillard. At this point, social theory appeared to have little future. But, new prospects opened, in turn, with the construction of postmodern theories of sociality, new approaches to reflexive modernization, risk society and globalization and exciting developments in political, cultural, media, feminist, and literary theory, as well as in the discipline of history. Today, these approaches and theories are beginning to impact upon the form and content of mainstream sociology which until now has tended to confront itself with a rather traditional, theoretical, conceptual and methodological vocabulary.

In the final chapter, we explored some of the new directions that new theory might take, and with this to call into question the changing basis of the 'social' today. The chapter presents a range of different theoretical approaches to the study of the contemporary world, and with this map out possible directions in which social theory and methodology might be developed. They are designed to orient critical thought to the study of major transformations that are taking place today, including the globalization or transnationalization of certain social and political relations, the heightened mediation of social life through new communication technologies, the increased power or 'agency' of technologies or objects and the emergence of increasingly fluid and transient forms of sociality. In this chapter, we have also focused on the intimate relation that has existed or perhaps still exists, between western modernity and the quest for power. In particular, we have mapped out a series of historical and political connection between republicanism and colonization. These connections in many respects underpin modern notions of citizenship rights, freedom notion and even the social, yet their social, political and philosophical dimensions have yet to be fully explored. For many writers, however, the question of colonization remains pivotal, not least, because republicanism is again a central question of the political debate and because aspects of republicanism have returned to haunt us. Beyond this attention is drawn to the continued existence of 'postcolonial societies' freed of their colonial status but not freed of their colonial structure, or which remain tied to a colonial model of the political in so far as freedom is conceived through an idealistic or romantic view of the nation-state. These colonies exist alongside or within new grey zone of globalization—zones which have all too easily fallen away from western consciousness and which today are scattered by increased poverty, corruption and violence. This list of transformation is certainly not exhaustive and there are other important developments not covered in this chapter. But, these discourses in Chapter 4 in no way seek to bring theoretical revolution or closure. Rather, their aim is to prompt further questioning and debate. For example, what new types of power are emerging in the course of contemporary social and political transformation? How theory and method might encounter those 'grey zones' of globalization that so rarely enter the sociological gaze? What is the future of the human subject and is it possible to conceive of a post-human conception of the 'social'? How might we think of gender against this backdrop of social-technical change? And, given the pace of change in contemporary world, what is the future of the theory and method, which have always been a patient and slow affair? Should they technologize themselves in order to keep pace?

Throughout the book, we have tried to answer such questions. Moreover, we have also concentrated on the crucial epistemological problem of the relation between sociological theory and method and the object to which the theory addresses itself. We have noted that the way a community of scholars attempts to resolve this problem has far-reaching consequences for the way it 'does' science in fact, for its definition of what is and what is not to be regarded as science or for that matter sociology. Kuhn has suggested that this situation can be described as one of incommensurable paradigms, which usually leads to the shifting of effective communication. Popper argues that in the contrary nothing is more fruitful than discussions with fellow scientists who view the world from an entirely different perspective.

This preface is not meant to summarize the arguments of the book. We only wish to say that though the chapters contained in the book were written in diverse contexts but they are bound a common thread of problems and ideas. They play their part in a single coherent, though as yet in complete endeavour.

The idea for writing this book emanated from the discussion with my teacher, Professor K.L. Sharma in the summer of 2004. I would like to thank Professor Sharma for welcoming my nascent ideas with much fervour and for supporting the writing through to its final stages. Developing this book has been an experience based on friendship and hardwork. Most of the chapters that form the essence of this book are co-authored by my colleague Dr Smita Verma. My interaction with her since 2005 led to many fruitful and vibrant deliberations on the project and it was then that I offered her to join me in this endeavour. I am really thankful to her for accepting my invitation.

Many others also encouraged and influenced me along the way. In particular, I would like to thank Shri Thakur Shashi Bhushan Verma and Smt Kanak Lata Verma to whom I hold in high esteem, for many stimulating conversations that inspired me to complete this task. I also owe a debt of gratitude to my wife Dr Neelam Pandey, and children Priyanka and Nishant, who patiently lived through every twist and turn of this project, and continue to be a source and inspiration and support. Last but not the least, I would like to thank Ms. Neha for helping me with the formatting and for reminding me time and again to complete the book. I specially thank my friends and students from BHU, Varanasi, JNU, New Delhi, and Lucknow University for giving me the support, suggestion and love, needed to do this work well.

Ajit Kumar Pandey

1

Methodology in Social Sciences

Mapping the Course of Development

The Positivist Tradition

The origins of sociology as a separate discipline are customarily traced back to the writings of Comte (1853) which are informed by a definite view of the logic of scientific method and the character of scientific knowledge. The hierarchy of the sciences expresses both an historical and a logical order of relationships between various fields of scientific endeavour. In the historical aspect, human knowledge in general, and the specific sciences in particular, pass through the successive phases of theological, metaphysical and positive thought. These processes of development, according to Comte, are primarily governed by a simple principle: those disciplines relating to phenomena furthest from man's own involvement and control develop first, and the history of science as a whole is one of a progressive movement inwards towards the study of man himself. The mechanism of scientific development provides the key to the logical relations between the sciences. The earliest sciences to come into being are those which lie below it, although its own concepts and generalizations are irreducible (Giddens, 1974). Sociology, which concerns itself with human social conduct, presupposes the laws of Biology, which apply to all organisms, while the latter in turn presumes the laws of Chemistry, etc.

The neatness of Comte's theoretical scheme believes the complexity of the problems which it conceals (Giddens, 1974). Comte's work both shares in and best exemplifies the views of the nature of science that dominated 19th century thought—which not only took scientific knowledge to be the paradigm of all valid knowledge but also saw in science the solution to the major practical problems facing mankind. It was fashionable at one time, Giddens says, to suppose that there were two Comtes: the another of the 'Positive Philosophy', the sober analyst of scientific history and method and the creator of the bizarre utopia of the 'Positive Polity'. But such an interpretation was the child of an age which had forsaken the 19th century vision of the transformative powers of scientific knowledge, and had tempered an acknowledgement of the achievements of natural science with a scepticism about whether these bore immediate consequences for social progress (Giddens, 1974: 2).

After Comte, very few philosophers or social thinkers willingly called themselves 'positivists', and there are evident differences between his views and those of others to whom the label has since been applied. The term has become one of opprobrium and has been used so broadly and vaguely as a weapon of critical attack both in philosophy and sociology, that it has lost any claim to an accepted and standard meaning. Moreover, philosophers and sociologists today have rather different points of reference in mind when they use the term. For many of the philosophers, it has become identified, not primarily with Comte at all, but with the 'logical positivism' of the 1930s although it is certainly not consistently used in the fairly restricted sense which it had when applied to certain of the conceptions originally developed by the Vienna Circle.

Since there is no longer much consistency in the general employment of the word, it would seem appropriate to attempt to impose some order upon the flux of differing usages. Positivism as a philosophy implies simply two main elements:

(i) *The rule of 'phenomenalism'* which asserts the uniqueness of experience as the basis of knowledge. Only that qualifies as 'knowledge', can in some sense, more or less directly, be related to a 'reality' immediately apprehended by the perceiver. This is often regarded as separable from the postulate of *'nominalism'*—that is to say, the notion that an abstract concept or generalization, such as may be involved in science, gives no extra, independent knowledge in the sense that, via its abstractions, it opens access to empirically inaccessible domains of reality (Kolakowski, 1972: 15–16; Giddens, 1974: 2). But actually these are merely different aspects of the fundamental supposition of the experiential foundation of all knowledge in sensorily apprehended reality.

(ii) Secondly, as necessarily following from the first proposition, the idea that judgements of value have no empirical content of a sort which renders them accessible to any tests of their validity in the light of experience. There is no kind of observation of the sensory environment which can have a direct bearing upon the content of value judgements or normative assertions (Giddens, 1974: 3).

Defined in this way, positivism certainly does not begin with Comte, but has a long history in Western philosophy. The implications which have been placed upon the views indicated above, the mode in which they have been expressed and the inferences which have been drawn from them, have been many and varied. Some of the problems raised by various competing and overlapping strands of positivistic thought in philosophy, however, are not as such relevant to the issues posed in sociological analysis. If 'positivism' has meant somewhat different things to philosophers and sociologists, this is partly because the introduction of positivistic assumptions into sociology creates a series of quite specific difficulties which cannot be resolved the level of generalized philosophical inquiry. Giddens statement in this regard deserves quote:

> "Positivism in philosophy in some sense revolves around the contention, or the implicit assumptions, that the notion and statements of science constitute a framework by references to which the nature of any form of knowledge may be determined. Positivism in sociology may be broadly represented as depending upon the assertion that the concepts and methods employed in natural sciences can be applied to form a 'science of man' or 'a natural science of society'. Since this, of course, relies upon some sort of stated or unstated views of the character of natural science it is obviously in the epistemological assumption of philosophical positivism". (Giddens, 1974: 3)

The 'positivistic attitude' in sociology may be said to comprise the following connected suppositions:

1. That the methodological procedures of natural science may be directly adapted to sociology. According to this standpoint, the phenomena of human subjectivity of volition and will do not offer any particular barriers to the treatment of social conduct as an 'object' on a par with objects in the natural world. Positivism here implies a particular stance concerning the sociologist as an observer of social reality.
2. That the outcome or end-result of sociological investigations can be formulated in parallel to those of natural science: that is to say, that the goal of sociological analysis can, and must be, to formulate 'laws' or 'law-like' generalizations of the same kind as those which have been established in relation to natural reality. Positivism here involves a definite view of the sociologist as analyst or interpreter of his subject matter.
3. That sociology has a technical character, providing knowledge, which is purely 'instrumental' in form; in other words, the findings of sociological research do not carry any logically given implications for practical policy or for the pursuit of values. Sociology, like natural science, is neutral in respect of values. From this aspect, positivism presumes a specific standpoint upon the sociologist as practically involved in the social order (Giddens, 1974: 3–4).
4. An empiricist epistemology, in which knowledge of an object consists in apprehending its essence by a process of abstraction (theorizing) from the concrete object, is appropriate for scientific sociology. Giddens adds that acceptance of any one of first three suppositions does not necessarily entail adoption of the other two.

The discipline of sociology through the work of Durkheim (1958), Booth (1892) and the Chicago School (Burgess and Bogue, 1964) in America developed in its own arena of knowledge—the arena of social facts, of social explanations that were required owing to the inadequacies of alternative based on psychology, economics, etc. Booth and other ecologists made an empirical study of the distribution of characteristics in the city, which showed them to have particular concentrations requiring a social, rather than a geographical, explanation.

The tradition that has emerged by the 20th century is one wedded to both the positivist idea of sociology as the scientific study of society and the empirical tradition of the collection and analysis of facts. This tradition has led a most profound influence upon the methods employed by researchers and also upon the type of theory that has developed.

The first element of the tradition as it finds expression in sociological activity has been analytical theories. These theories have been derived through a process of logical deduction rather than from a grounded empirical base within the society itself. The analytical theory consists of axiomatic statements that are true by definition and from which other statements are then derived. The resulting conceptual schemes have no direct empirical reference within society and are tested, if at all, once they have been fully articulated. The theory of social stratification advanced by Gerhard Lenski (1965) is based on an analytical distinction between the time when a society produces only enough goods and services to satisfy its needs and the time when a society produces a surplus of goods and services. The two propositions that lie at the base of the theory, therefore, are firstly that society must satisfy its basic necessities (survival component) and secondly that society then moves on to produce a surplus (the second stage of social development). Lenski postulates that during the first stage of development cooperation is of a functional consensus type (people need each other's help in order to survive and produce their basic necessities), but in the second stage, with society now moving into a situation of surplus, cooperation of this functional type gives way to one based upon coercion, which leads to conflict. The theory is clearly based upon a series of deductions following from the original analytic distinction.

Having formulated his model, Lenski then examined human societies along a continuum from the least technically advanced societies, such as hunting and gathering societies, to advanced industrial societies, in order to see whether inequalities increased as surpluses increased with improved technology and growing economic wealth, as predicted by his theory, and whether the nature of cooperation changed. The coercive-based system is one of inequalities, for the distribution of surpluses is unequal, dictated as it is by the holders of positions of power and influence. The relation between technology, size of the surplus and levels of inequality holds for Lenski in all societies until the most advanced stage of industrial societies is reached, when the trend appears to move into reverse and the inequalities begin to diminish.

(a) The method employed here for the empirical elaboration of the theory is essentially the case approach, which deliberately looks for cases that do not fit, and therefore, may discredit the theory. In the absence of deviant cases that theory can stand as a universal. Here, however, the deviant case of advanced industrial society poses two alternatives: either the theory needs reformulation or modification to account for the change observable or its postulates are wrong. Lenski opts for the first, and suggests features of advanced individual societies that lead to the change from the predicted pattern (Thorns, 1976: 12).

The analytic theory, like one developed by Lenski, only enters empirical data after the construction of the model; it does not generate the model out of the data itself, as advocated by proponents of Grounded Theory. The approach to verification via the case method has been one widely used by sociologists (Nadel, 1957; Wirth, 1948), who have constructed their theories at the level of total societies and then employed both comparative and historical methods to seek data that would demonstrate these applicability.

(b) The second powerful factor in the influence of positivism has been the adoption of the 'scientific method' which has been a somewhat stereotyped and mechanistic approach to sociological inquiry, divorced from the imaginative elements that have been so crucial to discovery within the realms of science. The philosophers of science and methodologists writing their 'methods' texts have identified five components of this scientific method (Gibson, 1960; Thorns, 1976):

(i) The first is *abstraction*: The real world is seen as very complex, so that in order to understand it, you must employ some form of simplification; this necessitates lifting out or abstracting certain key variables, in the same way as the scientist may explain the intricacies of the universe in terms of certain key factors.

(ii) The second component is the *construction of laws* or *general statements*: This task is seen as vital to the development of a cumulative body of knowledge and to the raising of the subject beyond a series of interesting and unique sets of observations.

(iii) The third is the use of *empirical evidence*: For the subjection of theories and conceptions to rigorous testing against the real world in controlled settings is seen to be necessary if statements are to move from a 'probationary' to an 'accepted' status. This component makes it necessary for sociology to develop its own experiments.

(iv) The fourth component is *ethical neutrality*, which raises the issue of value-neutrality of the subject—the pursuit of knowledge for its own sake rather than for explicit ideological ends.

(v) Finally comes *objectivity* that concerns the individual researcher's own biases and their control which may include their minimization. The scientific method gives rise to a particular set of procedures that are to be aimed at in the development of sociological research.

The first step lies in developing a research design that takes as its point of departure the existing body of theory or generalizations concerning the particular field of inquiry to be examined. This existing body of theory is made up of concepts; these being blended together to form a conceptual scheme around a particular area of sociological concern, e.g., social stratification, urbanization, ethnic relations, etc. The researcher formulates a hypothesis from the theory in the form of operational definitions and then tests it empirically within the real world. The subsequent analysis of the results leads to acceptance, rejection, or reformulation of the original hypothesis, so feeding back into the conceptual scheme and assisting in the development of the theory. This procedure is repeated until the theoretical model provides an empirically verifiable explanation of the social phenomenon under investigation (Thorns, 1976: 13).

The structuring of the research process in this manner requires the development of techniques of data gathering and analysis that permit the confirmation and rejection of hypothesis with some degree of certainty, and in a way that can be assessed by other researchers. This need has been met by the work of social statisticians. The three figures that stand out as being of particular influence are Bowley (1915), Pearson (1948) and Fisher (1960).

Bowley pioneered work on the sample survey in the early part of the 20th century. The method he developed was that of random sampling, and he devised it for his research into poverty which took him only two years, whereas the earlier study by Booth had taken seventeen years. Bowley was able to show that estimates of known accuracy could be made quite successfully from samples of the parent population if the sample was constructed according to certain principles. The most important of these concerned the elimination of the biases in the selection of sample members through the use of random selection. In this, every member of the population has a known and equal chance of selection.

Sampling, since Bowley's work in 1912–14, has been refined considerably, so that a whole range of sampling techniques are now available to the researcher, allowing him to control the selection of subjects and their distribution in the population. These controls are brought in through the use of stratification factors (such as age, sex, socio-economic class), multi-stage designs, and the multi-phase, sampling use in the 1971 UK census of population, where a sample was asked more detailed questions in addition to the general ones that were asked of all the population. The apparent growth in the accuracy of the estimates made from samples is not, however, without its attendant dangers. The chief one lies in the fact that the conditions under which samples can be constructed and the type of errors controlled are both strictly limited and closely defined by the type of sample design used. Basically, the controllable errors are only in the selection of cases or individuals to comprise the sample, not errors in such things as response patterns, accuracy of answers etc. The errors controlled through sampling, therefore, are only part of the total range of possible errors that can influence the research. Sampling is thus aimed at improving the reliability of the data collected rather than the validity of that data for the research question under investigation.

In the period lasting from the 1940s to the early 1960s, the use of sampling allied to the questionnaire or formal interview became the dominant mode of research—in fact to many the only method of research. Its protagonists did not use the methods of science so much as those of empirical logic to seek the establishment of causality in their work. Important in this search for cause was not only the work of empirical logicians like J.S. Mill (1862) but that of the social statisticians like Pearson (1948) and Fisher (1960) (Thorns, 1976: 15).

J.S. Mill (1862) has had a considerable influence upon the practice of social research, as can be seen by the recommendations of his canons of empirical logic within methodology textbooks as the means that should be used for developing sociological proofs. Mill outlines four principal methods by which cause-effect relationships could be determined. The first two of these—*the methods of agreement and differences*—are both based upon elimination. The method of difference is the more powerful, as it can isolate more clearly causal factors. The third, *the method of residues*, is of little value, as a considerable knowledge about society is required before it can be applied effectively. The final method *of concomitant variation*, however, has had wide usage, for it simply draws attention to things that vary together, and therefore, must be related in some way or other.

These methods are, in fact, an attempt to bring into sociological research a quasi-experimental method of discovery. Their advocates have looked towards the development of fully experimental methods within sociological research as the future goal. So far as such experimental methods have not been especially effective as a means of advancing knowledge. Because of the high nature of control required they have been extremely limited in both the areas of research in which they have been used and also in the type of subject chosen; there has been a particular emphasis upon school children and other such captive groups. The problem of how to establish causal connections is not so much solved as highlighted by the rules of empirical logic, and the basic rationale for proceeding via proofs of empirical relationships justified (Thorns, ibid.).

The development of this approach required the parallel development of techniques to allow the accurate measurement of the association of variables. Pearson's contribution to social statistics answered this need by providing a means of determining the degree of correlation or contingency between variables, thus solving one of the major difficulties. But it still left the question of what level of relationship was to be taken as significant. Here, Fisher provided the answer in the development of tests of significance. Fisher's initial assumption was that there was in fact no association between phenomena, so that all observed relationships were due to chance and chance alone. This assumption forms the basis of Fisher's null hypothesis, which states that no relationship exists between the studied variables. Consequently, the onus is put on the researcher to show that this is in fact incorrect. The rejection of the null hypothesis means that the relationship is not due entirely to chance factors, but this is only a step along the complex road of discovering what the relationship is in fact due to. Tests of significance, however, have for many become a central tool in the research process.

The approach to sociological research, via the rules of empirical logic and significance testing, is somewhat formal and mechanistic. Its dominance can be illustrated by the fact that half the articles appearing in the *American Sociological Review* between 1958 and 1967 employed statistical tests of significance (Morrison and Henkel, 1969). The role of such tests has increasingly come under the scrutiny and criticism by both statisticians and social researchers, particularly as regards the relation between statistical and substantive significance.

The question was first raised by Selvin (1957) when he mounted an attack upon the use of significance tests in non-experimental research. Selvin's position is that only when all important correlated biases have been controlled, is it possible to measure the influence of random errors by statistical tests of significance. This would mean that significance testing should become one of the last steps in the analysis of data and not, as is so often the case, the first step. Selvin does consider that such tests have a place in non-experimental research, but that conditions under which they can be correctly used seldom, apply owing to three main factors that together make it extremely difficult to remove all correlated biases (Thorns, 1976: 16–17).

(i) The first of these is the fact that samples are seldom large enough for the control of all extraneous variables.

(ii) The second that all the variables known to be relevant by the investigator may not for one reason or another have been included in the research design.

(iii) The third a possible interdependence between variables that does not allow one explanatory variable to be examined. Just as there are problems regarding the conditions under which the tests can be applied, there are problems with these interpretations. Selvin here attacks researchers for confusing statistical with substantive significance. He writes, for example, "A 1% difference may be significant at the 0.001 level of the sample is large enough yet such a small difference is essentially meaningless for sociology at present" (Selvin, 1957: 522–323).

The issue raised clearly here is that statistical significance on its own has little value. It has to be examined within the framework of the research to see whether it has also some substantive significance. Selvin's final criticism relates to random errors which are those specially controlled by significance tests. He argues that these enter into the research at points other than the selection of sample members, yet this is the only point that is controlled. He suggests that random errors may occur in response to interviewing, and in response to questions; in fact, each stage of the research process is as open to such errors as is the selection of cases.

Selvin's position has been countered by McGinnes (1958) and Kish (1959) among others. They consider that Selvin's problems arise from not distinguishing three types of statistical hypothesis:

(i) The 'absolute hypothesis' in which there are no conditions upon which the relationship depend;

(ii) The 'finitely conditional hypothesis' where the explanatory variables are dependent upon a number of other specified variables; and

(iii) The 'infinitely conditional hypothesis', where the explanatory variable is conditional upon an infinite number of variables.

They then suggest that Selvin's criticism is related only to the third hypothesis. They would not advocate the virtual abandonment of statistical significance testing, but rather its careful use under the appropriate conditions. They feel that adherence to Selvin's ideal norms, which confine the usage of tests to experimental situations, would stifle social research (Thorns, 1976: 17–18).

The research strategies so far examined have stemmed from a common origin in the desire to utilize and follow the 'methods of science' which would objectify and systematize the research process so that valid theories might be formulated. The consequence has been a form of enquiry stressing certain formal procedures around which the problem is examined at the stages of hypothesis formulation, empirical testing and analysis. The research strategies have been marked by the domination of the survey research, with emphasis upon identifying those variables that are seen to hold explanatory power with respect to particular social phenomena. This has led to a much greater concern with the reliability of the instruments and standardization of procedures for collection and analysis of the data than with the question of the validity of the data itself. How closely, for example, do the answers given to the interviewer reflect the respondent's actual behaviour in the situations examined by the survey?

The Ethnographic Tradition

The positivist tradition of research, with its increasing emphasis upon quantification and large-scale empirical investigation, has developed the ethnographic tradition which can be seen in the work of such scholars as Charles Booth with his *Poverty in East London* (1892–97) and the anthropologist Branislav Malinowski. Of these, the latter has had the most profound influence on this particular tradition. Malinowski developed the method of participant observation for the study of social situations in his own studies of the *Trobriand Islanders* (1922). He discovered that in order to understand something of the culture of this people, it was necessary for him to live with them for a period of time, to learn their languages and to gain access to their world of meanings. This method has since been widely employed in social anthropology and some areas of sociological research. Currently, its use has revived in sociological research, as it is a technique particularly suited to the contemporary phenomenological perspective (Bruyn, 1967).

The role of the observer poses a number of intrinsic problems, most of these relating to the existence of biases:

(i) The first problem is that observation and inference are very often linked, so that as we observe situations, we tend to categorize them according to our past experience and fail to appreciate new and unique features.

(ii) The second problem is that the observer is limited by his abilities to hear, see or appreciate all that is happening in a particular situation, so that his observations are always incomplete.

(iii) The final problem relates to the biases that are introduced through the interaction of the observer and those he observes. This is again a factor that it is difficult to measure, and it is often more extensive than the observer himself realizes (Thorns, 1976: 19).

The participant observer's second level of problems is that regarding the nature of his role vis-à-vis those he is studying. Should it be an open one, with his purpose fully explained, or should it be covert? The majority of participant observers have in fact chosen covert roles, ones which provide them with a legitimate reason for being present but not advertising the fact that they are social researchers. One such role, which has been quite often used, is that of local historian collecting material for a book on the area, group etc. Such an entry into a group was used by Whyte (1943) for his study *Street Corner Society*. Whyte's study also demonstrates the importance of sponsorship for the researcher: he was sponsored by DOC, the leader of the Italianite gang he studied, and without that support it is doubtful whether Whyte could have succeeded in completing his study. A further problem with the covert role also shown by Whyte's study is that the investigator has to wait for things to happen and information to emerge from the group. Once or twice, when Whyte deliberately tried to ask about things, he found little response, and in fact brought into question his own position in the group. The extreme case of the covert role would be an observer's secret entry into a closed group, the means used by Festinger (1956) for his study of a closed religious group. This may well be the only means of conducting some particular study, but does raise questions about the ethics of such procedures and of the rights of the respondents (Thorns, 1976: 20).

Participant observation has in the past been mainly used in social anthropological research, where it was first evolved; in community studies, which in many ways resemble the work of the social anthropologists in that the researcher is engaged in looking at the whole of the community and its interrelationships rather than trying to isolate independent and dependent variables; and in sub-cultural studies such as Whyte's, where the focus has been upon a particular group in an attempt to discover more of its social norms and distinctive patterns of behaviour. The popularity of the concept of participant observation led to the attempt in Britain by Madge and Harrisson (1939) to form a team of 'mass observers'—people from all over Britain drawn from different social groups who would provide a team of observers of major events. However, after one or two initial studies, the impetus was lost and the idea never developed any further.

Participant observation and survey methods have been contrasted by a number of writers to demonstrate that each method is concerned with different types of explanations and analyses. These attempts either argue in favour of a fusion of the two into a more comprehensive methodology or for the rejection of the survey approach. Bruyn (1967), for example, characterizes the participant observation method as one in which an inner perspective is gained as the observer is able to understand the people he is studying in terms of their own frames of reference rather than his own. Further, the observer's explanations are tied in directly to the events that he observes; his concepts sensitize areas rather than formalize them, helping the development of new insights as the study progresses. Finally, the knowledge gained allows a synthetic type of presentation; the observer is able to integrate the various aspects of the group or society he has been observing, since the total range of activities has been his area of concern rather than one particular aspect. The survey approach is seen in contrast to have an 'outer' perspective through the utilization of formal concepts and impersonal categories, those leading to an analytic explanation that is inevitably incomplete (Thorns, 1976: 21).

The resurgence of interest in, and emphasis upon, observation-based means of inquiry is a reflection of the increased concern with the subjective dimension of explanation. The positivist tradition has emphasized the objective character of knowledge to the almost virtual exclusion of the subjective elements. The movement in sociological perspectives in the 1960s and 1970s has all been in the direction of an increased awareness of, and concentration upon, the necessity to explore the self-conceptions and 'understandings' of the subject, and the primarily subjective character of knowledge.

The concern with the interaction between the observer and the observed that is seen to present problems for observational methods, as indeed it does for all methods, has led to the exploration of non-reactive means of data collection. These have concentrated upon devising ways of studying social phenomena without physical presence of the observer. The methods, which have been reviewed by Webb (1966), show quite a wide range of techniques.

One of the most important techniques is physical trace analysis, in which the researcher examines either the erosion of physical features, such as tiles in front of a display in a museum as an indication of its popularity, or the accumulation of material, such as objects left in a rented accommodation by tenants. Another technique is the examination of various types of documentary data, which can range from official records of governments and public agencies to the private records of individuals in the form of letters, diaries and autobiographies. Such data has been carefully used, for the purposes it was originally recorded and for which the researcher is using it are likely to be at odds, and, with personal documents, complex motives could have led to the choice of material to record and the interpretations placed upon events and activities. The final technique is that of non-participant observation, which is concentrated on particular facets of the situation and the respondents. One example of this is the study by Hall (1959) of physical spacing during different types of social interaction. He identified eight different distances adopted, from very close (3–6 inches) for 'soft-whisper' and top secret interactions, to the limits of 20–24 feet for more impersonal contacts. Such techniques as hidden recording devices have also been tried in an attempt to eliminate the physical presence of the observer, but these pose ethical problems. The lack of any great historical depth in the research for both the survey methods and, to a lesser extent, observational methods, has made it difficult to discover the antecedents of the current situation, or to use the information gained by research activities cumulatively as part of an ongoing and developing corpus of knowledge (Thorns, 1976: 21–22).

The first theme to emerge from the aforesaid review is the role of the positivist tradition and its influence in the form of the desire for the adoption of the 'methods of science'. This has meant, in practice, the devising of a particular mode of enquiry stressing the importance of concepts, hypotheses linked to defined variables, empirical testing and formal analysis. In conjunction with this process, social statistics have been used to aid both in the construction of the empirical test and in the analysis and interpretation of the results. Secondly, there is the alternative tradition, which has been strongly based in social anthropology and community studies, and has emphasized the total description and analysis of the social situations whether they be groups or societies. These two major themes have many sub-themes and variations, some of which the rest of the book aims at exploring, in so far as they constitute new trends in research methodology.

It is important to mention here how does Giddens distinguish three principal sets of issues specific to the importation of positivism into sociology, aspects of which most of the writings in subsequent chapters of the book are concerned.

Subjectivity and Its Connotation

Broadly speaking, there can be said to be two discrete traditions in social theory relating to the problems of method and to the identification of the 'subject matter' with which sociology is held to be concerned:

(i) One is quite evidently 'positivistic' in both the general and more specific senses of the term. This is precisely the tradition of social theory of which Comte stands as a prominent representative, but which stretches back well before him to Montesquieu and Condorcet and finds its most sophisticated defense later on in the 19th century, in Durkheim's work. In certain important respects, the French positivists were highly critical of British social theory, founded upon the model of orthodox political economy. But, although, the former insisted upon a 'holistic' conception of social reality, and the latter on the primacy of the 'individual', they shared common assumptions of a methodological sort, and the dominant strain in the 19th century British social thought may also be correctly designated as positivistic.

(ii) The social tradition in social theory—a complex issue of interweaving strands, but quite definitely in opposition to both French and British positivism—is that which arose in Germany in the latter period of the 19th century.

The complexity of this second tradition is well illustrated by the intellectual struggles which Max Weber was forced to undergo in order to achieve even the semblance of reconciliation between the differing fragments which were his theoretical inheritance. The conception of sociological and historical method which Weber worked out drew heavily from the writings of prior authors who rejected one or more of the four elements of positivism noted above; but he also attempted to synthesize these received views with others which were quite definitely positivistic. In Weber's thought, perhaps, the main axis of this confrontation is represented in his attempt, via neo-Kantian philosophy, to reconcile the 'subjectivism' and 'irrationalism' of the German historical school with the naturalistic views of Menger.

Weber's methodological essays deal with two overlapping themes: that of 'subjectivism' versus 'objectivism', and 'irrationality' versus 'rationality', in the explication of human conduct. In the essays on Roscher and Knies, Weber attempts to show that these authors confuse the two dimensions in such a manner as to obscure the logical distinctions presupposed by any form of sociological or historical study. From premise that human action necessarily is 'subjective' in character, they draw the conclusion that it possesses an 'irrational' or perhaps more accurately, an 'a-rational' quality in the sense that it is not specifically 'calculable' or 'predictable' in the way in which occurrences in the natural world are. This sort of viewpoint is linked with a rejection of 'causality' as relevant to the explanation of any form of conduct which is 'motivated conduct'. Weber questions this line of reasoning, by trying to recast the relationship between subjectivism and objectivism on the one hand, and irrationality and rationality, on the other.

Giddens (1974 : 6) states the essential basis of Weber's argument as follows:

> "We may, and must, accept that human action has a 'subjective' component which differentiates it qualitatively from the sphere of natural reality. But it is mistaken to suppose that recognition of the subjective character of action necessarily involves either the relinquishment of the possibility of confronting it 'objectively' as the natural scientist confronts natural reality, or the abandonment of causal explanation. The interpretation of human action in terms of motives can be causal interpretation precisely in so far as we are able to analyze it in terms of chains of rationality—that is to say, by linking motives or purposes to the means, whereby predictable: it is therefore erroneous to suppose that subjectivity may be equated with 'incalculability'".

Weber points out that the writers of the historical school assume that 'freedom of will' is ultimately the most fundamental factor separating the human universe from that of nature. In fact, Weber claims, the freer is an individual's action, the less of his act is conditioned either by internal impress of affect or external compulsion of some sort the more clearly it may be analysed in terms of a means-ends scheme of rationality and the more accurately its course and outcome may be predicted by the observer:

> "The more this is the case, the less room there is for any sort of romantic naturalistic conception of 'personality', that conception that paradoxically seeks the sacred quality of personality in an

'irrationality' based upon the dull, undifferentiated, vegetative 'foundation' of personal life". (Weber, 1974: 27)

It is precisely the rational character of 'freely willed' behaviour which distinguishes man from animals; not, as is proposed by these writers, some mystical quality of the irrational. 'Irrationality' of action in actually the trait by which we recognize the insane individuals whose behaviour is refractory to our interpretative 'understanding' and thereby is specifically 'incalculable' (Giddens, 1974: 6). Weber emphasizes that the interpretation of rational action depends upon the use of generalizations about typical processes of action—what he usually calls 'Erfahrungsregeln', or empirical rules. While these often remain unstated, and may not even be known to the actual individual whose behaviour is being analysed, no form of interpretative understanding can proceed without using them. The operation of 'free-will' which may be conceived to be realized to the degree to which an individual acts rationally in a given situation, in terms of the relating of means to ends thus presupposes that human behaviour conforms to 'laws', or ascertained regularities (Giddens, 1974: 7).

Giddens thus reaches the conclusion that, while the social sciences must of necessity to be founded upon a method—interpretative analysis of subjective meanings, or means-ends chain which is distinct from that employed in natural science, where 'understanding' in this sense is obviously impossible, this is not only compatible with causal generalizations about human behaviour, but presumes it. Since Weber places this standpoint within the context of neo-Kantian philosophy, following Windelband, Rickert and Simmel, his notion of the significance of theoretical generalizations in the social sciences takes a particular form. According to this conception, reality, whether natural or social, is extensively and intensively infinite; therefore, any approach to the analysis of a given event or phenomenon in reality must be selective, and guided by values, as stated in the principle of value-relevance (Wertbeziebung). It follows that the discovery of scientific 'laws' in no sense exhausts the analysis of the area of reality to which such laws apply. On the contrary, the more general the generalizations—the more successful it is in incorporating a range of occurrences which may be subsumed under it—the more abstract it is, and the less it tells us about the specific event or phenomenon in question. The more, because of particular values we hold which direct our interests along such a line, we are interested in a datum 'for its own sake', the more we are forced to complement analysis in term of generalization with the analysis (which again cannot be 'exhaustive') of historical individuals. In the social sciences, Weber holds, this sort of interest tends to be pre-eminent. Sociology is in a sense subordinate to history.

Schutz's *Der Sinnhafte Aufbau der Sozialen Welt* (1932) takes up and attempts to expand certain of the basic suppositions detailed in Weber's methodological writings. Given that his primary concern is to elaborate a conception of sociological method (Chapter 3), Schutz directs his attention mainly to effecting a critique of Weber's treatment of subjectivity and rationality. According to Weber's expositions of interpretative sociology, the aim of sociology is to analyse and explain social action through the study of the subjective meanings whereby individuals orient their conduct. But Schutz tries to show that Weber fails to pursue his arguments far enough. What he takes as the basic material of analysis, the subjective meanings of action, "by no means defines a primitive, as he thinks it does. It is, on the contrary, a mere label for a highly complex and ramified area that calls for much further study" (Schutz, 1972: 8). The constitution of 'meaning' in social action is problematic in a double sense: on the one side from the perspective of the analyst, who shares in the meaning-structure of the social world at same time as he seeks to detach himself from it, in order to observe it from the outside; and from the perspective of the social actors themselves, for whom meanings are not fixed and irreducible but are continually in a flux and in the process of being constructed and dissolved in an active fashion.

When Weber speaks of 'meaningful action', Schutz points out, he has in mind—as Giddens has described above—action which can be interpreted by the observer in terms of a means-ends scheme of rationality. This is shown by the fact that he places both affective responses and traditional conduct/behaviour governed by unthinking habit or custom, at the margins of action, which is meaningful and thus amenable to the method of interpretative sociology. Rational action serves Weber as the model for the study of social conduct. The upshot of this, according to Schutz, is that Weber confuses 'meaningful' with 'motivated' action..Schutz asserts that it is mistaken, to suppose that either emotional behaviour of habitual reactions are ipso facto devoid of meaning. In his discussion of interpretative sociology, Weber distinguishes between the 'direct understandings' and the 'explanatory understandings' of the subjective meaning of an observed action. The first refers to a situation in which the observer grasps the significance of the act directly, either because its rational content is immediately perceived by him, or because he has an emphatic understanding of it; the latter involves comprehending the motive which leads the individual to engage in the conduct in question, and is achieved by placing that conduct in the context of a broader complex of meanings (Giddens, 1974: 9). But this, Schutz argues, is a distinction which confuses more than it clarifies. When Weber speaks of 'direct understanding', he is certainly referring to the subjective experience of the actor; 'explanatory understanding' necessarily involves the analyst in considering far more than the subjective meaning with which the individual himself invests his action. If, however, we examine 'direct understanding' more closely, we find, that this also implies looking beyond what is designated by Weber. We see a man wielding axe, but in order to know that he is chopping wood, we have to locate what we observe in a wider context of meaning, which may not in fact be exactly the same as that attributed to his behaviour by the actor himself. We must distinguish the subjective from the objective context of meaning, a differentiation which cross-cuts that drawn by Weber. There is a certain logic in the distinction proposed by Schutz, but its import is quite different from that which he indicates: when we 'directly' understand the 'meaning' of the action of an individual, we do so within the framework of everyday life, participating in the action itself. Rather than, referring to a procedure which is to be employed by the scientist, Weber's 'direct understanding' merely concerns the sort of understanding which everyone makes use of in his day-to-day life; while this may adequately serve the practical demands of everyday social existence, it conceals a potentially complicated set of influences which themselves have to be examined" (Giddens, 1974).

According to Schutz, the main source of difficulty for sociology in the interpretation of meaning is that meaning is not simply constituted subjectively, but intersubjectively. It is not hard to see that his most fundamental problem, within the confines of the premises which he began from—a problem which he did not solve even to his own satisfaction—was that of bridging the apparently unfathomable gulf between subjectivity and intersubjectivity as parameters of existential knowledge (ibid.). Giddens (1974: 9–10) remarks:

> "For intersubjectivity is already presupposed in the analysis of the 'Lebenswelt' of the subject. In Schutz's sociological phenomenology, the matter does not, of course, present itself in the same form; but a practical dilemma arises in Schutz's separation of subjective and objective meaning. Schutz, however, bypasses the problem rather than solves it, objective meaning inhers in signs and expressions which are meaningful and intelligible in their own right—in their anonymous nature—regardless of whether anyone is thinking of them, regardless of whether anyone is using them (Schutz, 1974: 42–43). Thus, a term or phrase in a language has an objective meaning regardless of whether or not anyone happens to be uttering it at any particular time. Schutz holds that the objective meaning can be studied from two points of view—as constituted and 'given' (as in the case of the above mentioned example), and as in the process of becoming in the process of being constituted."

Schutz says that these considerations allow us to identify more clearly the defects in Weber's account of interpretative sociology. In speaking of the subjective meaning of action, Weber fails to treat 'action' within a time perspective. In this respect, W.F. Whyte's comment on Talcott Parsons' action theory—there is a stage, there is a set, but the actors do not move—could, following Schutz's critique, be equally well applied to Max Weber. Weber's analysis, Schutz points out, conflates action as a completed act in the latter's terms, an 'objectified act' and action as a flow of events. The theorem that the actor "attaches meaning to his action" is a metatheoretical expression; meaning is a reflexive mode of attending to experience, whether as a matter of forming, means-ends projects (subjective meaning), or as a matter of interpreting completed acts (objective meaning).

Giddens' following comments on Weber's methodology deserve quote in the context:

> "In Weber's writings, the question of rationality in social activity is one which continually appears, in several guises. The affirmation of the intrinsic rationality of conduct that is 'freely' directed by the individual is a major thesis in his analysis of his eminent precursors in the historical; school; although he also sought to place defined

limits upon the scope of reason in denying the possibility of rationality evaluating the ends of activity themselves. In constructing typological concepts for the study of society, he insisted that 'rational ideal types' setting out purely rational modes of action, must be the basis of interpretative sociology; the actual behaviour of individual is to be explained in terms of its deviation from rational conduct. The polarity if rationality and irrationality appears yet again in Weber's empirical sociology itself, in his many discussions on the increasing penetration of rationality into the various institutional spheres of modern society, and once more is offset by a contrast with 'unreason' (charisma). Even a cursory comparison of Weber's writings reveals that be uses the term 'rational' in a shifting and consistent way. Schutz's attempts to reformulate the Weberian treatment of subjectivity, as he recognizes, obviously has immediate implications for the notion of rationality of conduct" (Giddens, 1974: 10–11).

The course of sociological research has followed an opposite line to that advocated by Weber. Rather than finding it most useful to analyse social conduct by treating the 'non-rational' as a factor of deviation from the 'rational', in most of the available theories of social action and social structure, rational actions are assigned residual status (Garfinkel, 1974: 54). Neither of these propositions is satisfactory, and we have instead to discriminate different modes and aspects of rationality in conduct, no single one of which can be said to be more basic than the others. In fact, the numerous modes of rationality which Garfinkel distinguishes really divide into two main types: what Garfinkel calls 'scientific rationalities' and 'rationality of everyday life'. The mistake underlying most treatments of rationality in the social sciences is to suppose that the first can serve as a model for the study of the second. The essential core of Garfinkel's argument is that the ideal conduct of scientific inquiry far from embodying norms of rationality which can be applied usefully to the interpretative analysis of social conduct, has to be regarded as a separate and any every special type of activity (Giddens, 1974: 11).

Tribulations of Generalization

Few works dealing with problems of philosophy of the social sciences have stimulated as much controversy as Winch's concise work *The Idea of a Social Science* (1958). While Winch owes a debt to Wittgenstein, the book takes up similar questions of subjectivity and meaning to be dealt with against a different intellectual background by Weber and Schutz, but reaches conclusions which are substantially divergent from theirs. Neither Weber nor Schutz is of the view that a 'science of society' is possible. In their varying ways, they each emphasize the significance of the interpretative method as a necessary instrument of analysis in the social sciences and in doing so certainly recognize a major methodological division between social and natural science. But this does not compromise the possibility of establishing generalizations about social conduct which do not differ logically from those characteristics of natural science. Winch (1974), however, specifically rejects this view. He believes that philosophy stands in a different relationship to sociology than to natural science: "it is often supposed that newly developing disciplines with no settled basis of theory on which to build further research are particularly prove to throw up philosophical puzzles; but that this is a temporary stage which should be lived through and then shaken off as soon as possible. But it would be wrong to say this of sociology; for the philosophical problems which arise there are not tiresome foreign bodies which must be removed before sociology can advance on its own independent scientific lines. On the contrary, the central problem of sociology, that of giving an account of the nature of social phenomena in general itself belongs to philosophy" (p. 43).

Giddens has demonstrated the validity of this position, according to Winch, by considering Wittgenstein's notion of 'following a rule', and elucidating certain consequences which this has for sociological analysis:

> "Following a rule in linguistic usage must necessarily be a 'public' phenomenon, having reference to the responses of others, the notion of a rule is inseparable from a social setting in which that rules applied. The concept of following a rule Winch holds, gives us important insights into the nature of what Weber calls subjectively meaningful action. We can say, in fact, that meaningful action is that which is rule-governed, and this in turn shows us why we cannot generalize about human conduct in the same form as we can when dealing with phenomena in the natural world". (1974: 12–12)

In Winch's words, "the notion of a human society involves a scheme of concepts which is logically incompatible with the kinds of explanation offered in the natural sciences" (Winch, 1971: 72). Motives cannot be regarded (as Weber thought) as causal factors in human behaviour. To discover the motives of a given act is to understand it: understanding, when applied to human action, means nothing more or less than this. To say that a person was motivated to act in such way is to say that his behaviour is 'intelligible' or 'meaningful' in terms of the rules of conduct which pertain in the society of which he is a member. To interpret observed regularities in social conduct is not to offer the sort of law—like causal generalization familiar in natural sciences, but to inquire into the character of the rule to which it is oriented. These rules, not the producers of investigation of the sociologist, supply the criteria if identity whereby we judge two acts, of the same individual or of different individuals, to be 'the same'.

What Gellner (1974) refers to as the 'new idealism' has not been very favourably received by sociologists and his articles indicate some of the chief objection which has been raised (Giddens, 1974). As Gellner points out, in seeking to apply Wittgenstein's doctrine to the social sciences, Winch reverses the formula involved in the former philosophy of meaning: "Where Wittgenstein taught philosophers not to ask for the use, Winch advises social scientists not to look for the cause but for the meaning" (Gellner, 1974: 134–5). Winch does not see that this undermines Wittgenstein's philosophy itself; for it we accept that language and the social meaning it expresses, delimits the boundaries of 'our' world, but also assert that there exists a plurality of social contexts in which different rules of meaning have become elaborate, we are caught in a hopeless paradox. There are two ways out of this paradox; and it is not stretching Gellner's case too far to say that each of these is itself paradoxical:

(i) One is to suppose that there are criteria for judging the validity of propositions which stand outside variations in forms of language or conceptual structure. But this, by very nature, means abandoning Wittgenstein's original premise.

(ii) The other path which can be followed, the one taken by Winch, is towards a conceptual relativism. But this view cannot be reconciled with some essential aspects of sociological method and with certain basic features of social life itself. The latter, Gellner suggests, concerns the oppositions or contradictions which exist both within and between different societies or cultural milieu.

Giddens (1974: 14) considers "a zealous reforming movement which derives its proselytizing appeals from the conviction that existing rules of religious practice or meaning do not genuinely express revealed truth. A view which holds that meaning is wholly given in social usage cannot cope with such a circumstances; moreover, the type of situation illustrated by the case of the reforming zealot is not merely marginal in character—it exemplifies something which is generic to social life. This is an important sense again brings us back to questions of the nature of rationality, since the reformer may be declaring that existing beliefs/practices are irrational, in the light of the proper exegisis of doctrine".

For most modern thinkers, Gellner indicates, "relativism is a problem": for Winch and Wittgenstein it is a solution. Other thinkers start from the fact of the diversification of belief and morals, and try to find the touchstone of correct belief etc. This is the general form of the mainstream of modern western thought. But Wittgenstein and Winch arrive at relativism, they do not start from it, and they arrive at it as a solution to quite another problem, the problem of meaning. They say that meaning is not an echo, a reduplication, a structural mirroring of the thing meant, aided perhaps by the struts of a formal framework: it is the possession of a place, a role, in a 'language', a 'form of life', a culture (Gellner, 1974: 149–50). These relativities have to be treated as problematic, not only in relation to internal contradictions within any given society, but also in terms of what Gellner refers to as the 'unequal cognitive power' of different cultures. Gellner concludes that we must reject the view which presumes that any form of belief or 'rule of meaning' when interpreted within its social context is as valid as any other. (Giddens, 1974: 14)

Arguing that the "effectiveness of scientific industrial civilization and its diffusion are central facts of our time" which any adequate approach to the basic issues of sociological method must be able to encompass theoretically, Gellner reaches a conclusion which in fact forms something of a starting point for Touraine. Although Touraine's conception of 'action theory' borrows nothing from the sort of intellectual sources discussed by Gellner, questions of what significance must be given to the nature of 'meaning' in social action, and of the implications of this for causal generalization again appear as basic here. But Touraine is less concerned with philosophical problems underlying these phenomena than with deficiencies in existing forms of theoretical generalization in sociology.

Touraine's sociology of action (1974: 75–101) begins from the idea that human conduct is intrinsically 'meaningful' (Reynaud and Bourdieu, 1974: 101–13). Rather than discussing the nature of terms such as 'meaning', 'motive', 'purpose' etc., as applied to human behaviour in general, Touraine seeks to accomplish what Gellner says is taken for granted in Winch's analysis—the sources of the creation of new forms of meaning in society. Touraine's social 'action' has to be distinguished from Parsons' 'action theory' which belongs to a leading contemporary school of social theory that Touraine wishes to criticize—or to least, to show the limitations of Touraine—proposes that functionalism can be seen to have come into being at a particular stage in the development of modern society when, for definite reasons, men become preoccupied with the character of 'social cohesion' and the given existence of social norms. Touraine sets it out that action theory involves a different perspective; and in a specific sense, it implies a criticism of Weber's 'Verstehende Soziologie' as well as of functionalism. For, according to Touraine, we must abandon the conception that as Weber put it, "the individual is the 'atom', of sociological analysis", and recognize that 'subjectivity' and 'meaning' are not merely to be conceptualized as properties of the individual subject (Giddens, 1974). Touraine's 'historical subject' is not the individual actor. The values or symbolic systems (which includes language) embodied in social conduct at any point in time are not creations of any single individual nor can they said to represent some sort of aggregate of individual actions; nor are these values normally present in, or even necessarily accessible to the consciousness of the individual actor. The study of the historical subject involves analysing the emergent structure of a totalizing activity, the unity of the dialectical movements of historical action (Touraine, 1974: 105). The highly opaque style of expression which Touraine adopts—makes for a very real difficulty in elucidating the nature of the very concept of the 'historical subject'. Touraine emphasizes that the notion does not represent a return to outmoded conceptions of group mind or collective consciousness. The historical subject does not have a fixed empirical referent and is most aptly regarded as a methodological principle for understanding the 'unite totalisante' of social action as the creation of meaning. But neither does it imply a reversion to a philosophy of history: "when we speak of the historical subject of systems of action and projects, we do not construct a philosophy of history, but an historical sociology and more than, we build an understanding of the formation of social systems—which others study from the functional point of view. The historical subject is not a concrete totality, such as feudal society or industrial society; it is not therefore an interpretation of an analysis, a mode of analysing the normative orientation of conduct" (Touraine, 1974: 126).

Touraine suggests that the process of labour, such as conceived in Marxian theory, can be regarded as the exemplar of the creation of values by the activity of the historical subject. This should not be considered merely in terms of the material process of creation, whereby men modify their physical environment in such a way as to produce goods or commodities; rather the products of labour are the symbols or meanings which men bring into being in differentiating themselves from the senseless world of nature. According to Touraine, there are always two aspects of this: "The double exigency of creation and control". The point of reference is the source as involved in Schutz's distinction between subjective and objective meanings—what is created becomes externalized (objectified) as a reality outside the consciousness of the actor, and hence confronts him as phenomenon which may escape his control. The dialectic of subject and object, conceived of in these terms, represents a type of analysis that can be applied universally, but there are definite reasons, Touraine suggests, why modes of creation and control vary between different forms of society, and why action analysis should have a particular significance to industrial societies. For the advent of industrialism and secularized interpretation of the world which both precedes it and is furthered by it, allows men to free themselves from the constraints of previous ages, and to seek actively to control their destiny in ways foreign to the bounded and stable universe of traditional society.

Values, Interests and Scientific Knowledge

If Weber's methodological writings form the prop of most subsequent discussions of 'subjectivity' and 'objectivity' and 'meaning' by social scientists, they also constitute the classic point of reference for the problems of value interpretation. The famous 'Methodenstreit' is by now familiar to everyone; its much more recent successor 'Positivismusstreit' is less known outside the Germany. But some of the issues raised in the latter controversy are the same as those which were so vigorously debated over half century earlier, of course, within a rather different theoretical framework.

The contributions by Albert and Habermas represent part of the 'Positivismusstreit' debate, which had its immediate origins in the conference held by the German Sociological Association held in Tubingen in 1961 'On the Logic of Social Sciences' in which Popper presented his 27 theses on that topic. This was followed by a reply by Theodor Adorno, which however, instead of attaching Popper's stated position directly, set out an alternative one. Two anticipated confrontation between the two never got off the ground, and the 'positivism debate' really followed a subsequent intervention by Habermas in 1963, criticizing Popper's position. The aftermath was a similarly polemical paper by Hans Albert, stimulating a rejoinder from Habermas followed by a series of further interchanges between the two. The whole collections of papers, with new contributions from Adorno, were published as *The Positivist Dispute in German Sociology*. The curious thing is that the debate is, to quote Giddens, like 'Hamlet without the Prince'; for Popper insists that, not only are his 27 theses not discussed in the book, but that to call his views positivist betrays a complete misunderstanding of them (Adorno, 1970; Frisby, 1972; Popper, 1970).

Popper uses the term 'positivism' in a quite specific and precisely defined sense, whereas his opponents do not. Popper stresses:

> "I have fought against the aping of the natural sciences by the social sciences, and I have fought for the doctrine that the positivistic epistemology is inadequate even in its analysis of the natural sciences, which, in fact, are not carefully generalizing from observation as is normally believed but are essentially speculative and daring; moreover, I have taught, for more than 38 years, that all observations are theory—impregnated, and their main function is to

check and refute, rather than to prove our theories. Finally, I have not only stressed the meaningfulness of metaphysical assertions and the fact that I am myself a metaphysical realist, but I have also analyzed the important historical role played by metaphysics in the formation of scientific theories". (Popper, 1970: 262)

The main theme, however, which Adorno and Habermas wish to say, separates their standpoint from that of Popper, does not so much concern the matters referred to in the quotation, as the problem of the critical role of theory or perhaps more accurately, in their terms, the problem of the role of the critical theory. Now, once more, there are terminological difficulties here, since 'criticism' plays a fundamental part in Popper's idea as well. In opposition to those who have seen objectivity in science as resting upon some state of mind of the individual scientist confronting his subject matter, Popper treats this as possible only because of the 'public criticism' to which hypothesis are submitted, whereby they can be falsified. The process of conjecture and refutation is thus the central feature of Popper's epistemology as science (Giddens, 1974). But, this presupposes a relationship between the theory and criticism which Adorno and Habermas reject in attempting to set out their own notion of 'critical theory' particularly in a relation to the social sciences (discussed in detail in chapter on Sociology of Knowledge).

Habermas makes this clear in the article 'Rationalism Divided in Two'. His discussion, he says, is not directed towards analysing the procedures of research in natural sciences, nor even in what he calls 'behavioural-scientific sociology' but "exclusively towards the positivistic interpretation of such research processes" (Habermas, 1974: 195). Such an interpretation, according to Habermas, has the effect of closing off a whole range of problems from rational assessment, including the evaluation of the norms of scientific method itself. Habermas recognizes that Popper rejects 'empiricism'—which is actually 'positivism'—since he holds that, as it is expressed in the above quotation, "all observations are theory impregnated". What Habermas disputes are the further inferences which he believes Popper draws from this, and the unexamined nature of 'falsifiability':

"He rightly discredits every form of primary knowledge, but even mistakes can only be found to be such on the basis of criteria of

> validation. For their justifications, we must adduce arguments; but where then are we to look for these if not in precisely that dimensions—not of the origin but namely of the formation of knowledge—which has been ruled out? Otherwise the standard of falsification remains arbitrary. He assumes the epistemological independence of facts from the theories which should descriptively grasp these facts and the relations between them. Accordingly, tests examine theories against 'independent' facts. This thesis is the pivot of the positivistic problematic which Popper still retains". (ibid.: 200)

Giddens observes:

> "What Popper fails to do, according to Habermas, at least, is to reconcile the supposedly inherent 'uncertainty' of scientific information (i.e., its status never goes beyond that of 'not falsified') with the technical confidence with which it is everywhere applied in modern civilization. The 'technical-cognitive interests' which supply this confidence, and which therefore in a very significant sense determine the validation of scientific knowledge—validation in practice—remain unanalyzed in Popper's approach". (Giddens, 1974: 19)

It is over the significance of the question 'can rationalism be rationally justified'? That the views of Habermas and Adorno diverge from those of Albert and Popper. Albert seeks to attack the position adopted by Habermas in two primary respects: (i) First that Habermas himself relapses into naïve positivism at a very stage of his argument because, in stressing the role of 'technical-cognitive interests' in relation to the validation of scientific information, he confuses logical with the sociological questions in an illegitimate fashion. (ii) Secondly, that as a result of this confusion, Habermas avoids rather than solves he 'substantiation problem'. For Habermas, however, each of these points rests upon a misunderstanding. The main issue, as he sees it, escapes each of these observations. He does not wish to question the logical distinction between the genesis of ideas or theories and the mode of their revolution, nor to attempt to formulate a logical solution to the logical substantiation problem. Rather he wants to open up to rational criticism that area of analysis which he claims, since it defines the scope of reason in Popper's scheme is left purely residual—or alternatively, assumed a priority, which comes to the same thing. This is directly tied into the fact/value problem, since

Habermas wishes to disallow the separation between the 'is' and the 'ought' (ibid.: 20). Here lies the crux of Habermas' argument. Critical theory, as he conceives of it, means abandoning the idea that the parameters which define the character of scientific discourse may be identified with rational knowledge as such, and this in turn, entails the recognition that 'validation' is not limited to the technical procedures of scientific method. At this vital point in his discussion, however Habermas' exposition, never overtly transparent, slips into the sort of quasi-Hegelian murkiness which Albert rather understandably finds it difficult to penetrate (ibid.).

Giddens summarizes the substance of Habermas' position in the following lines:

> "Factual positions and value standards are not independent of one another, but are dialectically connected. Any form of evaluation of statements, regardless of whether or not they are factual in character, involves three elements—the 'descriptive', 'postulatory' and the 'critical'. Each of these presupposes the other two: the descriptive usage is in no way limited to a certain class of "facts". The postulatory usage covers the establishment of norms of standards of criteria and definitions of all types, no matter whether practical logical or methodological rules are involved. The critical usage employs arguments for considering, evaluating, judging and justifying the choice of standards … ." (Habermas, 1974: 216). Each description makes reference to standards of evaluation, and involves attitudes which are in need of justification and thus are open to criticism. When it goes beyond the sort of procedures applied in scientific method, criticism becomes the critique of ideology and seeks to evaluate historically created conditions in the context of historically generated values. It is in this latter dialectical fashion, that we can discern that science itself helped to create an outlook (positivism) which robs those who practice it of the capability of examining their own actively as ideological, i.e., in relation to the 'technical-cognitive interests' which shape it". (Giddens, 1974: 20–21)

The discussion of Husserl's work, by another Frankfurt philosopher Herbert Marcuse, is particularly interesting because it writes the theme of the limitations of scientific rationality with the phenomenological philosophy which was the proximate source of Schutz's attempt to reframe the basis of interpretative sociology.

Husserl identifies a process of the 'decomposition of reason' from the classical era up to the present age. The Greek concept of reason was founded upon a notion of the intellect as self-determining as controlling human destiny, within a universe that has an inherent rational structure; in other words, subjective or objective reasons are integrated. The consequences of this, as Marcuse presents Husserl's argument, is an identification of the real and the rational which transcends the given fact and indeed is thus set off against it; 'theoretical' and 'practical' reason are harmonized. Anthony remarks:

> "The triumph of scientific rationality, however, has dislocated science from the broader framework of ends which define the ultimate meanings of human existence. But transformation, as Marcuse puts it—'remains hidden to science itself', hidden and unquestioned. Reason looses its philosophical power and its scientific right to define and project ideas and modes of being beyond and against those established by the prevailing reality (Habermas, 1974: 229). The result is, in Habermas's terminology, the anatomy of 'technical-cognitive interests'—an apparent anatomy only, which actually legitimizes an impoverishment of human reason. Thus, here, we have almost come full circle: what seemed to Comte, and to most other 19th century thinkers, to be the highest and most complete attainment of man, in this perspective appears as a fundamental source of limitation upon the cognitive power of the human intellect". (Giddens, 1974: 21–22)

Several perspectives in sociology have attracted partisan cadres of advocates proclaiming them as candidates to replace the absolute paradigm. These include conflict theory, interaction theory, exchange theory, phenomenological and ethno-methodological theories, critical theory, neo-Marxist theory, postmodern theory, and post-structuralist theory. Each perspective emphasizes something real and significant about human interactions, but as candidate paradigms, each pretends to be more general than it is, and all would perpetuate the major flaw of the obsolete paradigm they propose to replace. They all exaggerate the autonomy of the human species. Each would perpetuate the no longer helpful aloofness of sociology from other disciplines that have crucially important things to say this changed world about the fundamental determinants of the besieged people's behaviour patterns. The present book will look into these in subsequent chapters.

References

Adorno, Theodor W., 1976, *The Positivist Dispute in German Sociology*, tr. by Blyn Adey and David Frisby, New York: Harper and Row.

Andreski, S., (ed.), 1971, *Herbert Spencer: Structure, Function and Evolution,* London: Johns Hopkins.

Aron, R., 1965, *Main Currents in Sociology Thought*, New York: Oxford University Press.

Bargstrom, G., 1969, *Too Many: A Study of the Earth's Biological Limitations*, New York: Collier-Macmillan.

Bates, M., 1955, *The Prevalence of People*, New York: Charles Scribner's Sons.

Beale, G., 1973, In Defence of Science, *New Society*, 26.

Bergstrom, G., 1972, *The Hungry Planet*, New York: Macmillan.

Booth, Charles., (ed.), 1892, *Life and Labour of the People in London*, London: Macmillan and Co.

Bowley, A.L., 1915, *The Measurement of Social Phenomena*, London: P.S. King and Son.

Brinton, C., 1950, *Ideas and Men: The Story of Western Thought*, New York: Prentice-Hall.

Brown, H., 1954, *The Challenge of Man's Future*, New York: Viking Press.

Bruyn, S., 1967, *The Human Perspective in Sociology*, New Jersey: Prentice-Hall.

Burgess, E.W. and Bogue, D.J. (eds.), 1964, *Contributions to Urban Sociology*, Chicago: University of Chicago Press.

Carneiro, R.L., (ed.), 1971, "The Evolution of Sociology", Selections from H. Spencer's *Principles of Sociology*, Chicago: University of Chicago Press.

Comte, A., 1853, *The Positivist Philosophy*, freely tr. by Harriet Martineau, 2 Vols.

Cottrell, F., 1955, *Energy and Society: The Relation between Energy, Social Change and Economic Development*, New York: McGraw-Hill Book Company, Inc.

David, Frisby, 1972, The Popper-Adorno Controversy: The Methodological Dispute in German Sociology, *Philosophy of Social Science*, Vol. 2.

Davis, K., 1959, The Myth of Functional Analysis as a Special Method in Sociology and Anthropology, *American Sociological Review*, 24: 761–69.

Day, L.H., 1964, *Too Many Americans*, Boston: Houghton Mifflin.

Dobzhansky, T., 1960, The Present Evolution of Man, *Scientific American*.

Durkheim, E., 1933, *The Division of Labour in Society*, tr. by G. Simpson, New York: Macmillan.

——, 1938, *The Rules of Sociological Method*, New York: The Free Press.

Ehrlich, P.R., 1968, *The Population Bomb*, New York: Ballantine Books.

Fallding, H., 1972, Only One Sociology, *British Journal of Sociology*, 23.

Festinger, L., 1956, *When Property Fails*, New York: Random House.

Fisher, R., 1960, *The Design of Experiments*, Edinburg: Oliver and Boyd.

Fromm, E., 1961, *Marx's Concept of Man*, New York: Frederick Ungar.

Garfinkel, Harold, 1974, "The Rational Properties of Scientific and Common Sense Activities" in A. Giddens (ed.), 1974, *Positivism and Sociology*, London: Heinemann, pp. 33–53.

Gellner, Ernest, 1974, "The New Idealism-Cause and Meaning in the Social Sciences", in A. Giddens (ed.), 1974, *Positivism and Sociology*, London: Heinemann, pp. 129–57.

Gibson, Q., 1960, *The Logic of Scientific Discovery*, London: Hutchinson.

Giddens, Anthony (ed.), 1974, *Positivism and Sociology*, London: Heinemann.

Gouldner, A.W., 1971, *The Coming Crisis of Western Sociology*, London: Heinemann.

Habermas, J., 1974, "Rationalism Divided in Two", in Giddens (ed.), 1974, *Positivism and Sociology*, London: Heinemann, pp. 195-223.

Hall, E.T., 1959, *The Silent Language*, New York: Doubleday.

Hanson, H.C. and Churchill, E.D., 1961, *The Plant Community*, New York: Reinhold Publishing Corp.

Hauser, P.M., (ed.), 1963, *The Population Dilemma*, Englewood Cliffs, N.J.: Prentice-Hall.

Hempel, C.G., 1959, "The Logic of Functional Analysis", in L. Gross (ed.), *Symposium on Sociological Theory*, New York: Harper and Row.

Hughes, Everett, 1961, Ethnocentric Sociology, *Social Forces*, 40.

Jarvie, I.C., 1965, "Limitations to Functionalism, and Alternatives to it in Anthropology", in D. Martindale (ed.), *Functionalism in the Social Sciences*, Philadelphia: American Academy of Political and Social Sciences.

Kish, L., 1959, Some Statistical Problems in Research Design, *America Sociological Review*, 24: 328–38.

Kolakowski, Leszek, 1972, *Positivist Sociology*, Harmondsworth: Penguin, pp. 15-16.

Lenski, Gerhard, 1965, *Power and Privilege*, New York: McGraw-Hill.

Madge, J. and Harrisson, T., 1939, *Britain by Mass Observation*, Harmondsworth: Penguin.

Malinowski, B., 1922, *Agronauts of the Western Pacific*, London: Routledge

Marcuse, Herbert, 1974, "On Science and Phenomenology", in A. Giddens, 1974, op. cit., pp. 225–39.

McGinnes, R., 1958, Randomization and Inference in Social Research, *American Sociological Review*, 23: 408–14.

Meadows, D.H., 1972, *The Limits of Growth*, New York: Universe Books.

Mill, J.S., 1862, *System of Logic*, New York: Harper and Bros.

Morrison, D.E. and Henkel, R.E. 1969, Significance Tests Reconsidered, *American Sociologist*, 4.

Nadel, S.F., 1957, *Theory of Social Structure*, London: Cohen & West.

Odum, E.P., 1971, *Environment, Power and Society*, New York: John Wiley.

Oosting, H.J., 1956, *The Study of Plant Communities*, 2nd ed., San Francisco: W.H. Freeman and Co.

Paddock, W. and Paddock, P., 1967, *Famine 1975*, Boston: Little, Brown and Company.

Parsons, Talcott, 1948, *The Structure of Social Action*, UK: Allen and Unwin.

Pearson, K., 1948, *Karl Pearson's Early Statistical Papers*, Cambridge: Cambridge University Press.

Popper, Karl, 1959, *The Logic of Scientific Discovery*, New York: Basic Books.

——, 1968, *Conjectures Refutations: The Growth of Scientific Knowledge*, New York: Harper and Row.

Reynaud, Jean-Daniel and Bourdieu, Pierre, 1974, "Is a Sociology of Action Possible", in Anthony Giddens (ed.), 1974, op. cit., pp. 105–15.

Rose, E.A., 1927, *Standing Room Only*, New York: The Century.

Sax, K., 1955, *Standing Room Only*, Boston: Beacon Press.

Schutz, Alfred, 1972, *The Phenomenology of the Social World*, London: Heinemann, 8.

——, 1974, "Subjective and Objective Meaning", in A. Giddens (ed.), 1974, op. cit., pp. 33-52.

Selvin, H.C., 1957, A Critique of Test of Significance in Sociological Research, *American Sociological Review*, 22.

Snow, C.P., 1969, *The State of Siege*, New York: Scribner Publication.

Spencer, H., 1904, *An Autobiography*, New York: D. Appleton.

Taylor, L.R. (ed.), 1970, *The Optimum Population for Britain*, London: Academic Press.

Thorns, David C., (ed.), 1976, *New Directions in Sociology*, New Jersey: Rowman and Littlefield.

Touraine, Alain, 1974, "The Raison d'etre of Sociology of Action", in A. Giddens (ed.), 1974, op. cit., pp. 115–29.

——, "Towards a Sociology of Action", in A. Giddens (ed.), 1974, op. cit., pp. 75–101.

Webb, E. 1966, *Unobtrusive Measures*, New York: Rand-McNally.

Weber, Max, 1949, *The Methodology of the Social Sciences*, Chicago: University of Chicago Press.

——, 1974, "Subjectivity and Determinism", in A. Giddens (ed.), 1974, op. cit., pp. 23-31.

Whelpton, P.K., 1939, Population Policy in the United States, *Journal of Heredity*, 30: 401–6.

Whyte, W.H., 1943, *Street Corner Society*, Chicago: University of Chicago Press.

Wirth, L., 1948, Urbanism as a Way of Life, *American Journal of Sociology*, XLIV, 1–24.

2

Sociology of Knowledge

A Perspective for Evaluating Positivistic Method

All the major contributors in the 19th century to the incipient sociology of knowledge were doubtful about the possibility of including natural science within its scope. This may be seen in the writings of Emile Durkheim and Karl Marx. Durkheim attempted to provide a sociological account of the genesis of man's basic categories of thought and his forms of reasoning. He argued, for instance, that ideas of time and space, force and contradiction vary from one group to another and within the same group from one period to another. For Durkheim, the existence of such cultural variation showed that our basic categories and our rules of logic depend, to some extent, on factors that are historical and consequently social (Durkheim, 1915: 12–13). This appears to make an analysis of the cognitive content of science distinctly possible, because it seems that the conclusions of every particular intellectual community will be constrained at least partly by such factors as their cultural resources, the structure of their social group and their place in the wider society. But, although Durkheim does not abandon this general position, he does modify some of its details so as to remove scientific knowledge from the analytical consideration (Mulkay, 1979).

In the first place, he takes steps to avoid a completely relativist position, in which the social origin of categories and forms of reasoning could be seen to render them wholly arbitrary so far as their application to nature is concerned.

> "From the fact that the ideas of time, space, class, cause or personality are constructed out of social elements, it is not necessary to conclude that they are devoid of all objective value. On the contrary, their social origin rather leads to the belief that they are not without foundation in the nature of things". (Durkheim, 1915: 19)

Durkheim reaches this conclusion by postulating a unity between the physical and social worlds. Thus, a group's conception of time, he suggests, will be derived from these social rhythms of its collective life. But these social rhythms will be linked to, and in a sense part of, more inclusive periodicities in the physical world. The physical and social words constitute one overall realm of natural phenomena. Accordingly, in Durkheim's view, it follows that conceptions arising out of social regularities will be applicable to parallel regularities in the physical world. However, Durkheim's argument here is extremely general. It applies equally to all human groups. It establishes, at most, only that all socially derived categories will have some, unspecified degree of objectivity. The problem remains of how to judge between divergent accounts of the physical world offered by the members of different social groups. Durkheim does not appear to recognize this difficulty explicitly. But it becomes clear in his account of social evolution that he can and does employ a more discriminating criterion of objectivity. He argues that objectivity becomes increasingly attainable as social evolution unfolds and as science replaces religion as the basis for human thought about the natural world.

> "the essential ideas of scientific logic are of religious, i.e., social origin but science gives them a new elaboration; It purges them of all accidental elements; in a general way, it brings a spirit of criticism into all its doings, which religion ignores; it surrounds itself with pre-cautions to 'escape precipitation and bias' and to hold aside the passions, prejudices and all subjective influences. Having left religion, science tends to substitute itself for this latter in all that which concerns the cognitive and intellectual functions". (Durkheim, 1915: 429)

Durkheim describes at a rather general level the social conditions which he believes are responsible for this fundamental transition in human thought. His central claim is that the growth in size of human societies and their progressive internal differentiation increasingly liberate intellectual from social constraint. Scientific thought is an outcome of this liberation and its conclusions are, therefore, comparatively unaffected by direct social influences. Religious thought about the natural world, originating in cohesive, small-scale societies, was permeated by categories and presuppositions derived from social life. But as societies become more complex and the form of social solidarity becomes less restricting, so it is increasingly possible for certain sectors of society to refine their conceptions and their techniques of observation in accordance with the actual realities of the natural world. The concepts and conclusions of science, he maintains, are increasingly adopted because they are true and not simply as is primarily the case with religious beliefs because they are collective (Durkheim, 1915: 437).

A sociological analysis of science is possible, then for Durkheim; but in a more limited form than is the case for areas of intellectual endeavours (Mulkay, 1979). In principle, we can show how certain social developments have brought about the emergence of science; we can investigate whether the scientific community has certain distinctive features which make possible the institutionalization of scientific method and the virtual elimination of bias, prejudice and intellectual distortion; and we can observe how the minority views of the scientific specialist are received by the other sections of highly differentiated societies. All this we can do, and perhaps more. But we cannot give a sociological account of scientific knowledge because, to the extent that it is truly scientific, it is independent of its social context. Genuine sciences, such as astronomy, physics and biology, are based on observable facts about the physical world. The conclusions of these sciences are derived from the facts, instead of being imposed upon them. Science represents phenomena not in terms of culturally contingent ideas, but in terms of their inherent properties (Durkheim, 1938: 35).

The Durkheim's aforesaid verdict with respect to science is relatively unambiguous. In contrast, Marx's view of science as a social phenomenon emerges in a piecemeal fashion in the course of his wide-ranging examination of consciousness, ideology and modes of production. His conclusions about science are, therefore, less clear-cut and there have been somewhat different interpretations of how far he saw social factors as determining the content of science. Consequently, it will be necessary to look briefly at two different approaches, both of which claim to be forms of Marxist analysis. There are numerous important writings on science in the Marxist tradition, which I have too little space to examine here, for example, Marcuse (1962) and Habermas (1972). I will focus on those relevant features of Marx's work about which there is little disagreement.

The history of mankind takes place within the natural setting provided by the objective world—a setting which is continuously transformed by human actions. By acting on the natural world, man produces the means of his own existence. The repetitive relationships between people, which grow out of this productive economic activity, are fundamental to all societies constituting the major influence upon their overall structures and their mental productions. In the course of acting upon the natural world, man generates knowledge about the world. This knowledge is formulated in response to the interests and economic concerns of various social groups; and is constrained by the ideological assumptions current within particular modes of production. Such knowledge is used to manipulate natural phenomena and to support, or, in certain circumstances, to transform existing social relationships (Mulkay, 1979: 5).

The growth and elaboration of scientific knowledge of the natural world was greatly stimulated by the emergence of capitalist society. The economic tasks faced by the bourgeoise in the 17th and 18th centuries drew attention to certain technological issues, which stimulated an increasingly practical approach to questions of natural philosophy on the part of the intellectual representatives of this class. In due course, the new natural philosophy began to generate practically effective scientific knowledge, which was used by the capitalist class as a direct means of economic production. As scientific knowledge improved production, so more resources were made available for the support of scientific investigation. Consequently, throughout the 19th century, science has become intimately bound up with the capitalist economy and continuous technological innovation which capitalism appears to require.

> "The bourgeoise has created massive and more colossal forces than have all preceding generations altogether. Subjection of nature's

> forces to man, machinery, application of chemistry to industry and agriculture, steam navigation, electric telegraphs what early century had even a presentiment that such productive forces slumbered in the lap of social labour?". (Marx and Engel, 1965: 47)

Thus capitalism needs and promotes "the development of the natural sciences to their highest point" (Marx, 1973: 409).

Initially, natural sciences, like capitalism itself, were liberating force, setting men free from superstition and the ideological confusions of religions thought. But, in due course, science necessarily became an exploitative resource for the bourgeoise. Particularly within the realm of industrial production, science contributed significantly to the dehumanization of man (Marx, 1974: 97). Objective scientific knowledge was increasingly used to create economic and administrative technologies which restricted narrowly the actions and initiatives available to their 'operatives' (Mulkay, 1979: 6).

> "The unity of thought and action, conception and execution, hand and mind, which capitalism threatened from its beginnings, is now attacked by a systematic dissolution employing all the resources of science and the various engineering disciplines based upon it. The subjective factor of the labour process is removed to a place among its inanimate objective factors. To the materials and instruments of production are added 'labour force,' another 'factor of production' this is the ideal towards which management uses and shapes every productive innovation furnished by science". (Braverman, 1974: 171–72)

The central theme, then, of the Marxist analysis of science is to see the latter as a social creation and to stress that its consequences, its uses and the direction in which it develops, can only be understood in relation to the wider social context (Mulkay, 1979). There are some similarities with Durkheim; science is viewed from an evolutionary perspective as being set in motion by changes in the structure of society and as undermining the effectiveness of the religions beliefs, which helped to hold together pre-capitalist social forms. But Marx goes farther than Durkheim, although by no means far enough, towards analysing the production of science in complex differentiated societies. This is possible for Marx because he avoids Durkheim's reliance on an inherently ambiguous notion of simple 'correspondence' between concepts and thought, on the one hand, and general features of 'social structure', on the other. Marx offers in addition a dynamic account of social processes which can be used to describe some of the links between science and society. In particular, he stresses that societies are composed of relatively distinct groupings, the members of which have opposing interests as well as an unequal capacity for controlling the actions of others. Consequently, the direction taken by modern science, its rapid rate of growth and the manner of its application in industry and government can be seen to have been largely determined by the technological objectives of particular dominant group, namely, bourgeoise. The bourgeoise has been the one group in capitalist society able to deploy surplus product to generate new scientific knowledge directly relevant to its own objectives.

But, what of the form and content of scientific knowledge? In the following passage, Marx seems to come close to arguing that the very laws of natural sciences are mainly a device for achieving socially contingent objectives. Under capitalism, he claims:

> "nature becomes purely an object for mankind, purely a matter of utility; ceases to be recognized as a power for itself; and the theoretical discovery of autonomous laws appears merely as a ruse so as to subjugate it under human needs, whether as an object of consumption or as a means of production". (Marx, 1973: 410; also see Mulkay, 1979)

This reading of Marx has been developed most fully within the Russian Marxist tradition. For example, in a famous paper, Boris Hessen (1931) tries to interpret Newton's 'Principia' within a Marxist framework. He presents evidence to show, first of all, that there was a close identity between the central technical problems facing the entrepreneurs of the capitalist economy during Newton's period and the major scientific problems formulated by natural philosophy at that time (Merton, 1970; Mulkay, 1979). He also tries to show that these same technical problems provided the focus of Newton's influential work. Consequently, Newton's work can be seen partly as an indirect response from the intellectuals of the bourgeoise class to difficulties arising in the course of economic production. However, the content of Newton's 'Principia' cannot be explained quite as simply as that. Although the economic factor is fundamental to materialist conception of history, this does not mean in Hessen's view that it is the sole determining influence upon any particular set of ideas. Accordingly, he attempts to complete his analysis of Newton's work by showing how Newton drew selectively upon the cultural resources available to a member of his class, for example, in the form of political, juridical, philosophical and religious beliefs, and by showing how these ideological elements influenced and limited Newton's thought.

Although Hessen strongly urges that science is not a passive contemplative acceptance of reality, but a means to effect its active reconstruction; he manages to reconcile this view with commitment to the Marxist-Leninist notion "that genuine scientific knowledge of the laws of the historical process leads with irrefutable iron necessity" to certain political conclusions (Hessen, 1931: 211). Hessen's position is not without ambiguity or irony. However, we should not intend to examine further Hessen's essay or to assess its merits and defects. It merely serves here to illustrate that Marx can be interpreted in a strong sense, i.e., as implying that the content of established scientific knowledge should be treated to a considerable extent as the outcome of specifiable social processes. On the whole, however, academic sociology has not adopted the reading of Marx. Merton, for example, having noted that Marxist analysis, allows the different spheres of mental production varying degrees of independence from the economic base, decides that Marx and Engels regard science as having a greater degree of independence than any other realm of thought. The following passage is quoted as crucial evidence for this interpretation:

> "With the change of the economic foundation the entire immense superstructure is more or less rapidly transformed. In considering such transformations the distinction should always be made between the material transformation of the economic conditions of production which can be determined with the precision of natural science, and the legal, political, religions, aesthetic or philosophic—in short, ideological forms in which men become conscious of this conflict and fight it out". (Marx, 1904: 12; Merton, 1973)

But this passage is not viewed on its own. It is interpreted in the light of what Merton regards as the overall trend in Marx's treatment of science.

> "One line of development of Marxism, from the early "German Ideology" to the latter writings of Engels, consists in a progressive definition and delimitation of the extent to which the relations of production do in fact condition knowledge and forms of thought". (Merton, 1973: 14)

Merton's final reading, therefore, is that although the focus of attention of natural science may be socially determined, this is true neither of its conceptual apparatus nor of its substantive conclusions. Marx and Engles are seen as granting science a status quite distinct from that of ideology.

It might be objected at this point that Merton is unlikely to be an accurate interpreter of Marx, given that his own theoretical frame of reference, that of functional analysis, is so different (Mulkay, 1979). Whether this is true or not, Merton's interpretation of Marx, which is also his own view, is important if only because Merton's work has exerted such a pervasive influence on the sociological analysis of science. Moreover, it is worth noting that many authors strongly committed to a Marxist analysis of science have reached similar conclusions. To illustrate this point Mulkay (1979) discusses briefly an essay by Rose and Rose (1976). These authors certainly pay more attention than does Merton to Marx's idea that science generates its own ideology. They emphasize that 'scientism' or 'positivism' has become so dominant in present-day industrial societies that any knowledge-claim which falls outside its scope is widely regarded as necessarily vacuous. They write that:

> "science becomes an ideology and scientists the ideologists. How does this work? As the material world controls the limits of an interpretation of the scientist in his own work, the answer lies, as Marx and Engels saw, outside the precise research area, where the scientist, freed from such constraints, talks pure ideology. In the name of science, invoking neutrality, technique and expertise, the scientist supports the ruling strata". (Rose and Rose, 1976: 8–9)

In this passage, the authors make a distinction between the technical knowledge-claims a scientist makes within his own research network and the claims he makes in other social contexts. They suggest that the former are normally controlled by the nature of the physical world. It must be recognized, of course, that scientists will sometimes be influenced by social pressures to purpose unjustified knowledge-claims. But, as long as there is no interference from outside with the technical criteria of adequacy applied by the research community, these socially generated claims will be judged to be inadequate by other specialists and they will be rejected. Thus, within a specific research area, those knowledge-claims which come to be accepted as valid can be seen to be non-ideological. They provide an accurate account of certain features of the physical world and their content is accordingly independent of participants' social relationships and vested interests. However, in other social contexts, the situation is quite different. Non-scientists, and indeed specialists in other areas, seldom have the technical competence to assess the adequacy of a particular scientist's claims. It follows that he will be able to use specialized knowledge so as to furnish an apparent technical rationale for policies which express his own social interests as well as the interests of other groups on whose behalf he is acting.

Claims made by scientists in the wider social context, then, will often be ideological; but this will be obscured by their technical content and by scientists' ability to invoke the objective facts of the natural world as leading inevitably to certain economic, political and social conclusions. This is the kind of analysis which is generated by Roses' Marxist approach. It is clearly different in emphasis from that of Merton and Durkheim, and directs our attention to important questions which are largely ignored by the latter. Yet the Roses' reading of Marx appears to coincide with that of Merton on one critical issue. For them, as for Merton, Marxist analysis recognizes that scientists' knowledge-claims within their precise research areas are non-ideological.

Despite important analytical differences, therefore, the writers we have examined so far, with the possible exception of Hessen, have agreed on at least the following points: (i) that science flourishes in large-scale, industrial (capitalist) societies and that within such societies, scientists create distinct communities which regulate the production of certified knowledge; (ii) that although the rate of growth, the focus of attention and the use made of scientific knowledge are in large measure socially determined, its content is independent of social influences; and (iii) thirdly, that scientific research communities are likely to have special social characteristics which reduce the impact on members' technical work of such distorting factors as bias, prejudice and irrationality, and which, are therefore, crucial in enabling scientists to generate objective knowledge. It would even be possible to bring Hessen into the fold if we were to allow a distinction to be made between the situation obtaining within the capitalist society and that characteristic of socialist societies. For, Hessen retains the notion that ineluctable laws of nature are available within the Marxist-Leninist framework. His main theme, therefore, be interpreted as a claim that Newtonian science was partly pseudo-science, distorted by the social relationships of capitalism and due to be replaced by the truly scientific and determinate formulations forthcoming within socialist society (Hessen, 1931: 211–12).

Other Variants: Mannheim and Stark

Now, it is important to examine the work of two more major contributors—Karl Mannheim and Werner Stark—to the sociology of knowledge, which will enable us to make explicit some of the philosophical assumptions which underlie the tendency to regard science as a special kind of sociological problem.

Karl Mannheim

Mannheim's sociology of knowledge includes a number of ideas taken directly from Marxism; for example, a belief in the importance of economic interests and class groupings and in the ideological character of much social thought. In the course of his work, Mannheim tried to extend the Marxist notion of the 'existential base' to cover generations, sects and occupational groups. He also supplemented the concept of 'ideology' with an associated concept of 'utopia' and provided historical documentation of the connections between thought and social factors by means of several empirical studies. But, the Marxist strain in his work was combined with elements taken from the German academic tradition of New-Kantian thought (Mannheim, 1952: 5). One of the main ideas which he adopted from this tradition was that a radical distinction had to be made between the methods and concepts of the natural sciences on the one hand and those of the social sciences and historical thought, on the other. This has been widely discussed in relation to the writings of Dilthey and others

(Outhwaite, 1975). Here Mulkay's mention of some of the points emphasized by Mannheim deserves quote. In the first place, Mannheim says, the phenomena of the material world and the relationships between them are seen as being invariant (Mannheim, 1936: 116). Mannheim regularly refers to the natural world, and to the concepts appropriate to its study, as being 'timeless and static'. Valid knowledge about such objective phenomena, he maintains, can be obtained only by detached, impartial observation, by reliance on sense data and by accurate measurement (Mannheim, 1952: 4–16; 1936: 168–69). Because the empirical relationships of the natural world are unchanging and universal, the criteria of truth by which knowledge-claims are to be judged are also permanent and uniform (1936: 168). It follows that natural science develops in a relatively straight line, as errors are eliminated and a growing number of truths are discerned. In short, scientific knowledge evolves through the gradual accumulation of permanently valid conclusions about a stable physical world.

Cultural products, however, cannot be investigated properly by methods of detached observation or by means of static concepts. For correct categorization and understanding of cultural phenomena necessarily involves the interpretation of participants' meanings; and meanings cannot be simply observed like objects in the external world. Each historical period and each social group has its own distinctive values and meanings. Each analyst begins from his own culturally specific framework of meanings. Accordingly, no product of human culture can be analysed adequately from a timeless perspective. The interpretation of meanings is essentially dynamic. It must deal with the unique features of each cultural epoch and must be undertaken anew by the representatives of every succeeding historical period (Mannheim, 1952: 61). Moreover, there can be no such thing as detached uniform observation of cultural products. Their meaning must be acquired, instead, by means of involvement and sympathetic understanding (Mannheim, 1936, 1970).

In accordance with this characterization of the sciences and the contrasting cultural disciplines, Mannheim continually treats the advanced physical sciences as a special case from the perspectives of the sociology of knowledge:

> "Are the existential factors in the social process merely of peripheral significance or do they penetrate into the perspective of concrete

> particular assertions? The historical and social genesis of an idea would only be irrelevant to its ultimate validity if the temporal and social conditions of its emergence had no effect on its content and form. If this were the case, any two periods in the history of human knowledge would only be distinguished from one another by the fact that in the earlier period certain things were still unknown and certain errors still existed which, through later knowledge were completely corrected. This simple relationship may to a large extent be appropriate for the exact sciences". (1936: 271)

In the light of several statements of this kind and in view of the importance for the whole of Mannheim's thought on the distinction between natural science and socio-historical thought, virtually, all interpreters have regarded him as being entirely consistent and unambiguous in treating scientific knowledge as beyond the scope of sociological analysis (Mannheim, 1952: 29; Merton, 1973: 21; Bloor, 1976: 8). However, if we read Mannheim with particular care, we will observe that, on at least a few occasions, he seems to become weaker on this point. For example, he follows the quotation given immediately above with the following qualification: "although indeed today the notion of the stability of the categorical structure of the exact sciences is, compared with the logic of classical physics, considerably shaken" (Mannheim, 1936: 271). In this passage, Mannheim seems to be questioning his own characterization of scientific knowledge as timeless and immutable. His uncertainty on this point becomes most noticeable when he is dealing with epistemological issues and he finally offers a resolution of the problem in epistemological terms (Mulkay, 1979: 12).

The basic epistemological problem faced by Mannheim, as well as by Durkheim, is that of relativity. The sociology of knowledge asserts that all 'social thought', i.e., all thought outside the exact sciences, is relative to a particular social position or undertaken from a particular perspective or formulated in accordance with certain social interests. Thus, in this sphere, there appear to be no generally applicable criteria for judging the validity of any specific assertion. But, clearly, the sociology of knowledge is itself part of this intellectual domain. Therefore, it seems to follow that there is no way of assessing the validity of its own claims—including the central claim that all social knowledge is existentially determined. Mannheim, of course, wishes to reject this conclusion and he tries to show that the assertions of the cultural sciences, although different in kind from those of the exact sciences, can still furnish true knowledge. In seeking to establish this point, Mannheim is almost, but not quite, led to revise his epistemological assumptions about the natural sciences.

Mannheim does not abandon science entirely as a subject for sociological investigation and in a few pages of *Ideology and Utopia* he interprets the rise of science broadly along Marxist lines (1936: 165–69). He argues that the methodology adopted by the advanced sciences was a by-product of the *Weltanschauung* of the ascendant bourgeoise. The worldview of this class, which he describes as 'democratic cosmopolitanism', denied the value of personal, qualitative 'knowledge'. Only formulations which were universally valid and necessary were allowed to stand as genuine knowledge.

> "Similarly, every kind of knowledge which only certain specific historical social groups could acquire was distrusted. Only that kind of knowledge was wanted which was free from all the influences of the subject's *Weltanschauung*. What was not noticed was that world of the purely quantifiable and analyzable was itself only discoverable on the basis of a definite *Weltanschauung*. Similarly, it was not noticed that a *Weltanschauung* is not of necessity a source of error, but often gives access to spheres of knowledge otherwise closed". (Mannheim, 1936: 168)

As the bourgeoise achieved positions of social and political pre-eminence, so scientific knowledge and its associated epistemology came to pervade and to dominate intellectual life. Consequently, Mannheim maintains, virtually all knowledge-claims have come to be measured against the particular epistemology derived from the dominant form of scientific knowledge.

> "The particularity of the theory of knowledge holding sway today is now clearly demonstrable by the fact that the natural sciences have been selected as the ideal to which all knowledge should aspire. It is only because natural science, especially in its quantifiable phases, is largely detachable from the historical-social perspective of the investigator that the ideal of true knowledge was so construed that all attempts to attain a type of knowledge arriving at the comprehension of quality are considered as methods of inferior value". (1936: 290–91)

In response to this situation, Mannheim tries to formulate an alternative epistemology which is appropriate for qualitative, existentially determined knowledge and which is in accordance with the conclusion of his own version of the sociology of knowledge.

In Mannheim's view, the sociology of knowledge has shown that the positivist epistemology of bourgeoise society is itself partial and the product of a particular, limited *Weltanschauung*. This epistemology is therefore inadequate in the sense that it fails to recognize its own limitations and its own dependence on historically specific assumptions. Accordingly, its application must be confined in future to the special realm of knowledge about the physical world, to which alone it is appropriate, and it must be supplemented by a broader epistemology which recognizes the partial character of all human perspectives. It has become possible for us today, in a way which was impossible before the advent of the sociology of knowledge to treat situationally detached knowledge as a marginal and special case of the situationally conditioned. From this epistemological position one assumes "the inherently relational structure of human knowledge (just as the essentially perspectivistic nature of visually perceived objects is admitted without question). It is not intended to assert that objects do not exist or that reliance upon observation is useless and futile but rather that the answers we get to the questions we put to the subject matter are, in certain cases, in the nature of things, possible only within the limits of the observer's perspective" (1936: 300). This does not mean that we are abandoning the notion of 'objectivity' or the possibility of establishing 'facts'. Rather it means that our conception of objectivity has to change (Mulkay, 1979: 14).

There is no need to deny that people can often reach what they take to be 'objective' conclusions about particular phenomena, i.e., conclusions, which are verifiable by the application of established procedures. Yet epistemologically these objective conclusions must be regarded as incomplete, as the product of a specific perspective and as open to revision in new social situations where other perspectives are brought to bear. In the case of different observers working within a common frame of reference, objectivity must be conceived as the application of agreed criteria of adequacy to particular knowledge-claims (1936: 300–1). When participates have different perspectives, however, objectivity can only be attained in 'a more roundabout fashion'. Mannheim continues to treat objectivity as being indistinguishable from intellectual agreement, but argues that the latter will be possible only in so far as the results of each perspective are translated into the other and reconciled, usually at a more general level. This notion of divergent frames of reference becomes central to his new epistemology. Mannheim writes of two alternative versions of his theory of knowledge, but both versions depend on this principle of resolving the differences of specific perspectives within a more comprehensive formulation. Where some choice has to be made between perspectives, pre-eminence is given to that "which gives evidence of the greatest comprehensiveness and the greatest fruitfulness in dealing with empirical materials" (1936: 301). Thus, the old static epistemological conception of true statements corresponding to the realities of a directly observable world has been abandoned for most realms of thought and perhaps for thought in its entirety.

> "We will have to reckon with situational determination as an inherent factor in knowledge, as well as with the theory of relationism and the theory of the changing basis of thought. We must reject the notion that there is a 'sphere of truth in itself' as a disruptive and unjustifiable hypothesis. It is instructive to note that the natural sciences seem to be, in many respects, in a clearly analogous situation". (1936: 305)

This last sentence brings us back to the 'marginal, special case' of science. It is followed in Mannheim's text by a single page discussing certain developments in modern physics which were then quite recent. The point of the discussion is to show that the established certainties of classical physics appeared at that time to be giving way to a much more 'relativist' framework of ideas. Mannheim notes that in quantum mechanics, it had come to be regarded as impossible to conceive of measurements independently of the actions and techniques involved in measuring. He points out that empirical relationships at the sub-atomic level were thought to be inherently indeterminate and that traditional notions about particles having a specific location and a definite and ascertainable trajectory of movement had now been abandoned. And, of course, he mentions Einstein's theory of relativity and the way in which it brought the position of the observer into the very equations of physics (1936: 305–06).

Mannheim suggests that this trend of thought in natural science is, in its 'unformulated relationisms', surprisingly similar to his own. At this point in the argument it seems possible that Mannheim will be led to reject his previous neo-Kantian portrayal of scientific knowledge as composed of universal and static truths. It seems possible that he will go on to claim that knowledge of the physical world, like that of the social, depends on the kinds of questions that we pose, on the purposes of the knowers and on their socially derived perspectives. There would be no epistemological inconsistency for Mannheim in adopting this position. For his relational epistemology provides for the 'objectivity' of socially derived knowledge-claims; and it is no less convincing to claim that active commitment to a partial perspective will reveal truth about the physical world than it is to make the same claim regarding the social world. Furthermore, this line of reasoning would have enabled Mannheim to avoid treating one major area of knowledge as a partial exception to his general epistemological principles and it would have enabled him to undertake a sociological analysis of that recent and puzzling transformation in modern physics (Mulkay, 1979: 15-16).

Yet, despite these potential advantages, Mannheim draws back from the conclusion that scientific knowledge is in any way socially contingent. He does not take the decisive step of claiming that his alternative epistemology fits the physical sciences in exactly the same way as it does the historical disciplines. He is careful to state that the two realms are no more than analogous. Their appropriate epistemologies are parallel but distinct. The relationism of physical science is best seen as a special case of the general principle of relationism. What he seems to mean by this that whereas the knowledge available to observers in the socio-historical sphere is necessarily related to their social position, cultural background, group interests and so on, the knowledge attainable by observers of the physical world is necessarily constrained only by their position in time and space. Thus, Mannheim reaches a final position from which both types of knowledge are seen as inherently limited and revisable; but he maintains the distinction between the two spheres by claiming that the limitations or constraints essential to each intellectual domain are quite different in character.

Mannheim conclusively has done three things in his discussion of epistemology: (a) He has tried to restrict the scope of the positivist epistemology to the sphere of natural science. (b) He has tried to outline an alternative relational epistemology for socio-historical existentially determined thought. (c) He has raised the possibility that the old epistemology is not even entirely adequate for the advanced physical sciences. But he has resolved his doubts about the status of scientific knowledge without seriously challenging the orthodox epistemology and consequently, without opening the door for a full-fledged sociology of science (Mulkay, 1979: 16). One reason why Mannheim went no further in this direction may well have been that he was entirely dependent on the work of historians of science for his own views about scientific development. Therefore, he had to wait for suitable studies in the history of ideas to emerge, and these studies did not come until long after his death. But, in addition, there is the fact that so much of Mannheim's thought was formulated in terms of the epistemological distinction between scientific and socio-historical knowledge.

W. Stark

Mulkay (1979) has suggested that some passages in Mannheim's writings contain the term of a new philosophical view of science—one more favourable than the standard view to the possibility of a sociological approach to scientific knowledge. But these passages have generally been missed or they have been interpreted so as to make them entirely consistent with Mannheim's more frequently expressed idea that science constitutes a special epistemological and hence sociological case. Since Mannheim, this latter view has to become firmly entrenched in the sociology of knowledge. This is well exemplified in the writings of Werner Stark which appeared 20 years or so after the publication of *Ideology and Utopia* (Mannheim, 1936). In Stark's account of the sociology of knowledge, there is no longer any questioning of the status of scientific knowledge. Mannheim's epistemological reservations have been forgotten and arguments, which remained largely implicit in Mannheim, are marshalled clearly and explicitly by Stark to exclude science from sociological consideration.

Stark begins by stating what he regards as a necessary assumption about the physical world is that it has a fundamental permanence. There is inherent in the natural world, he suggests, a determinate state of affairs which scientists can observe and represent with increasing accuracy and completeness. Because physical scientists can achieve an abiding correspondence between an invariant nature and their own formulations, they are able to establish their distinctive degree of intellectual consensus. Scientific consensus is a product of the objectivity of scientific knowledge. This situation, however, does not apply in so-called sciences. Like Mannheim, Stark believes that there is a fundamental difference between those concerned with society. The facts of society are made, and ever re-made by us, whereas the facts of nature are not. They are data in a more stringent meaning of the term (Stark, 1958: 165).

The second major contention in Stark's analysis seems initially to be slightly at odds with the first. For having maintained that there is a straightforward, unproblematic correspondence between true scientific knowledge and invariant natural phenomena, he suggests that another reason why knowledge of the physical world is cumulative and reliable is that such knowledge is always formulated within a perspective organized in terms of technical efficiency.

> "Whereas man has more than once shifted his vantage point for the consideration of social facts so that these facts appear to him in ever new, and often surprising, outlines, he has always kept to the same spot for surveying the facts of nature ... so that latter facts have always offered to him the self-same surface. He has merely learned to look more closely. Whether he likes it or not, he must, under all circumstances, pursue, among others, the economic and technological values, the value of science". (1958: 166)

The dependence of scientific knowledge on a particular perspective on, or attitude towards, the natural world appears at first sight to weaken the belief in the certainty and definitive character of that knowledge. Scientific knowledge seems to have become to some extent socially contingent. But Stark resolves this problem by postulating that the central value guiding man's attempts to understand the natural world has necessarily always been the same. Not only have men always sought to understand nature in order to exert control over natural processes but, in Stark's view, there is no alternative stance available to them. Thus, the factual content of science is beyond the scope of sociological inquiry because it is universal. It is the product of the cumulative application of a uniform perspective to determine natural world (Mulkay, 1979: 18).

Stark maintains that there is 'cause for rejoicing' in the fact that the main movements in the sociology of knowledge have agreed in all essentials with his characterization of science (1958: 167), and he quotes such diverse authors as Marx, Lukacs, Mannheim, Alfred Weber and Merton to illustrate this agreement. This is clear from the discussion above that there has been less certainty among sociologists of knowledge about the nature of science than Stark seems to imply. Nevertheless, Mulkay thinks that he is substantially correct if he is taken to mean that most writers in this field have operated within the limits of single, standard philosophy of scientific knowledge. It is largely because sociologists of knowledge have been unable to offer a serious alternative to the standard epistemological view of science that they have been propelled into a position from which scientific knowledge and the intellectual activities of scientists have to be treated with special deference (Agassi, 1963: 1–23).

Both Mannheim and Stark began their attempts to establish the distinctive character of scientific knowledge with a statement of what has been called the 'principle of the uniformity of nature'. They maintained that the phenomena and relationships of the material world differ from those of the social world in being invariant and stable. In their view, this is substantiated by the fact that the basic conclusions of physical science, its laws of nature, are always and everywhere the same. Although the principle of uniformity was regarded by these sociologists of knowledge as a 'necessary and crucial assumption' in any attempt to understand the nature of science, it has attracted little attention in the debates which provide material for our analysis. Fortunately, however, the principle has been examined rather carefully by Hanson (1969). He shows that its use in the sociology of knowledge has been based on a misunderstanding and that it is a shaky foundation on which to build one's sociological endeavours.

Hanson asks the questions: How do we obtain the knowledge that nature is regular, uniform and constant? How do we know that the principle of uniformity is true? There are only two ways in which its truth could be established, he suggests, either by formal or by empirical means. Clearly, the principle of uniformity is not intended as a mere formalism. It is meant to convey something factual about the material world. Consequently, the principle of uniformity must be established empirically. But if this is so, we are faced with a vicious circle. For, if the principle is true, it must be presupposing in every empirical procedure—including that by which we hope to prove the truth of the principle itself. If the principle is not assumed, we cannot establish its validity by generalizing from empirical evidence. Unless the principle is assumed to operate, there is no way in which we can infer it from particular observations.

> "Hence, to gain knowledge of the truth of these principles by experiment and observation is to presupposing in the search the very existence of that for which we are in search. If the principles are true, we cannot learn of it empirically for the essence of the principles is that their truth is presupposed in every empirical enquiry". (1969: 408)

Hanson goes on to show with various specific examples that the principle of uniformity is vacuous in the sense that it makes no definite assertion at all. It seems that modern philosophical analysis reveals the principle of uniformity to be no more than a rather misleading formulation of what is meant by the term 'law of nature'. The principle of uniformly is not an aspect of the natural world but rather an aspect of scientist's methods for constructing their accounts of that world. It cannot be used, therefore, as grounds for treating the generalization of natural science as definitive representations of a stable and uniform physical reality.

Fact and Theory

Belief in the inherent stability and uniformity of the physical world has often been linked to a particular view of the relationship between fact and theory in science. From this orthodox position it is assumed that certain objects and processes exist in the physical world, that certain events occur consistently and that certain stable relationships persist: these objects, processes, events and relationships constitute the facts which science has to describe accurately and explain convincingly. This is the argument of Mulkay and for the purposes of his argument, there is no need systematically to distinguish particular facts and specific observations from general relationships, between observable phenomena and the empirical generalizations which express such relationships. These facts are seen as being theoretically neutral. Therefore, they can be expressed in a language which is independent of theory and formulated in a way which simply represents the observable realities of the physical world. Once firmly established, facts remain unaffected by interpretative advances. Indeed, as long as there have been no observational errors, they can undergo no change of content or meaning and they can be used, therefore, to discriminate objectively between theoretical alternatives.

It is accepted, of course, that successful theories usually generate new observations and new facts about the physical world. However, once such facts have been properly confirmed, they are thought to acquire an intellectual autonomy which enables them to remain unaffected even by the wholesale refutation of the analytical scheme which gave them birth.

> "an experimental law, unlike a theoretical statement, invariably possesses a determinate empirical content which in principle can always be controlled by observational evidence ... even when an experimental law is explained by a given theory and is thus incorporated into the framework of the latter's ideas ... two characteristics continue to hold for the law. It retains a meaning that can be formulated independently of the theory, and it is based on observational evidence that may enable the law to survive the eventual demise of the theory". (Nagel, 1961: 83–86)

This two-tier view of scientific knowledge, taken for granted by most sociologists of knowledge, has given rise to a number of intractable philosophical difficulties. In seeking to resolve these difficulties philosophers have gradually evolved a new account of the relationship between fact and theory which has major implications for the scope of sociological analysis.

It has sometimes been maintained that when we conceive of scientific knowledge as composed of separate theoretical and factual prepositions, we are making use of a distinction between observable objects and unobservable or theoretical objects. Factual prepositions deal with the relations between observable objects, which are explained by statements involving such unobservable objects as electrons, quarks and genes. The nature of observable objects is ascertainable by direct experience and, assuming that proper experimental precautions are taken, can be established with great confidence. But, the character of theoretical objects is known only indirectly and must, therefore, be treated as inherently speculative. Theoretical objects are perhaps no more than convenient fictions. Electrons, for example, are to be regarded as hypothetical constructions derived from our experiences with real objects like cathode ray tubes and galvanometers. Accordingly, the notion of "electron can be abandoned if it proves unfruitful in the long run or incompatible with newly observed facts; and the propositions in which it features can be recast. In contrast, we can hardly deny the existence of such objects as cathode ray tubes or galvanometers; and our direct knowledge of these objects, although it can always be made more precise, is not open to doubt or repudiation to anything like the same extent".

Although this argument makes a plausible appeal to common sense it is certainly incomplete. For example, it deals only with objects and fails to cover the referents of scientific concepts concerned with relationships or processes. But, more important, there are also strong reasons for the distinction between observable and unobservable objects as untenable. The central assumption is that we can distinguish unambiguously between observing an object directly and merely inferring its characteristics from its effects. But seeing an object directly is thought to involve photons moving from the object in question and impinging on the retina of the observer. As soon as we think in their terms, the notion of 'direct observation' starts to lose its clarity and thereby its usefulness in separating fact from theory. The vagueness of the distinction is also highlighted by considering how little is the difference between seeing directly and observing with a magnifying glass, and between the latter and using a small telescope (Smart, 1973). Yet we are required by this thesis to regard the objects revealed by the telescope as different in kind from those visible to the naked eye. Furthermore, we cannot avoid the problem simply by classifying 'seeing through a telescope' as direct observation. For we are then faced with such anomalies as the failure of those scholastics who peered through Galileo's telescope to see the objects which were so obvious to the disciples of Copernicus. No clear distinction has been made between observable and unobservable objects; and consequently the distinction cannot be used to strengthen the two-tier or standard view of scientific knowledge (Mulkay, 1979: 31).

> "If observability is merely a matter of degree, then there seems to be no plausible way of drawing a sharp line on this basis between objects which do and objects which do not exist. Under the

influence of these considerations, most philosophers have given up the attempt to distinguish observable from unobservable on this basis and focus instead on the terminological distinction". (Grandy, 1973: 3)

Now, therefore, we focus on the question of whether a difference can be established between theoretical and observational terms.

The debate about the nature of scientific terms has been concerned particularly with the meaning of theoretical concepts. The central problem has arisen as a consequence of taking factual statements as unproblematic except in the 'trivial' sense of depending on careful, accurate observation and as conceptually distinct from those of theory. Thus, if statements of fact are independent of scientific theories and can be used as a neutral check upon them, and if theoretical propositions go beyond the established facts, what reference in the real world can be attributed to theoretical claims and the terms in which they are formulated? For instance, if the factual statements of geneticists about the colours of successive generations of sweet peas are quite separate from theoretical propositions about genes, about which we can obtain no direct evidence, can the latter claims be said to have scientific meaning? Furthermore, if the statements in which terms like 'gene' occur have no meaning, if they are not synthetic propositions, how can we maintain that they are true or false? And, if theoretical claims are neither true nor false, they can hardly be regarded as furnishing valid knowledge.

There is some overlap between this conception of the problem and that which seeks to distinguish between kinds of scientific objects. This second formulation, however, points in a more promising direction. Whilst it appears that theoretical terms do not correspond to a special type of entity and that theoretical concepts seem to have a different kind of meaning from those used to report observations, it cannot be denied that the use of theoretical terms is peculiarly characteristic of science and that they must therefore be meaningful in some way (Mulkay, 1979: 31-32).

One response to this problem is to accept that scientific theories have no direct meaning and to regard them simply as formal systems. Theoretical terms come to be seen, therefore, merely as logical devices for deriving new observational statements from established facts and as acquiring 'indirect meaning' through their linkage with factual statements (Carnap, 1939). But this answer raises further difficulties. In the first place, it is difficult to reconcile the relatively trivial role assigned to theory by this interpretation with the fact that theoretical work is regarded as of fundamental importance by practising researchers and the fact that theorists receive by far the greatest honour and respect among scientists (Hagstrom, 1965). Thus, this attempt to describe the structure of scientific knowledge, although, succeeds in portraying its factual basis in a way which supports the standard view of science, does so at the cost of treating its theoretical component as largely redundant and of implying that scientists themselves are generally mistaken about the relative value of the contributions to knowledge made by theorists and observers. Clearly, an account of scientific knowledge which made sense of scientists' own high regard for theory would be preferable.

A move in this direction was made with the recognition that it was in practice extremely difficult to distinguish observational terms, whose meaning was 'derived from experience', from speculative theoretical terms. For instance, there seems little point in insisting that they are two meanings of the term 'mass': one observable (as in the observed mass of a volume of gas) and one theoretical (as in the mass of the constituent molecules, which are individually unobservable yet which in sum determine the observable mass). Accordingly, it has increasingly come to be accepted that the distinction is arbitrary and as inherently ambiguous as that between observable and unobservable objects (Carnap, 1966). One major reason why it has proved so difficult to separate observational from theoretical terms is that terms seem to acquire their meaning, not as isolated units which in the case of observational terms can be referred to corresponding physical entities, but as elements within wider linguistic frameworks (Mulkay, 1979: 32).

> "It is not correct to speak, as is often done, of the experiential 'meaning' of a term or a sentence is isolation. In the language of science, and for similar reasons even in pre-scientific discourse, a single statement usually has no experiential implications. A single sentence in a scientific theory does not, as a rule, entail any observation sentences; consequences asserting the occurrence of certain observable phenomena can be derived from it only by conjoining it

> with a set of other, subsidiary, hypotheses. On the latter, some will usually be observation sentences, and others will be previously accepted theoretical statements. Thus, for example, the relativistic theory of the deflection of light rays in the gravitational field of the sun entails assertions about observable phenomena only if it is conjoined with a considerable body of astronomical and optical theory as well as a large number of specific statements about the instruments used in those observations of solar eclipses which serve to test the hypothesis in question". (Hempel, 1965: 112)

If this is so, and if observational terms have no experiential meaning apart from their location in a broader conceptual and propositional scheme, it is simply impossible to identify a separate class of factual statements constituting the bedrock on which scientific knowledge is built.

The way in which particular observational terms acquire their meaning from a cluster of associated propositions and concept has been made especially clear by Hesse (1974). She begins with the assumption that every physical situation is indefinitely complex. Each new situation is in detail different from each other. This leads to a loss of information in every application of observational terms, which leaves room for changes in classification to take place under certain circumstances. Many of the observational categories used in science, as well as in everyday life, are learned in complete empirical contexts, where a direct association is established between selected aspects of the situation and a certain term. But complete fluency in the use of descriptive terms is not obtained by means of direct association alone. Learning a language also involves learning certain generalizations or 'laws' containing its terms. These laws are always linked together in symbolic networks. Knowledge of the laws and networks is required in order to identify proper occasions for the use of a physical predicate; such knowledge enables the user to apply the terms 'correctly' in situations other than those in which they were learned initially (Mulkay, 1979: 32).

For example, a person may learn to observe and identify the planet—Venus—partly by means of the 'law' that "stars twinkle in the night sky but planets do not". The law can then be used as a resource for observing other planets and may lead to the 'correct' identification of Mars and so on. Of course, in applying this 'law', a newcomer may make what is regarded by a more experienced observer as a mistake. He may think that he is observing a planet, when what he is 'really' seeing is a star. If the more experienced observer wishes to correct the mistake, he may merely suggest that if his companion looks more carefully he will see that the celestial object in question is actually twinkling. But if his companion is not convinced thus easily, it may be necessary for the experienced observer to draw extensively upon his knowledge of astronomical parallax, upon theories of gravitation and optical transmission, and so on, in order to show that the object simply cannot be another planet for as it were, the whole science of celestial mechanics would be overturned. The logic of this procedure is to take the current knowledge system and its laws as given and explicitly to decide what it is we are observing in the light of the requirements of the system. Thus, the meaning of the observational term 'planet' is derived from its use within a network of related terms and propositions, and is not established simply by direct reference to a series of isolated empirical instances which can be identified independently of this cluster of interpretative resources. As Hesse (1974) herself emphasizes, this account of scientific knowledge involves a far-reaching reinterpretation of the theory/observation distinction.

There are considerable implications for the standard view of science in this abandonment of the orthodox distinction between theoretical and observational terms. In the first place, if all terms obtain their meaning through their location in a framework of concepts and propositions, then it seems that no statement of the fact is theoretically neutral. Scientists do not have access to independent findings against which to check theoretical alternatives. They can never step entirely outside their own analytical scheme, for to do so would deprive their concepts and their propositions of meaning. Thus, all empirical statements are 'theory-laden' (Ryle, 1949). Furthermore, it follows that, in so far as the analytical framework alters, so does the meaning of observation statements (whether particular findings or empirical generalizations) formulated within its frame of reference.

> "no feature in the total landscape of functioning of a descriptive predicate is exempt from modification under pressure from its surroundings. That any empirical law may be abandoned in the face of counter examples is trite, but it becomes less trite when the

> functioning of every predicate is found to depend essentially on some laws or other and when it is also the case that any 'correct' situation of application may become incorrect in order to preserve a system of laws and other applications. It is in this sense that I shall understand the theory dependence or 'theory ladenness' of all descriptive predicates". (Hesse, 1974: 11)

We appear, then, to have reached a conclusion which rejects two basic assumptions of the standard view of science, that is, we have concluded that the factual claims of science are neither independent of theory nor stable in meaning. Even when the symbols on the page of a scientific textbook remain unchanged over a fairly long period, the meaning in the eyes of the research community may well be in continual flux as the interpretative context of research evolves. In addition, it follows that the meaning of given factual statements will often differ for different sections of the scientific community; for instance, for researchers as against school teachers and for members of separate specialties, depending on how far these social groupings operate with divergent interpretative frameworks. Thus, not only is the factual 'basis' of science theory – dependent and revisable in meaning, but it also appears to be socially variable (Mulkay, 1979: 35).

The revised perspective on the relations between fact and theory has several strong interpretations (Feyerabend, 1975), as well as numerous weaker versions (Scheffler, 1963). Before we discuss in more detail the characteristics of these strong and weak versions, we would like to focus on the ways in which linguistic frameworks may affect the formulation of factual propositions. There is an influential empiricist tradition which treats facts as things or events out there to be observed and appropriately described. Thus, facts are thought to exist, even though we may not have words with which to express them. In order to appreciate the limitations of this view, it is useful to ask, as Hanson (1969) does: what do the facts 'out there' look or sound or feel like? Could one photograph fact? It is evident that a photograph, no matter how clearly focused, cannot present us with facts until we begin to select from it certain elements and to formulate them in linguistic form. The argument here parallels that taken from Hesse above. The facts represented in the photographs are those features which can be so expressed (Strawson, 1959) ; and what can be so expressed depends on the linguistic and other symbolic resources available. In other words, the nature of our language will tend to favour certain kinds of statement, whilst prohibiting others. Some of the work in cognitive anthropology is worth considering here (Frake, 1961; Hoijer, 1964). This argument is as applicable to the vocabularies of science as to any other language system. Hanson says:

> "Our types of notation in physics may occasionally render us insensitive to features of material world. I am not saying that there are aspects of protozoa, and subatomic entities that elude description in the languages available to us. My point is only that it is not logically impossible that there might be. And if this point is sound we can see that it is not logically impossible that we might have come to think about the physical world very differently from the way we actually think. Given the same physical world we might have come to speak of it differently. In other words, the logical and grammatical traits of our several scientific languages, notations and symbol—clusters may affect how we see the world, or what we understand to be the facts about the world". (1969: 182–83)

Hanson stresses that it is impossible to demonstrate this thesis other than logically. For it follows from the thesis itself that one cannot prove it empirically by presenting a fact which is beyond the scope of our linguistic resources. It should also be noted that no claim is being advanced that linguistic frameworks alone determine the content of factual statements. As Scheffler (1967) points out, scientists using an identical, conceptual scheme can perfectly well formulate contradictory hypotheses. Nevertheless, it is clear that linguistic frameworks in science usually devised in conjunction with substantive models or interpretations (Bohm, 1965); and that the latter do influence the content of factual statement in a fairly direct manner.

> "It follows that although the same categorization allows the expression of alternative hypothesis, these hypotheses will nevertheless confer alternative meanings on the categorization in question. If I can indeed formulate the denial of my hypothesis in terms of categorization by which it is expressed, I cannot accept such denial without altering the very meaning of this categorization, for such acceptance effects a change in my language system". (Scheffler, 1967: 46)

Although linguistic frameworks are necessary for the statement of facts, they give no hold on the external world until they are used to formulate some positive account of certain facets of that world. Only when this has been done, can the observer attribute significance to his observations and thereby state them as meaningful propositions (Mulkay, 1979: 36). This is nicely illustrated by Darwin's failure to recognize that one of his experiments had revealed what would now be seen as an important empirical regularity.

> "Having crossed snapdragons and produced hybrid varieties, Darwin found what he called 'prepotency' and what Mendel called 'dominance' in the first generation offspring. What is more he obtained both parental types in the second generation of hybrids, actually counted the number of each kind, and found 88 of the prepotent type, and 37 of the other. This result is not significantly different from a Mendelian 3:1 ratio, but Darwin did not know how to attribute meaning to it". (Glass, 1953: 152)

Mendel himself was able to transform similar findings into a statement of empirical regularity, at least partly because he had clear expectation in mind which enabled him to regard the approximate numbers occurring in actual experiments as crude expressions of an idealized theoretical relationship (Fisher, 1936).

The aforesaid distinctions have focused on the fact that the traditional distinctions between observable and unobservable entities, and between factual and theoretical statements, are impossible to maintain without considerable qualification. The most we can do is to distinguish roughly between propositions which are closer to particular evidence and those which are used in a more general sense. But all factual claims, whether very specific statements or relatively general propositions, are theory-laden. Technical terms and the more commonsense terms and propositions, which scientists regularly use, acquire their scientific meaning from the linguistic, theoretical and perhaps social context in which they are embedded. The meaning of scientific observational categories and factual claims must be conceived in terms of the position they occupy in a theory. Every fact is a fact for or against theory (Hanson, 1969: 216–17). This interpretation of the relationship between fact and theory in science unlike the standard view has the advantage of being consistent with the great importance that scientists themselves attach to theoretical work. It also has major implications for the sociology of knowledge as Nagel and others have noted:

> "The import of every observation statement is therefore determined by some theory that is accepted by the investigator so that the adequacy of a theory cannot be judged in the light of the theory-neutral observation statements. Accordingly, if these claims are sound, they apparently lead to a far-reaching 'relativism of knowledge', to a scepticism concerning the possibility of achieving warranted knowledge of nature that is much more radical than the relativism associated with the views of Karl Mannheim and other sociologists of knowledge". (1971: 18)

It is hardly surprising, therefore, that this account of scientific knowledge, certainly in its stronger forms, generates philosophical difficulties similar to those faced by Mannheim.

First, in some versions, scientific knowledge comes close to appearing empirically vacuous. The idea that factual reports are formulated in terms of their associated theoretical or metaphysical presuppositions seems to imply that each theory can only be tested in its own terms, yet that within its own terms it is immune from refutation. Any particular observation will have no meaning until it has been theoretically interpreted. However, the meaning supplied by the theory can only serve to confirm that theory. It seems only too easy to dismiss any observation which appears to depart from expectation by asserting, perhaps in a more refined form, that: "if it departs from expectation, then it is either an incorrect observation or it is an observation of the wrong type" (Mulkay, 1979: 38). Within this view of science, although an analytical framework may generate such severe internal inconsistencies that its adherents adopt some alternative scheme, it can never be unequivocally refuted by means of empirical evidence (Kuhn, 1962; Lakatos, 1970).

In addition, there is the related problem of 'incommensurability'. If the meaning of scientific terms and propositions depends on the whole belief system within which they are presented, then, it is different to see how any two theories can be regarded as rivals or their factual claims as incompatible. Scientists working within different schemes will be investigating different worlds; and although their statements may sometimes appear superficially to be identical when taken in isolation, their meaning within divergent frames of reference will not actually be the same. Furthermore, genuine communication will be possible only among those who share a common framework, within which given statements are understood in the same way. Kuhn (1962) has argued that these interpretative frameworks are community-based and that inability to communicate effectively is experienced only intermittently, whenever a research community's paradigm disintegrates under the pressure of internally generated inconsistencies. It is, however, just as plausible to argue that each individual scientist develops a unique perspective on his research area (Ravetz, 1971; Gilbert, 1976a) and that, if the meaning of particular assertions depends on the whole framework of belief, each scientist must be "trapped in the web of his own meanings" (Scheffler, 1967: 46).

This kind of difficulty closely resembles that posed by Mannheim in his attempt to devise a new epistemology for social knowledge. Like Kuhn, Mannheim assumed that agreement about facts can usually be reached fairly easily by those operating within a shared framework of meanings. But when divergent perspectives are involved between which some choice must be made, there is in Mannheim's view no alternative but to try to translate the 'opposing' perspectives to a higher level of common meaning, in such a way that the greatest fruitfulness in dealing with empirical materials is achieved. The new philosophy of science goes further than Mannheim, as Nagel notes, not only in arguing that man's view of the physical as well as the social world depends on shared meanings, but also in stressing the difficulty of translating from one network of meanings to another and of achieving a common understanding of what is to count as 'empirical material' (Mulkay, 1979: 38).

This strong alternative to the standard view, although it has been gaining ground since the 1950s, is still a minority position among philosophers of science. Indeed, meanings of the latter have devoted considerable effort to amending, without entirely relinquishing, the orthodox account of fact and theory in response to the major points raised by its more radical critics. It seems, however, that the various moderate, compromise views which have resulted still differ sufficiently from the standard view to warrant a reappraisal of the sociology of scientific knowledge.

Certain of the ideas which have been discussed above have come to be generally accepted, even by those who do not wish to abandon totally the orthodox position. In particular, it is accepted "that the sense and use of predicates employed in the sciences, including those employed to report allegedly observed matters, is determined by the general laws and rules into which these predicates enter" (Nagel et al., 1971: 19–20). It follows that all factual statements are corrigible in principle, that their connection with the external world is problematic and mediated by theoretical presuppositions, and that their meaning is subject to change as the analytical context itself develops. All this is accepted. What is challenged is that the meaning of factual propositions is "determined by the totality of laws and rules of application belonging to the corpus of assumptions of a science at a given time" (Nagel et al., 1971: 20). Scheffler makes the same point, denying that meanings are "so interlocked that a change in any one affects all the rest within a given language system" (1967: 59). In other words, it is being suggested that the cohesion, the connectedness, of scientific knowledge systems has been exaggerated; and also that it is this misapprehension which has given rise to the philosophically unacceptable assertion of incommensurability and of empirical vacuity. Once we recognize, it is argued, that each conceptual framework does not constitute a seamless web, then we can avoid being driven to these indefensible conclusions (Edge and Mulkay, 1976).

Mulkay (1979), with the help of the example taken from the field of radio astronomy, has shown that single group of scientists can have access to various bodies of theoretical resources which are not closely connected; and that factual statements although undoubtedly theory-laden, do not derive their meaning exclusively from that framework of assumptions which gave them birth. Similar conclusions are reached by Nagel and others in the course of an examination of some of Newton's researches, into optics. Nagel and others note that Newton's observational terms, acquired at least part of their meaning from various laws in which they were embedded and which Newton took for granted. But, he argues, the conceptions used by Newton in interpreting his findings were in no way assumed in the design and execution of his experiments.

> "This shows that an experiment intended to ascertain on what factors the occurrence of a certain phenomenon depends can be described so that the statement of the observations made is neutral as between alternative theories which may be proposed to explain the phenomenon, even though the descriptive statement will indeed presuppose various theories, laws, and other background information that are not in dispute in the given inquiry". (Nagel et al., 1971: 26)

Thus, once we allow that the networks of assumptions and concepts used in scientific research are neither completely determinate in meaning nor wholly unified, it becomes possible to escape from the 'stultifying circularity' according to which factual statements are linked indissolubly to a particular framework of preconceptions. It does not seem possible for scientists sometimes to devise independent checks for specific factual claims; although it is clear that this can only be done by treating other sets of assumptions as unproblematic, at least for the moment. Similarly, it may well be that the problem of incommensurability has been exaggerated. The example of Newtonion optics seems to show that scientists can agree about the theoretical basis for a given set of empirical results, without thereby committing themselves necessarily to identical interpretations of those results. If this is so, then, at least some degree of communication is possible between participants operating with divergent analytical frameworks (Grandy, 1973). This is what Kuhn, in reflecting on his critics, has come to call for 'partial communication' (Lakatos and Musgrave, 1970).

The aforesaid discussions simply establish the fact that in abandoning the standard view, one does not necessarily have to adopt an extreme interpretation of scientific thought as composed of closed, self-perpetuating meaning systems. Even the more moderate analyses of facts and theories that have been described above depart significantly from the standard view. Gone is the simple notion that science is built upon a growing corpus of neutral facts. Gone also is the idea that well-established facts are unrevisable and that, consequently scientific knowledge accumulates in a relatively straightforward fashion. Nevertheless, although, the notion of 'fact' has been made more provisional and although facts must be seen in relation to specific intellectual frameworks, it would be wrong to conceive of scientists generally as treating their observational or theoretical knowledge as merely hypothetical and in constant danger of collapse. In fact, one important factor contributing to the impressive intellectual development of modern science has been the capacity of its adherents to forget their background assumptions and to concentrate on using these assumptions to undertake detailed empirical exploration (Mulkay, 1978: 41). Kuhn is surely correct in stressing that modern science is unusually free, compared with other areas of intellectual endeavour, from debates about fundamentals. Most scientific research is carried out in a context in which a whole series of assumptions are so firmly entrenched that their revision or refutation is virtually unthinkable. For instance, in the discovery of quasars (not pulsars), astronomers were faced, implicitly, with a choice between either recognizing the existence of extraordinary objects 100 times more luminous than previously known radio galaxies, for which no remotely satisfactory theoretical account was available, or with revising views about 'redshifts' and stellar spectra which provided the basis for whole areas of astronomy and its techniques (Edge and Mulkay, 1976). It is clear that very few astronomers seriously considered the latter course, even after years of interpretative failure.

It is only against the background furnished by such well-entrenched assumptions that scientists are able to formulate meaningful and detailed hypotheses about the world. For each researcher and for each research community only a limited number of issues are normally treated as empirically open. We must not, however, fall into the trap of trying to distinguish, by means of inherent characteristics, those analytical resources which are entrenched from those which are taken as contingent. To do this would be very similar to trying to distinguish observational statements unambiguously from theoretical statements. It must not be forgotten that the meaning of a scientific preposition varies with the intellectual context in which it is used. This is not merely to say that some prepositions become more firmly entrenched as a research area matures, although this does not tend to happen. It is to suggest, in addition, that specific scientific formulations can be employed in various different ways at the same point in time.

'Observation' in Science

From within the standard view of science, observation is thought to be scientifically adequate in so far as such distorting influences as bias, intellectual prejudice and emotional involvement have been removed. Proper scientific observation occurs when the observer allows himself to be impressed by an objective reality. This view is consistent with the fact that natural philosophers at the birth of modern science, eliminated from consideration secondary, subjective qualities such as taste, smell and colour and concentrated on "objective, measurable attributes, such as motion and magnitude" (Burtt, 1924). Thus observation in science has been seen as a plain recording of the unembroidered evidence of the senses and as being quite separate from the creation of meanings. Much recent work in the philosophy of science has been devoted to formulating an alternative account of scientific observation which is more consistent with the revised conception of the nature of scientific theory. In devising this account philosophers have drawn heavily on the conclusions of experimental psychologists about human perception in general.

One fundamental conclusion arising from work in psychology is that observation can never be as passive as the standard view requires. We never simply receive and register inputs from the external world. Instead we can act upon that world so as to create a series of discernible but never changing cues about its characteristics; and in the very act of perception, the observer interprets these cues in terms of the cultural resources he brings to bear. For example, in artificial situations, where we are required to observe solely by means of touch, we construct or infer the structure and composition of objects placed in our hands by performing a series of observations such as pressing, turning and balancing. As a result of such active manipulation, we are generally able to place objects into categories and to produce statements about their overall shape and general attributes which go well beyond our actual contact with them. When asked to report what we have observed, we tend to describe the inferred structure in terms of the conventional categories available to us. We do not, and almost certainly could not, describe our complex series of hand movements nor the fragmented tactile sensations produced by those movements. Our piecemeal explorations of the objects occur only on the fringes of awareness. We regard ourselves as having observed the relatively invariant structure which we have inferred out of a limited range of sensations (Mulkay, 1979: 43).

Studies conducted by experimental psychologists seem to show that direct observation, whether scientific or otherwise, involves us in more than merely registering and reporting "the unembroidered evidence of the senses". The observer has no alternative but to embroider the evidence of his sense for he receives from them no stable nor complete record of objects or processes in the physical world. Instead, he receives, as a consequence of his own action upon that world, a series of continually changing cues about its characteristics. With the help of these cues, the observer is able to perform inferential work, often quite complex even in the everyday world, which enables him to decide what it is that he has observed.

> "The perceived picture is therefore not just an image or reflection of our momentary sense impressions, but rather it is the outcome of an ever changing construction. Such a construction functions in effect, as a kind of 'hypothesis' compatible with the observed invariant features of the person's overall experience with the environment in question". (Bohm, 1965: 203)

The same conclusion is reached by Bruner in the course of his influential studies of perception/observation. He states clearly that we must no longer think of observation as providing us with a representation of the real world:

> "What we generally mean when we speak of representation or veridicality is that perception is predictive in varying degrees. That is to say, the object that we see, can also be felt and smelled and there will somehow be a match or congruity between what we see, feel and smell. Or in still different terms, the categorical placement of the object leads to appropriate consequences in terms of later behaviour directed towards the perceived object. It appears as an apple and indeed it keeps the doctor away if consumed once a day. The meaning of a thing, thus, is the placement of an object in a network of hypothetical inference concerning its other observable properties, its effects, and so on veridicality is not so much a matter of representation as it is a matter of what I shall call model building". (1974: 10–11)

In this quotation Bruner shifts between behavioural and a linguistic definition of veridicality. In some contexts a behavioural definition seems reasonably appropriate, particularly when one is considering perception by animals, for instance. In the case of animals, observation leads to behaviour without the mediation of words. In human perception, however, the linguistic element is prominent; at least partly because human observation often leads to statements about what was observed, in accordance with which action is initiated. Scientific observation, in particular, is necessarily expressed in terms of words or equivalent symbols. Scientific knowledge consists of propositions about the world, formulated in the conventional forms of a specific language system. Observation, which is not contained in some kind of observation report and not formulated in terms of general categories, is irrelevant to the purposes of science (Ravetz, 1971). In contrast, a representation pure and simple, in the visual form of a photograph or retinal image, contains in itself no linguistic component. A retinal image makes no assertions about the world. Yet what we see, what we observe, has a crucial bearing on our propositional knowledge. If seeing were a purely visual phenomenon, unaffected by the categories that the observer has at his disposal, nothing that we saw with our eyes would be relevant to what we know about the world (Mulkay, 1979).

> "So our visual sensations must be cast in the form of language before they can even be considered in terms of what we know to be true. Until a visual sensation can be so considered, it is not observation". (Hanson, 1969: 127)

Even if one wishes to claim that human beings do sometimes register the external world without the mediation of linguistic categories, even if one regards some human perception as equivalent to that of other animals, it is difficult to maintain that this kind of observation is relevant to science. Scientific knowledge deals with what Ravetz (1971) has called "intellectually constructed classes of things and events", i.e. with general classifications which are defined by certain properties of their members. Particular things and events are classified (conceptualized) on the basis of how far they display the features of a particular class. And, the observational reports which enter the body of scientific knowledge are couched in terms of these categories.

Scientific observation, then, is fundamentally dependent on language. For most purposes, we can think of observation as the act of locating things and events by means of categories; and such categories acquire their meaning by implying that certain statements will be found to apply to that which has been observed. Thus, if a physicist sees an object as an X-ray tube, he thereby assumes that specific propositions will apply to this object; for instance that under certain conditions fluorescence will appear around the anode at high voltages. Similarly, if an astronomer identifies an object as a pulsar, he assumes that it will move around the heavens on sidereal time, that the pulses of electro-magnetic radiation which it emits will be regular and of short duration and so on. It is clear that these verbal assertions are somehow implied in the act of observation, for if they were found subsequently not to apply, it would follow necessarily that the observed object was not really an X-ray tube or not really a pulsar. This is what Bruner means when he writes that observation involves placing an 'object' in a network of hypothetical inference. Here, there is a clear correspondence between Bruner's conclusion and the general proposition argued earlier. But, the argument has now been extended explicitly to cover observation. Observation involves the application of categories to sense impressions. Categories, however, only have meaning within a network of related concepts and propositions. Consequently, observation consists in the interpretation of sense impressions in terms of a linguistic and theoretical framework.

This does not mean that scientists first obtain various kinds of sensations and then apply concepts and interpretations to them. Concepts and theories are always present in the very act of scientific observation (Harris, 1970). It is appropriate to quote Duhem here. His following passage illustrates how this is particularly clear in the advanced physical sciences, where observation is mediated through a complex vocabulary of symbolic resources:

> "Go into this laboratory; draw near this table crowded with so much apparatus: an electric battery, copper wire wrapped in silk, vessels filled with mercury, coils, a small iron bar carrying a mirror. An observer plunges the metallic stem of a rod, mounted with rubber, into small holes. The iron oscillates and by means of the mirror tied to it, sends a beam of light over a celluloid ruler, and the observer follows the movement of the light beam on it. There, no doubt, you have an experiment; by means of the vibration of this spot of light, this physicist minutely observes the oscillations of the piece of iron. Ask him now what he is doing. Is he going to answer: 'I am studying the oscillations of the piece of iron carrying this mirror?' No, he will tell you that he is measuring the electrical resistance of a coil. If you are astonished and ask him what meaning these words have, and what relation they have to the phenomena he has perceived and which you have at the sometime perceived, he will reply that your question would require some very long explanations, and he will recommend that you take a course in electricity". (Duhem, 1962: 145)

It is clear that the trained observer and the untrained observer in this instance do not see the same things on the same events. The interpretative constructions through which we observe the world generate expectations about the cues to be received in various types of physical setting. These expectations make us either more or less sensitive to different kinds of cues and they can be thought of as providing interpretative sets which enable us to translate expected cues fairly smoothly into firm observations (Bruner, 1974). Thus, what we observe depends in large measure on what we 'know' and therefore expect, about the world around us. Observation is "shot through with interpretation, expectation, and wish" (Scheffler, 1967: 22). The importance of his general point to scientific research has, of course, been argued emphatically and documented extensively by Kuhn (1962). In Kuhn's view, scientific observation far from being an unselective and unstructured encounter with a series of unfamiliar flashes, sounds and bumps, is a precisely calculated creation of these flashes, sounds and bumps of a particular kind. Science differs from commonsense knowledge, not in the elimination of preconceptions, but in the precision with which some of these preconceptions are formulated and the detail with which they are used to guide observation. "Sometimes, as in a wave-length measurement, everything but the most esoteric detail of the result is known in advance and the typical latitude of expectation is only somewhat greater" (Kuhn, 1962: 53).

A similar characterization of this aspect of science was developed sometime ago by Duhem. He pointed out that ordinary testimony, based on the observational "procedures of everyday life, can achieve a very high level of reliability. In a certain street of the city and near a certain home, I saw a white horse: that is what I affirm with certainty" (Duhem, 1962: 163). But this comparative certainty is attained by restricting one's reports to relatively gross features of what is observed and by omitting the complex detail. In contrast, scientists try to deal in a precise manner with a complexity and minutiae of details which would defy description, if the scientist did not have at his service the clear and concise symbolic means of representation and measurement furnished by mathematical theory (Duhem, 1962: 164). Because scientific research is constructed and the resultant observations are expressed in terms of precise symbolic formulations, scientists are able to probe the physical world in intricate detail. Without the resources of a mathematically formulated theoretical language, an account of any routine experiment would fill a whole volume with the most confused, the most involved and the least comprehensible recital imaginable (Kuhn, 1963). Duhem's general conclusion will surprise many scholars even today.

> "The uninitiated believe that the result of a scientific experiment is distinguished from ordinary observation by a higher degree of certainty. They are mistaken, for the account of an experiment in physics does not have the immediate certainty, relatively easy to check, that ordinary, non-scientific testimony has. Though less certain than the latter, physical experiment is ahead of it in the number and precision of the details it causes us to know: therein lies its true and essential superiority". (1962: 163)

This is a far cry from the traditional view that science has evolved observational procedures which effectively eliminate uncertainty.

Scientific observations, then, are typically construed in terms of an established and complicated repertoire of interpretative formulations. In order to obtain precise observations and detailed distinctions, scientists necessarily take for granted a wide range of background assumptions. These are normally used as unproblematic resources for organizing observation and for giving it scientific meaning (Mulkay, 1979: 48). As Kuhn puts it "most of scientific research consists in fitting observations into the conceptual boxes provided by professional education. Yet Kuhn is surely wrong, Mulkay comments, in claiming that in great majority of specific areas of study there is only one cluster of concepts, only one paradigm or exemplar, available" (1979). There is tendency in the literature to exaggerate the degree of intellectual rigidity or cohesion in science (Merton, 1973). It is in fact far from unusual to find that there are several candidate schemes in use in any particular area and that the research scientist's central dilemma is precisely that of choosing between these schemes (Lakatos, 1970). Nevertheless, Kuhn is clearly right in stressing that scientific discovery is often associated with the failure to match actual observations with symbolically generated expectations. When this happens, when what we expect to observe patently fails to occur, it seems likely that scientific observation comes closest to resembling the account embedded in the standard view of science. In such circumstances, to return to Duhem's aforesaid quotation, the scientist may abandon the notion that he is measuring the electrical resistance of a coil and revert to describing in gross terms the oscillations of a piece of iron carrying a mirror.

> "these observational situations have a point to them just because they contrast with our more usual cases of seeing. The language of shapes, colour patches, oscillations, and pointer readings is the language appropriate to the unsettled experimental situations where confusion and perhaps even conceptual muddlement dominate. And the seeing that figures in such situations is the sort where the observer does not know what he is seeing. He will not be satisfied until he does know, until his observations cohere and intelligible as against the general background of his already accepted and established knowledge. And it is this latter kind of seeing that is the goal of observation. For it is largely in terms of it, and seldom in terms of merely phenomenal seeing, that new inquiry will proceed". (Hanson, 1969: 108–9)

It is important to quote here the Mulkay's observation: "what Hanson here calls 'phenomenal seeing' is not a mere registering of the external world. Even phenomenal observation is an interpretative act, but one in which generally available cultural resources are utilized in place of specialized technical vocabulary. Thus, another way of saying that scientist does not know what he is seeing is to say that the formulation of his observations in the crude terminology of everyday life is normally deemed to be inadequate in the social context of physical research. However, such a formulation may well be entirely appropriate in the optician's testing room, in the psychologist's laboratory, or when theoretically generated expectations no longer appear to hold. It seems, therefore, that what is to count as an accurate observation of physical phenomena will vary from one social setting to another" (Lewis, 1956: 52).

It appears, then, that observation of the physical world has at least the following features, none of which is consistent with the standard view of science. It is an active process, in the sense that the observer creates and responds to a dynamic sequence of cues. It involves categorization, in that cues are used to place hypothesized objects and events in terms of pre-established sets of concepts. It is inferential, that is, the observer necessarily generalizes from a range of cues which is always 'incomplete' in order to establish what it is he perceives. Observation is not separate from interpretation; rather these are two facets of single process. In most scientific research, observation is intimately guided by and expressed in terms of a complex repertoire of symbolic formulations. These give rise to comparatively precise expectations in relations to which observations can be assigned their scientific significance. The quantified language of science as well as its controlled experimental procedure produce exceptionally detailed and diverse empirical evidence. But neither the certainty of these observations nor the correctness of their formulation is in any way guaranteed. Nor is there any 'one right way' of reporting the results of given observation. Judgements of observational adequacy seem to vary, like the meaning of propositions, according to the interpretative and social context.

The Assessment of Knowledge-Claims

In the philosophical debate about the criteria used to certify scientific knowledge, most attention has been given to the principles involved in validating theoretical claims. Popper is not unrepresentative in suggesting that it is scientists' way of choosing between theories which make science rational (Popper, 1963: 215). Despite philosopher's emphasis on theory, it is clear that most practising scientists are also required, and probably more frequently, to make judgments about the accuracy or reliability of particular observational reports. It may initially seem surprising, therefore, that there has been so little concern with the criteria by which specific data are judged, especially in view of the fact that 'agreement with the data' has been so frequently proposed as a fundamental principle for the assessment of theoretical claims (Frank, 1961). However, one reason for concentrating rather more on theoretical than on observational criteria is that observation is itself 'theory-laden'. Consequently, when general criteria are used to judge the accuracy of particular observational reports, they are interpreted in terms of specific theoretical assumptions and specific analytical context.

Mulkay (1979) explains the example of the criterion of 'replicability':

> "There can be no doubt that scientists often use a notion of this kind in deciding whether or not particular experimental claims should be accepted (Ravetz, 1971). Empirical re ults which cannot be reproduced under specific conditions are usually regarded as

> untrustworthy. However, the application of such a rule to specific instances is far from unproblematic; for what counts as following a rule cannot be ascertained from inspection of the rule itself (Wittgenstein, 1953). What is to count as a 'replication' depends on scientists' theories about the phenomena under study and on their view of the factors which may influence the observational situation. Consequently, as theoretical frameworks evolve and experimental techniques develop, so the way in which the general criterion of *'replicability'* is applied in any given area necessarily alters". (1979: 52)

When we look at closely at the observational criterion of 'replicability', we find that it is almost a mere formality. It has not content until it is put into practice in particular scientific context. It can perhaps best be thought of as a recommendation that scientists ought to try to produce numerous 'equivalent' observations in connection with any given problem. But replication introduces no new criteria by which experimental results can be judged. Nothing more is involved in replication than the normal procedures of interpreting findings in accordance with other evidence and in the light of analytical conceptions. If this illustration is at all representative, it seems that the kind of observational criteria discussed in the philosophical literature obtain their meaning from the theoretical or interpretative context in which they are applied. Now, it is time to examine the principles by which theories are thought to be validated.

Numerous criteria appear to be cited by scientists in assessing relatively generalized or theoretical knowledge-claims; criteria such as agreement with evidence, simplicity, accuracy, scope, fruitfulness and elegance. One of the main difficulties with these principles is that they deal with quite different dimensions. How, then, is it possible for scientists to combine them in a manner which is not arbitrary and which provides the common criteria required by the standard view? For instance, how is the requisite of accuracy to be reconciled with that of simplicity? How much inaccuracy will we allow in order to achieve a given level of simplicity, and why? Such questions are undoubtedly resolved in practice. Thus, "physics is filled with laws that express proportionality, such as Hooke's law in elasticity or Ohm's law in electrodynamics. In all these cases, there is no doubt that a non-linear relationship would describe the facts in a more accurate way, but one tries to get along with a linear law as much as possible" (Frank 1961: 14). In these instances, generalizations are stated in such a way that accuracy and agreement with the evidence are to some extent sacrificed in order to achieve a convenient level of simplicity and to facilitate certain kinds of mathematical computation. But, the balance between these different dimensions, which is achieved in any particular set of formulations, is clearly not given by the physical world. It is rather a conventional arrangement which differs over time and from one group of scientists to another (Ravetz, 1971; Lakatos, 1976). This does not mean that the ways in which criteria are combined are entirely arbitrary. But it does mean that different procedures, and therefore different knowledge-claims, would be acceptable in different interpretative contexts (Mulkey, 1979: 52-53).

In short, the criteria used in evaluating theoretical claims, like those applied to particular observational reports, seem to vary in meaning in accordance with the context in which they are used. They cannot be regarded, therefore, as providing a means of assessing knowledge-claims which is independent of specific analytical commitments.

This conclusion applies just as much to the criterion of 'consonance with observation' as to the other more obviously conventional criteria. There was a time when it was thought that scientific theories or generalizations were accepted when they could be proved to be true, that is, in agreement with the observational facts (Frank, 1961). Thus scientific knowledge-claims were seen as claims to have established the truth (Shepherd and Johnson, 1976). But this view has been shown to be inadequate in the course of the philosophical debate about induction. It is inadequate because, logically, it is impossible to prove any general, law-like proposition by means of evidence about particular instances. General propositions cannot be induced from a particular set of observations with certainty, because each general proposition necessarily goes beyond the cases already observed, to include others about which there is at present no evidence. In other words, the universal generalizations of science must be seen as being imaginatively hypothesized, or extrapolated, from essentially incomplete sets of observations. Moreover, such universal propositions can never be subsequently proved, even by means of the most extensive and detailed series of successful predictions. For, there can be no complete guarantee that the next test will not produce such disagreement between prediction and observational results that the universality of the proposition will have to be abandoned. This argument presupposes that observations are not completely determined by the theory they are intended to test.

It has, therefore, been suggested, particularly by Popper (1959, 1963) that the major criterion of theoretical adequacy in science is and should be the ability of a claim to withstand attempts at falsification. This argument seems initially plausible because, in principle, although an immense number of positive observations is insufficient to prove a generalization, one negative observation seems enough to disprove it. However, this thesis would only hold in relation to isolated theoretical propositions which could be compared with absolutely unproblematic observations. As soon as we take into account that any theoretical proposition is linked to, and depends upon others, that observation is itself an interpretative act and that some theoretical assumptions must be made in order to establish the meaning of an observation, the appealing simplicity of the criterion of 'resistance to falsification' is lost. We are never in a position where we can measure an isolated and simple theoretical statement against an unmediated natural world. Instead we formulate and compare complex networks of theoretical and observational statements, and we seek to establish as consistent an account overall as possible of the phenomena with which we are concerned. We never, therefore, propose a theory in such a way "that Nature may shout 'No'. Rather, we propose a maze of theories, and Nature may shout INCONSISTENT" (Lakatos, 1968: 162). The most that scientists can achieve, then, is a high level of consistency among the various components of their analytical framework.

One clear implication of this philosophical debate is that scientific knowledge is inherently inconclusive. For it is impossible to move conclusively from reports about particular samples of things and events to statements about general classes of things and events (Ravetz, 1971). It seems to follow that, because formally valid demonstrations yielding certainty are unattainable in science, scientific knowledge-claims are assessed not for their truth but for their capacity to meet the requirements of a particular interpretative context. Such contexts in science contain at least following two general requirements: (a) first, consistency with other knowledge-claims, which may vary in their level of generality and in the degree to which they are firmly established; and (b) secondly, conformity to conventional standards of adequacy, for example, in connection with quantitative precision, rigour of argument, range of evidence, etc., which are regarded by the members of a 'research community' to be appropriate to a given class of problems (Mulkay, 1979: 54-55). The relevance of prior knowledge-claims to the assessment of subsequent claims has already been demonstrated sufficiently. There are also examples of variation in the conventional criteria of mathematical rigour and experimental accuracy. It is worth emphasizing the limitations of these two elements as bases for assessing new knowledge-claims. Prior claims can give us no certainty when we use them to screen subsequent claims, because all scientific claims are inherently inconclusive. Criteria of adequacy are no more certain, for they cannot even be established by normal scientific procedures, i.e., by means of argument based on controlled observation. This is partly because they are often difficult to make explicit, being akin to the tacit knowledge which is passed on by craftsmen through personal contact—a characteristic which helps to explain why philosophers have not succeeded in studying them in any detail. It also means that they are not easily subject to critical public evaluation via journals. Thus, while criteria of scientific adequacy operate as resources for judging knowledge-claims, their own 'adequacy' can only be established in a most indirect and uncertain manner (Ravetz, 1971).

It is important to note Mulkay's observations on this issue:

> "an item can appear to satisfy current criteria of adequacy as an observational or theoretical claim and yet be rejected on grounds of inconsistency with established knowledge. Consistency of this latter kind is crucial in determining whether or not a particular claim is rejected. Nevertheless, at least in mature fields, there is always a close connection between the body of established knowledge and the criteria of adequacy used by the practitioners. The range and complexity of such criteria of operative in any field reflect the structure of the interpretative scheme in use. Consequently, although it is possible to distinguish certain general classes of criteria, the members of any one class are realized in different ways in each area of research". (Mulkay, 1979: 55)

Ravetz identifies two broad types of criteria of adequacy: those relating to processes of inference and those relating to evidence. The latter are more varied than the former.

> "for they control not only the conditions of the production of data and information but also the strength and fact of the evidence in its particular context. It will frequently be necessary for some of the evidence to be explained and defended explicitly; and these subsidiary arguments must also meet criteria of adequacy appropriate to their function. Thus the complexity of a solved problem is matched by that of the set of relevant criteria of adequacy; and that set will depend closely on the field of enquiry. Hence it is impossible to produce an explicit list of adequacy applying to a wide class of problems". (Ravetz, 1971: 154–55)

It follows from this analysis that criteria of adequacy will change and evolve as the technical culture alters in which they are embedded. "A scientific problem, unlike a textbook exercise, carries with it no guarantee that there exists a 'correct' solution against which those actually achieved can be tested" (Ravetz, 1971: 149). (Although in a situation resembling Kuhnian normal science, the existence of such solutions may be assumed by participants). Thus, any significant knowledge-claim is likely to entail some revision of criteria of adequacy, as well as involving alteration to the current theoretical framework. Edge and Mulkay (1976) have illustrated this point with an example taken from radio astronomy as under:

> "When the first reports of celestial radio emission were published in the 1930s, they were virtually ignored by physicists and by astronomers. There were sound reasons for this. In the first place, there was Plank's law of black-body radiation from which it could be inferred that radio emission from celestial objects would not be detectable. Secondly, there was the apparent anomaly that the sun, despite being a dominant source of electromagnetic-radiation at visual wave-lengths, was reported to be a relatively weak source of such radiation of radio wave-lengths. Thirdly, the early findings in radio astronomy seemed to show that there were effectively two separate universes: the traditional one made up of an almost completely distinct collection of objects detectable only by radio techniques. As a result of these and other apparent anomalies, optical astronomers on the whole were unwilling to pay much attention to the early knowledge-claims of radio astronomers. These claims were too difficult to reconcile with well established optical knowledge. And in addition, they did not satisfy the standards of precision or rigour required by the community of optical astronomers. Consequently, it was possible for astronomers to dismiss

these startling assertions until the evidence on which they were based was 'adequate' that is comparable to the results of optical work". (Mulkay, 1979: 56)

"In the long run, Mulkay adds, of course, optical astronomers did change their interpretation of many celestial phenomena in response to the findings of radio astronomers. Theorists were the first to respond favourably, partly because, being less involved in observation, they were less committed to the criteria of adequacy governing optical observation. They were able to recognize that this kind of knowledge-claim had to be judged initially by different, and less demanding, standards. Close collaboration in observational work however, occurred very seldom until radio astronomers had achieved standard which approximated to the established criteria of optical adequacy. These latter criteria had been evolved within the long tradition of optical research and were appropriate for current visual techniques. But they were quite inappropriate when applied to the crude initial observations by radio methods, at least in the view of radio astronomers. It is clear that the first knowledge-claims to be proposed by the latter were inconsistent with both the established astronomical framework of interpretation and the associated criteria of observational adequacy. For their claims to be considered, not only was it necessary to accept that the body of optical knowledge might need extensive revision, but also that the very criteria by which an astronomical knowledge-claim could be deemed worthy of investigation might have to be set aside. In case of major claims like this, it is quite misleading to think in terms of assessment by the application of clear and predetermined criteria. Rather the knowledge-claim, if it signifies at all, implies that the cultural resources available for purposes of assessment are themselves in need of amendment". (Mulkay, 1979: 56–57)

Because the evaluation of scientific knowledge-claims is highly complex, involving a subtle balance of tacit criteria of adequacy with estimates of consistency, significance and analytical import, it tends to be a somewhat prolonged process—except in cases where claims are universally ignored as trivial or unanimously rejected as inconceivable. In the course of this process, knowledge-claims move through a sequence of phases, within which their content and their meaning are continually reinterpreted in accordance with the demands of different interpretative and social contexts.

One social context through which almost all significant scientific knowledge-claims pass is that of evaluation on behalf of a professional journal. But publication in a journal in no way establishes that a claim has been accepted by the scientific community. The assessment carried out at this juncture is relatively routine. Seldom is any attempt made to reproduce experimental data; and complex arguments are not usually examined in great detail. In short, the knowledge-claim is subject at this stage to a fairly superficial and preliminary appraisal of adequacy, consistency and significance (Mulkay and Williams, 1971; Ravetz, 1971; Mulkay, 1979). However, a much more stringent selection procedure comes into operation after the claim has become publicly available. For it is now treated by other researchers as a symbolic resource. As this point, each interested researcher asks, in effect. "How far does this contribution help me to produce 'better' solutions to my own problem?" It seems that the answer to this question is usually negative, for the great majority of published reports receive little attention in the subsequent literature. Thus claims which are found wanting are seldom publicly refuted. They are usually ignored instead. A relatively small proportion of knowledge-claims however are noticed and used widely by other researchers. But the elements which are regarded by others as the most significant parts of a claim are not necessarily the same as those intended by its author; nor is the claim necessarily interpreted in the same way. As a knowledge-claim becomes divorced from its original context, it is subject to varying reinterpretations even while remaining within one area of investigation.

> "When a solved problem has been presented to the community, and new work is done on its basis, then the objects of investigation will necessarily change, sometimes only slightly, but sometimes drastically. In a retrospect on the original problem even after a brief period of development, its argument will be seen as concerning objects which no longer exist. There is then the question of whether it can be translated or recast so as to relate to the newer objects descended from the original ones, and still be an adequate foundation for a conclusion. If not, then the original conclusion is rejected as dealing with non-objects or as ascribing false properties to real objects. But if such a translation or recasting is possible then the original solved problem is seen to have contained some element which is invariant with respect to the changes in the subjects of investigation". (Ravetz, 1971: 189)

> "It is this informal process of selection that directs the course of scientific development and that transforms those few formulations which withstand reinterpretation and which continue to generate 'successful' conclusions into the major intellectual achievements in science". (Toulmin, 1968 quoted in Mulkay, 1979: 58)

Those select few assertions which are found to be capable of wide-ranging and fruitful elaborations are passed from one research area to another and eventually reach the scientific textbook and the historical record. These influential formulations are undoubtedly part of scientific knowledge. There is, however, no clear distinction to be made between those claims which contribute to knowledge and those which do not, apart from their interpretation and use in a particular context; for a claim unambiguously rejected by one research community can be treated by another as a valid and fundamental assertion.

Furthermore, the meaning and content of these formulations does not remain stable. They undergo what Ravetz has called a 'process of standardization' (1971: 199–208). Ravetz argues that a claim must be standardized if it is to become a fairly general component of scientific knowledge. If an assertion remains attached to its original problem, it will not outlive the solution of that problem. But in so far as it is divorced from that problem, it must be stated in some standard form which can be employed for various new purposes and in diverse scientific contexts. In this process, however, some of the original content is lost. Meaning is lost by translation in science as well as in literature. Points of obscurity and conceptual difficulties are overlooked. The limitations of underlying assumptions are forgotten. And the balance and emphasis of the original formulation are altered to meet the needs of new areas of application. In addition, because the knowledge, technical skills and standards of adequacy of the various audiences involved are likely to be quite diverse, the standardized version must be considerably simplified. This process reaches its climax in the passage of certified knowledge from the research community to the school curriculum and the popular text; but there are merely the most obvious parts of a continuous sequence of reinterpretation and change of meaning.

> "the content of a standardized fact may decay, almost without limit; the degree of sophistication and of faithfulness to its original which

is necessary for its adequate performance of its function will depend very strongly on its use. Also, it can be seen that a version of a standardized fact which is good enough for one function can be quite inadequate for another; and since any standardized fact performs a variety of functions, it will naturally appear in a variety of versions". (Ravetz, 1971: 202)

Conclusively, scientific knowledge-claims are not assessed by means of invariant, universal criteria. Although certain broad conceptions have been identified in the philosophical literature as common bases for accepting or rejecting claims, these conceptions are necessarily interpreted by scientists in terms of particular theoretical ideas and specific analytical repertories. The rules of evidence, criteria of consistency, and so on, in science are not rigid. They are certainly flexible enough to allow scientists considerable leeway in interpreting evidence so as to support well-entrenched assumptions. Moreover, the standards applied in the selection of knowledge-claims are not inherent in the phenomena of the physical world. All claims are judged according to conventional criteria of adequacy, which vary over time and from one group or social context to another, and partly in terms of their consistency with an ever changing interpretative framework. Any significant claim is likely to entail some revision of current criteria of adequacy, as well as implying that the established corpus of knowledge is inadequate in some way. Consequently, the assessment of such claims within a research speciality tends to occur relatively slowly, and is often characterized by marked opposition, as members explore the implications of the claim. Therefore, the process of assessment is also a process of reinterpretation. Similarly reinterpretation or meaning-change occurs, in accordance with different criteria of adequacy and different analytical purposes, whenever assertions enter another research area or move altogether outside the research community. In short, it seems that scientific knowledge is not stable in meaning, not independent of social context and not certified by the application of generally agreed procedures of verification.

Sociological Insinuations

In so far as the arguments presented above and in the literature on which it draws are deemed to be valid, the epistemological barrier to a sociological analysis of scientific knowledge has been removed;

although many practical difficulties shall remain. Sociologists of knowledge treated science as beyond the scope of this analysis because it was thought to be a special kind of knowledge. This is true in some respects, for instance, to the extent to which it has achieved intellectual supremacy in the modern world. Thus, when they stressed that science and scientific community were special social phenomena, thinkers like Durkheim and Mannheim were undoubtedly correct. But this view of scientific knowledge required them to place a strict limit on their conception of the social character of science. In the first place, they saw that science played an important part in modern society because the provision of objective knowledge had many social side-effects, not the least of which was the displacement of religion noted by Durkheim. Secondly, science was sociologically significant because scientists seemed not only to have devised a research method which progressively revealed the realities of the external world, but also to have evolved an appropriate form of social organization which kept their knowledge exceptionally free from distortion by social and personal influences. It was this social aspect of science which particularly interested Merton. But sociological analysis had to stop there. Thus, we find Mannheim eagerly accepting that the findings of physics are relative to the observer's position in time and space, but drawing back from the possibility that they might in some sense be socially relative. Sociological analysis could not go this far, for science was not simply one social construction among others; it was "real, certain, indubitable and demonstrable knowledge of an objective world" (Popper, 1963: 93). Sociology could deal either with the social conditions which helped to reveal or to hide the objective world or with the social consequences of objective knowledge. Sociology could say nothing about the form or content of scientific knowledge itself, because the conclusions of science were thought to be determined by the physical and not the social world (Mulkay, 1979: 60).

There are good grounds for rejecting the aforesaid portrayal of science. In particular, the central assumption that scientific knowledge is based on a direct representation of the physical world has been criticized from several directions. For instance, factual statements have been shown to depend on speculative assumptions while observation has been shown to be guided by linguistic categories. And, the acceptance of knowledge-claims has been shown to involve indeterminate and variable criteria. Scientific knowledge, then, necessarily offers an account of the physical world which is mediated through available cultural resources and these resources are in no way definitive. The indeterminacy of scientific criteria, the inconclusive character of the general knowledge-claims of science, the dependence of such claims on the available symbolic resources all indicate that world could be analysed perfectly adequately by means of language and presuppositions quite different from those employed in the modern scientific community. "Therefore, there is nothing in the physical world which uniquely determines the conclusions of that community" (Mulkay, 1979: 61). It is, of course, self-evident that the external world exerts constraint on the conclusions of science. But this constraint operates through the meanings created by scientists in their attempts to interpret the world. These meanings are inherently inconclusive, continually revised and partly dependent on the social context in which interpretation occurs. If this view, which is central to the new philosophy of science, is accepted, there is no alternative but to regard the products of science as social constructions like other cultural products. Accordingly, there seems every reason to explore how far and in what ways scientific knowledge is conditioned by its social milieu, how change of meaning is brought about and how knowledge is used as a cultural resource in various kinds of social interaction. It is, no doubt, possible that this revised view is fundamentally wrong and its conclusions merely a result of defective philosophical analysis. If this is so, the attempt to explore the social construction of scientific knowledge will probably flounder. But not to make the attempt, at a time when the earlier set of philosophical ideas appears clearly to be inadequate is an indefensible position (Mulkay, 1979: 60-61).

There is a crucial distinction made by many sociologists of knowledge between scientific and social/historical thought. The latter was regarded as amenable to sociological analysis because it is related to a particular social context and undertaken from a particular, historically unique perspective. The knowledge gained is restricted by and formulated in terms of the observer's necessarily limited interpretative framework. Another way of putting this is that the answer obtained depends on the questions posed and on the questions presuppositions. Particular assertions can only be understood in the light of these background assumptions and any attempt to assess their validity must utilize specific rather than generally applicable criteria. Owing to the diversity and evolution of interpretative frameworks, meanings are 'made and even re-made' in the course of social life and past contributions are continually reinterpreted. These, then, are the main characteristics attributed by sociologists to social constructions, i.e., to mental products having their origin in the social as opposed to the physical world. They were thought to indicate that only socially variable knowledge of this kind was open to sociological analysis, because only here did participants' socially derived perspectives appear to penetrate into the meaning and evaluation of particular assertions. However, the similarity between this characterization of social thought and the newer philosophical account of science is very obvious. If the revised view of science is accepted, the basis for the traditional distinction between scientific and social thought is eliminated, as is the exclusion of scientific knowledge from sociological interpretation (Barnes, 1974). Of course, we would hardly expect any other conclusion, for one of the central claims of the revised views is that scientific assertions are socially created and not directly given by the physical world as is supposed by many of the positivists. It is not implied that there are no differences at all between the analysis of the physical and the social worlds; only that at this level of generality, the distinction traditionally used in the sociology of knowledge no longer seems to apply.

The implications of this conclusion are considerable, for it enables us to ask (i) to what extent presuppositions which are widespread in modern society have been implicit in scientific research and moulded its findings; (ii) how do the scientists decide on the adequacy and significance of knowledge-claims; (iii) whether their assessments are as disinterested as has been customarily supposed; and (iv) how is the meaning of scientific assertions reinterpreted in different social situations and whether, for instance, such reinterpretation can serve as a source of social power? In general, we can assess how far detailed sociological investigation of the social life of science provides support for the revised philosophical view; and we can explore what difference the revised view makes to our understanding of the social relationships involved in the creation of scientific knowledge.

The sociology of knowledge critique, best represented in the contemporary scene by the work of Kuhn, thus challenges 'sociology's dominant' sub-community—the positivists—on many fronts and on many fundamental issues. Among the ones we have discussed the more important would include the following:

(a) Denial of the notion of absolute truth.

(b) Denial of the cumulative nature of scientific advance.

(c) Denial of universal demarcation criteria.

(d) Denial of the claim that there can be a conclusive disproof of a theory.

(e) Affirmation of the fundamentally social nature of science.

(f) Affirmation of the notion that paradigms define 'facts'.

References

Agassi, J., 1963, *Towards an Historiography of Science: History and Theory*, Vol. II, New York: University Press.

Barnes, B., 1974, *Scientific Knowledge and Sociological Theory*, London: Routledge and Kegan Paul.

Bohm, D., 1965, *The Special Theory of Relativity*, New York: Benjamin.

——, 1975, "The Social Function of Cognitive Structure", in K. Knorr, H. Strasser and H.G. Zilian (eds.), *Determinants and Controls of Scientific Development*, Dordrecht, Holland: Reidel.

Braverman, H., 1974, *Labour and Monopoly Capital*, New York and London: Monthly Review Press.

Bruner, J.S., 1974, *Beyond the Information Given*, London: Allen and Unwin.

Burtt, E.A., 1924, *The Metaphysical Foundations of Modern Science*, London: Routledge and Kegan Paul.

Carnap, R., 1939, *Foundations of Logic and Mathematics*, Chicago: University of Chicago Press.

——, 1966, *Philosophical Foundations of Physics*, New York: Basic Books.

Duhem, P., 1962, *The Aim and Structure of Physical Theory*, New York: Atheneum.

Durkheim, E., 1915, *The Elementary Forms of Religious Life*, London: Allen and Unwin.

——, 1938, *The Rules of Sociological Method*, Glencoe Ill: The Free Press.

Edge, D.O. and Mulkay, M.J. 1976, *Astronomy Transformed*, New York: Wiley Interscience.

Frake, C.O., 1961, "The Diagnosis of Disease among the Subanum of Mindanao", *American Anthropologist*, Vol. 63.

Feyerabend, P., 1975, *Against Method*, London: NLB.

Fisher, R.A., 1936, "Has Mendel's Work been Rediscovered?" *Annals of Science*, Vol. I.

Frank, G.P., 1961, *The Validation of Scientific Theories*, New York: Collier.

Gilbert, G.N., 1976(a), "The Transformation of Research Findings into Scientific Knowledge", *Social Studies of Science*, Vol. 6.

——, 1976(b), "The Development of Science and Scientific Knowledge: The Case of Radar Meter or Research", in G. Lemaine (ed.), *Perspectives on the Emergence of Scientific Disciplines*, The Hague and Paris: Mouton.

Glass, B., 1953, "The Long Neglect of a Scientific Discovery: Mendel's Laws of Inheritance", in G. Boas (ed.), *Studies in Intellectual History*, Baltimore, Maryland: Johns Hopkins Press.

Grandy, R.E., 1973, *Theories and Observation in Science*, Englewood Cliffs, N.J.: Prentice-Hall.

Habermas, J., 1972, *Knowledge and Human Interest*, London: Heinemann.

Hagstrom, W.O., 1965, *The Scientific Community*, New York: Basic Books.

Hanson, N.R., 1965, *Pattern of Discovery*, Cambridge: Cambridge University Press.

——, 1969, *Perception and Discovery*, San Francisco: Freeman, Cooper.

Harris, E.E., 1963, "The Function of Measurement in Modern Physical Science", in H. Woolf (ed.), *Quantification*, New York: Bobbs-Merrill.

——, 1970, *Hypothesis and Perception*, London: Allen and Unwin.

Hempel, C.G., 1965, *Aspects of Scientific Explanation*, New York and London: The Free Press.

Hesse, M., 1974, *The Structure of Scientific Inference*, London: Macmillan.

Hessen, Boris, 1931, "The Social and Economic Roots of Newton's Principia", in N.I. Bukharin et al. (eds.), *Science at the Crossroads* (2nd ed., 1971), London: Frank Cass.

Hoijer, H., 1964, "Cultural Implications of Some Navaho Linguistic Categories", in D. Hymer (ed.), *Language and Culture in Society*, New York and London: Harper and Row.

Kuhn, T.S., 1962, *The Structure of Scientific Revolutions*, Chicago and London: University of Chicago Press (enlarged in 1970).

——, 1963, "The Function of Measurement in Modern Physical Science", in H. Woolf (ed.), *Quantificaton*, New York: Brbbs-Merrill, pp. 31-61.

Lakatos, I. and Musgrave, A. (eds.), 1970, *Criticism and Growth of Knowledge*, Cambridge: Cambridge University Press.

Lakatos, I., 1968, Criticism and the Methodology of Scientific Research Programmes, *Proceedings of the Aristotelian Society*, Vol. 69.

——, 1970, "Falsification and the Methodology of Scientific Research Programmes", in I. Lakatos and A. Musgrave (eds.), *Criticism and Growth of Knowledge*, Cambridge: Cambridge University Press.

——, 1976, *Proofs and Refutations*, Cambridge: Cambridge University Press.

Lewis, C.I., 1956, *Mind and the World Order*, New York: Diverse Publications.

Mannheim, Karl, 1936, *Ideology and Utopia*, New York: Harcourt, Brace and World.

——, 1952, *Essays on the Sociology of Knowledge*, London: Routledge and Kegan Paul.

Marcuse, H., 1962, *One-Dimensional Man*, London: Routledge and Kegan Paul.

Marx, Karl, 1904, *The Contribution to the Critique of Political Economy*, Chicago: C.H. Kerr.

——, 1973, *Grundrisse*, Harmondsworth: Penguin.

——, 1974, *Economic and Philosophic Manuscripts of 1844*, Moscow: Progress Publishers.

Marx, K. and Engel, F., 1965, *Manifesto of the Communist Party*, Moscow: Progress Publishers.

Merton, R.K., 1970, *Science, Technology and Society in 17th Century England*, New York: Harper and Row.

——, 1973, *The Sociology of Science*, Chicago and London: University of Chicago Press.

——, 1975, "Structural Analysis in Sociology", in P. Blau (ed.), *Approaches to the Study of Social Structure*, New York: The Free Press.

Mulkay, M.J., 1976, "Norms and Ideology in Science", *Social Science Information*, Vol. 15.

——, 1979, *Science and the Sociology of Knowledge*, London: George Allen and Unwin.

Mulkay, M.J. and Williams, A.T., 1971, A Sociological Study of a Physics Department, *British Journal of Sociology*, Vol. 22.

Nagel, E., 1961, *The Structure of Science*, London: Routledge and Kegan Paul.

Nagel, E., Bromberger, S. and Grunbaum, A., 1971, *Observation and Theory in Science*, Baltimore and London: Johns Hopkins Press.

Outhwaite, W., 1975, *Understanding Social Life*, London: Allen and Unwin.

Popper, Karl R., 1959, *The Logic of Scientific Discovery*, New York: Harper and Row.

——, 1963, *Conjectures and Refutations*, London: Routledge and Kegan Paul.

Ravetz, J.R., 1971, *Scientific Knowledge and Its Social Problems*, Oxford: Clarendon Press.

Rose, H. and Rose, S. (eds.), 1976, *The Political Economy of Science*, London: Macmillan.

Ryle, G., 1949, *The Concept of Mind*, London: Hutchinson.

Scheffler, I., 1963, *The Anatomy of Inquiry*, New York: Knopf.

Shepherd, J. and Johnson, R., 1976, *Science and Rationality*, Manchester: University of Manchester, Department of Liberal Studies in Science, Siscon Pamphlet.

Smart, J.C., 1973, "The Reality of Theoretical Entities", in R.E. Grandy (ed.), *Theories and Observation in Science*, Englewood Cliffs, N.J.: Prentice-Hall.

Stark, Werner, 1958, *The Sociology of Knowledge*, London: Routledge and Kegan Paul.

Strawson, P.F., 1959, *Individuals*, London: Methuen.

Toulmin, N.J., 1968, *Foresight and Understanding*, New York: Harper and Row.

Wittgenstein, L., 1953, *Philosophical Investigations*, Oxford: Blackwell.

3

Appraising Positivism

Phenomenology and Ethnomethodology

Methodology has split the social scientists into two schools of thought:

1. One of these holds that the methods of the natural sciences are the only scientific ones and that they alone, therefore, have to be applied in their entirety to the study of human affairs. Failure to do so, it has been maintained, prevented the social sciences from developing systems of explanatory theory comparable in precision to those offered by the natural sciences and makes debatable the empirical work of theories developed in restricted domains such as economics.
2. The other school unfolds in the opinion that there is a basic difference in the structure of the social world and the world of nature. This led to the conclusion that the methods of the social sciences are different from the natural sciences. In support of this position, the following arguments were proffered:
   (i) the social sciences are ideographic, characterized by individualizing conceptualization and seeking singular assertory propositions, whereas the natural sciences are nomothetic, characterized by generalizing conceptualization and seeking general apodictic propositions;
   (ii) the natural sciences have to deal with constant relations of magnitude which can be measured and can perform

experiments, whereas, neither measurement nor experiment is practicable in the social sciences;

(iii) the natural sciences have to deal with material objects and processes, whereas the social sciences with psychological and intellectual ones; and

(iv) therefore, the methodology of the natural sciences consists in explaining and that of the social sciences in understanding.

Most of these highly generalized statements are untenable under closer examination for several reasons:

(i) Some proponents of the characterized arguments had a rather erroneous concept of the methods of the natural sciences.

(ii) Others were inclined to identify the methodological situation in one particular social science with the method of the social sciences in general.

(iii) Because history has to deal with unique and non-recurrent events, it was contended that all social sciences are restricted to singular assertory propositions.

(iv) Because experiments are hardly possible in cultural anthropology, the fact was ignored that social psychologists can successfully use laboratory experiments at least to a certain extent.

(v) Finally, these arguments disregard the fact that a set of rules for scientific procedure is equally valid for all empirical sciences whether they deal with objects of nature or with human affairs. Here, the principles of controlled inference and verification, by fellow scientists and the theoretical ideals of unity, simplicity, universality, and precision prevail (Schutz, 1970: 2).

This unsatisfactory state of affairs results mainly from the fact that the development of the modern social sciences occurring during a period in which the science of logic was mostly concerned with the logic of natural sciences. In this monopolistic imperialism the methods of natural sciences were declared to be only scientific ones and the particular problems encountered by the social scientists in their academic work were ignored. However, the social scientists tried to develop their own conceptions of what they believed to be the methodology of the social sciences. But these efforts were without sufficient philosophical knowledge; as a result, they stopped their attempts when they reached a level of generalizations which appeared to justify their deeply felt conviction that the goal of their enquiry could not be assured by the adopting the methods of the natural sciences without modification or implementation. It is a fact that their arguments are frequently ill-founded, their formulations were insufficient, and that many misunderstandings obfuscate the controversy. Not what social scientists said but what they meant is therefore the main concern of phenomenologists.

At this juncture of analysis, it is important to present a logical debate between positivists (Nagel, Hempel and Kauffmann) and Alfred Schutz, the phenomenologist, on the concept and method in social sciences.

Phenomenology and Positivist Method: A Debate

The writings of the Felix Kauffmann, Ernest Nagel and C.G. Hempel criticized many fallacies in the arguments proposed by social scientists and prepared the ground for another approach to the problem. We concentrate on Nagel's criticism of the claim made by Max Weber and his school that the social sciences seek to understand social phenomena in terms of meaningful categories of human experience and that, therefore, the 'casual functional' approach of the natural sciences is not applicable in social reality. Nagel holds the opinion that the Weberian school maintains that all socially significant human behaviour is an expression of motivated psychic states that in consequence the social scientist cannot be satisfied with viewing social processes simply as concatenations of externally related events, and that the establishment of correlations or even of universal relations of concomitance cannot be his ultimate goal. The Weberian school advocates for the construction of 'ideal types' on 'models of motivations' in terms of which a social scientist seeks to understand overt social behaviour by imputing springs of action to the actors involved in it (Schutz, 1970: 3).

Nagel, in his criticism of the Weberian school, maintains that:

1. These springs of action are not accessible to sensory observation. It follows that the social scientist must imaginatively identify himself with the participants and view the situation which they face as the actors themselves view it. Surely, however, we need not undergo other men's psychic experiences in order to know that they have them or in order to predict their overt behaviour.

2. The imputation of emotions, attitudes and purposes, as an explanation of overt behaviour, is a two-fold hypothesis: (a) it assumes that the agents participating in some social phenomena are in certain psychological states, and (b) it assumes also definite relations of concomitance between such states, and between such states and overt behaviour. Yet none of the psychological states which we imagine the subjects of our study to possess may in reality be theirs, and even if our imputations should be correct, none of the overt actions which allegedly issue from those states may appear to be understandable or reasonable.
3. We do not understand the nature and operations of human motives and their issuance in overt behaviour more adequately than the external causal relations. If by meaningful explanation we assert merely that a particular action is an instance of a pattern of behaviour which human beings exhibit under a variety of circumstances and that, since some of the relevant circumstances are realized in the given situation, a person can be expected to manifest a certain form of that pattern, then there is no sharp gulf separating such explanations from those involving merely external knowledge of causal connections. It is possible to gain knowledge of the actions of men on the evidence supplied by their overt behaviour just as it is possible to discover and know the atomic constitution of water on the evidence supplied by the physical and chemical behaviour of that substance. Hence, the rejection of a purely objective or behaviouristic social science by the proponents of 'meaningful connections' as the goal of social sciences is unwarranted (Nagel, 1952: 43–44).

Schutz, despite his disagreement with the aforesaid Nagel's objections to Weberian methodology, agrees with Nagel and his school on three points:

(i) All empirical knowledge involves discovery through processes of controlled inference and it must be statable in propositional form and capable of being verified by anyone through observations but not as Nagel (1952: 56) does that this observation has to be sensory in the precise meaning of this term.
(ii) Theory means in all empirical sciences the explicit formulation of determinate relations between a set of variables in terms of which a fairly extensive class of empirically ascertainable regularities can be explained.

(iii) Neither the fact that these regularities have in the social sciences a rather narrowly restricted universality nor the fact that they permit prediction only to a rather limited extent, constitutes a basic difference between the social and natural sciences, since many branches of the latter show the same features (Schutz, 1970: 4–5).

It seems to Schutz that Nagel misunderstands Max Weber's postulate of subjective interpretation. Nevertheless, he is right in stating that the method which would require that the individual scientific observer identifies himself with the social agent observed in order to understand the motives of the latter, or a method which would refer the selection of the facts observed and their interpretation to the private value system of the particular observer, would merely lead to an uncontrollable private and subjective image in the mind of this particular student of human affairs, but never to a scientific theory.

Schutz goes on to say:

> "But I do not know of any social scientist of stature who ever advocated such a concept of subjectivity as that criticized by Nagel. Most certainly, this was not the case of Max Weber". (ibid.: 5)

Schutz holds the opinion that the social scientists are prevented from grasping the points of vital concern to them by this basic philosophy of sensationalistic empiricism or logic positivism which identifies experience with sensory observation and which assumes that the only alternative to controllable and therefore, objective sensory observation is that of subjective and therefore uncontrollable and unverifiable introspection. In order to account for his own position, Schutz (1970: 5-7) proposes to defend a few rather simple propositions:

1. The primary goal of the social sciences is to obtain organized knowledge of the social reality. 'Social reality', to Schutz, is the sum total of objects and occurrences within the social-cultural world or experienced by the commonsense thinking of men living their daily lives among their fellow men, connected with them in manifold relations of interaction. It is the world of cultural objects and social institutions into which we all are born, within which we have to find our bearings, and with which we have to come to terms. From the outset, we, the actors on the social scene, experience the world we live in as a world both of

nature and of culture, not as a private but as an inter-subjective one, i.e., a world either actually given or potentially accessible to everyone; and this involves intercommunication and language.

2. All forms of naturalism and logical empiricism simply take for granted this social reality, which is the proper object of the social sciences. Inter-subjectivity, interaction, intercommunication and language are simply presupposed as the un clarified foundation of these theories. They assume, as it were, that the social scientist has already solved his fundamental problem, before scientific enquiry starts. To be sure, while Dewey (1934, 1950, 1965) emphasized with a clarity that all enquiry starts and ends within the social cultural matrix, Nagel is fully aware of the fact that science and its self-correcting process is a social enterprise (Nagel, 1952: 53). But, the postulate of describing and explaining human behaviour in terms of controllable sensory observation stops short before the description and explanation of the process by which scientist B controls and verifies the observational findings of scientist A and the conclusions drawn by him. In order to do so, B has to know what A has observed, what the goal of his enquiry is, why he thought the observed fact worthy of being observed, i.e., relevant to the scientific problem at hand etc. This knowledge is commonly called understanding. The explanation of how such a mutual understanding of human beings might occur is apparently left to the social scientist. But, whatever his explanation might be, one thing is sure, that such an inter-subjective understanding between scientist B and scientist A occurs neither by B's observations of A's overt behaviour nor by introspection performed by B, nor by identification of B with A. This means, in the language dear to logical positivism, that so-called protocol propositions about the physical world are of an entirely different kind from protocol propositions about the psycho-physical world.
3. The identification of experience with sensory observation in general and of the experience of overt action in particular (and that is what Nagel proposes) excludes several dimensions of social reality from all possible inquiry.
4. In terms of commonsense thinking, in everyday life, men have knowledge of these various dimensions of the social world in

which they live. To be sure, this knowledge is not only fragmentary, since it is restricted principally to certain sectors of the world, it is also frequently inconsistent in itself and slows all degrees of clarity and distinctness from full insight or 'knowledge about', through 'knowledge of acquaintance' or mere familiarity, to blind belief in things just taken for granted. In this respect, there are considerable differences from individual to individual and from social group to social group. Yet, in spite of all these inadequacies, commonsense knowledge of everyday life is sufficient for coming to terms with fellow men, cultural objects social institutions, or in brief, social reality. This is so because the world (the natural and the social one) is from the outset an inter-subjective world and because, our knowledge of it is in various ways socialized. Moreover, the social world is experienced from the beginning as a meaningful one. We experience our fellow man's action in terms of his motives and goals. And, in the same way, we experience cultural objects in terms of the human action of which they are the result.

5. The fact that in commonsense thinking we take for granted our actual or potential knowledge of the meaning of human actions and their products, as Schutz suggests, precisely what social scientists want to express if they speak of understanding or 'Verstehen' as a technique of dealing with human affairs, Schutz adds.

Verstehen as the Experiential Form of Commonsense Knowledge of Human Interaction

"Verstehen is, thus primarily not a method used by social scientist, but the particular experiential form in which commonsense thinking takes cognizance of the social cultural world. It has nothing to do with introspection; it is a result of processes of learning or acculturation in the same way the commonsense experience of the so-called natural world. Verstehen is, moreover, by no means, a private affair of the observer which cannot be controlled by the experiences of other observers. It is controllable at least to the same extent to which the private sensory perceptions of an individual are controllable by any other individual under certain conditions. Predictions based on Verstehen are continuously made in commences thinking with high success". (Schutz, 1976: 103–9)

Both defenders and critics of the process of Verstehen maintain that Verstehen is subjective. The critics of understanding call it subjective because they hold that understanding the motives of another man's action depends upon the private, uncontrollable and unverifiable institution of the observer and refers to be his private value system. Weber and his school however call Verstehen objective because its goal is to find out what the actor means in his action in contrast to the meaning which this action has for the actor's partner or a neutral observer. This is the origin of Weber's famous postulate of subjective interpretation. The whole discussion, Schutz (1970: 9) speaks, suffers from the failure to distinguish clearly between Verstehen:

(i) as the experiential form of commonsense knowledge of human affairs,
(ii) as an epistemological problem, and
(iii) as a method peculiar to the social sciences.

Verstehen as an Epistemological Problem

In the aforesaid paragraphs, we have already focused on how Schutz looks at Verstehen as the way in which commonsense thinking finds its bearing within the social world and comes to terms with it. Therefore, now, we shift to the epistemological question: how is such understanding or Verstehen possible? Alluding to a statement Kant made in another context, Schutz suggests that it is a 'scandal of philosophy' that so far a satisfactory solution to the problem of our knowledge of other minds, and, in connection therewith, of the inter-subjectivity of our experience of the natural as well as the socio-cultural world has not been found and that until rather recent times, this problem has even escaped the attention of the philosophers (Schutz, 1970: 10). Schutz further adds:

> "But the solution of this most difficult problem of philosophical interpretation is one of the first things taken for granted in our commonsense thinking and practically solved without any difficulty in each of our everyday actions. And since human beings are born of mothers and not concocted in retorts, the experience of the existence of other human beings and of the meaning of their actions is certainly the first and most original empirical observation man makes". (Schutz, 1970: 10)

On the other hand, philosophers like James, Bergson, Dewey, Husserl and Whitehead agree that the commonsense knowledge of everyday life is unquestioned but always questionable background within which enquiry starts and within which alone it can be carried out. While it is this 'Lebenswelt' within which, according to Husserl, all scientific and even logical concepts originate, it is the social matrix within which, according to Dewey, unclarified situations emerge, which have to be transformed by the process of inquiry into unwarranted assertability. Likewise, Whitehead has pointed out that it is the aim of science to produce a theory which agrees with experience by explaining the thought objects constructed by commonsense through the mental constructs or thought objects of science. Thus, for all these thinkers, any knowledge of the world, in commonsense thinking as well as in science, involves mental constructs, syntheses, generalizations, formalizations and idealizations, specific to the respective level of thought organization. The concept of nature, for instance, with which the natural sciences have to deal, is an idealizing abstraction from the Lebenswelt and abstraction which, on principle and of course, legitimately excludes persons with their personal life and all objects of culture which originate as such in practical human activity. Exactly this layer of the Lebenswelt, however, from which the natural sciences have to abstract, is the social reality which the social sciences have to investigate (Schutz, 1970: 10–11).

Verstehen as a Method

This insight sheds light on certain methodological problems peculiar to the social sciences. Schutz says that the assumption that the strict adoption of the principles of concept and theory formation prevailing in the natural sciences will lead to reliable knowledge of social reality is inconsistent in itself. If a theory can be developed on such principles, then it will not tell us anything about social reality as experienced by men in everyday life. Here, Nagel himself admits "it will be highly abstract and its concepts will apparently be remote from the obvious and familiar traits found in any society" (1952: 63). Schutz, on the other hand, says:

> "a theory which aims at explaining social reality, has to develop particular devices foreign to the natural sciences in order to agree with the commonsense experience of the social world. This is

indeed what all theoretical sciences of human affairs—economics, sociology, the sciences of law, linguistics, cultural anthropology, etc.—have done. This state of affairs is founded on the fact that there is an essential difference in the structure of the thought objects or mental constructs formed by the social sciences and those formed by the natural sciences. It is up to the natural scientist alone to define, in accordance with the procedural rules of his science, his observational field, and to determine the facts, data and events within it, which are relevant for his problem or scientific purpose at hand. Neither are those facts and events pre-selected nor is the observational field pre-interpreted. The world of nature, as explored by the natural scientist, does not mean anything to molecules, atoms and electrons. But, the observational field of the social scientist—social reality—has a specific meaning and relevance structure flow to human beings living, acting and thinking within it. By a series of commonsense constructs, they have pre-selected and pre-interpreted this world which they experience as the reality of their daily lives. It is these thought objects of theirs which determine their behaviour by motivating it. The thought objects constructed by the social scientist, in order to grasp this social reality, have to be founded upon the thought objects constructed by the commonsense thinking of men living their daily life within their social world. Thus, the constructs of the social sciences are constructs of the second degree, i.e., constructs of the constructs made by the actors on the social scene, whose behaviour the social scientist has to observe and explain in accordance with the procedural rules of his science" (Schutz, 1970: 11–12).

Thus, according to the phenomenological school of thought, the exploration of the general principles according to which man in daily life organizes his experiences, especially those of the social world, is the first task of the methodology of the social sciences. Schutz has also briefly mentioned only a few problems involved in the phenomenological analysis of the so-called natural attitude by which the aforesaid task can be done.

"The world is from the outset experienced in the pre-scientific thinking of everyday life in the mode of typically. The unique objects and events given to us in a unique aspect are unique within a horizon of typical familiarity and pre-acquaintanceship. Starting form here, it can be shown that whether I do one or the other, and also which traits on qualities of a given object or event, I consider as

> individually unique and which as typical, depends upon my actual interest and the system of relevances involved, briefly upon my practical on theoretical 'problem at hand'. This problem at hand originates, in turn, in the circumstances within which I find myself at any moment of my daily life and which I propose to call my biographically determined situation. Thus, typification depends upon my problem at hand for the definition and solution of which the type has been formed. It can be further shown that at least one aspect of the biographically and situationally determined systems of interest and relevance is subjectively experienced in the thinking of everyday life as systems of motives for action, of choices to be made, of projects to be carried out, of goals to be reached. It is the insight of the actor into the dependencies of the motives and goals of his actions upon his biographically determined situation which social scientists have in view when speaking of the subjective meaning which the actor 'bestows upon' or 'connects' with his action. This implies that the actor and he alone, strictly speaking, know what he does, why he does it and when and where his action starts and ends". (ibid.: 12–13)

Schutz's following narrations deserve special mention here:

> "But the world of everyday life is from the outset also a social cultural world in which I am interrelated in manifold ways of interactions with fellow men known to me in varying degrees of intimacy and anonymity. Phenomenologist holds the view that to a certain extent sufficient for many practical purposes, I understand their behaviour, if I understand their motives goals, choices and plans originating in their biographically determined circumstances. Yet only in particular situations, and then only fragmentarily, can I experience the other's motives, goals, etc., briefly, the subjective meanings they bestow upon their actions, in their uniqueness. I can, however, experience them in their typicality. In order to do so, I construct typical patterns of the actors' motives and ends even of their attitudes and personalities of which their actual conduct is just an instance or example. These typified patterns of others' behaviour become in turn motives of my own actions, and this leads to the phenomenon of self typification will known to social scientists under various names". (ibid.: 13)

Here, what Schutz submits, in the commonsense thinking of everyday life, is the origin of the so-called constructive or ideal types, a concept which as a tool of the social sciences has been analysed by Hempel. But, at least at the commonsense level, the formation of these types involves neither intuition nor a theory if we understand these terms in the sense of Hempel's statements (Hempel, 1952: 76–80). There are also other kinds of ideal or constructive types those formed by the social scientist, which are of a quite different structure and indeed involve theory. But Hempel has not distinguished between the two.

Commonsense Knowledge of Everyday Life is Socialized

- It is, first, structurally socialized since it is based on the fundamental idealization that if someone is to change places with his fellow men, he would experience the same sector of the world in substantially the same perfectives as the fellow-man does, our particular biographical circumstances becoming for all particular purposes at hand irrelevant. Schutz calls this idealization that of the reciprocity of perspectives.
- It is then genetically socialized, because the greater part of our knowledge, as to its content and the particular forms of typification under which it is organized, is socially derived, and this in socially approved terms.
- It is also socialized in the sense of social distribution of knowledge, each individual knowing merely a sector of the world and common knowledge of the same sector varying individually as to its degree of distinctness clarity acquaintanship or mere belief.

These principles of socialization of commonsense knowledge, especially that of the social distribution of knowledge, explain at level partially what the social scientist has in mind in speaking of the functional-structural approach to studies of human affairs. The concept of functionalism in the modern social sciences refers to the socially distributed constructs of patterns of typical motives, goals, attitudes and personalities, which are supposed to be invariant and are then interpreted as the function or structure of the social system itself. The more these interlocked behaviour patterns are standardized and institutionalized, i.e., the more their typicality is socially approved by laws, folkways, mores and habits, the greater is their usefulness in commonsense and scientific thinking as a scheme of interpretation of human behaviour (Schutz, 1970).

These are the outlines of a few major features of the constructs involved in commonsense experience of the inter-subjective world in daily life, called 'Verstehen'. They are the first-level constructs upon which the second-level constructs of the social sciences have to be created. But here a major problem emerges as observed by Schutz. On the one hand, it has been shown that the constructs on the first level, the commonsense constructs, refer to subjective elements, namely, the Verstehen of the actor's action from his, the actor's point of view.

> "Consequently, if the social sciences aim indeed at explaining social reality, then the scientific constructs on the second level, too, must include a reference to the subjective meaning an action has for the actor. This is, I think, what Max Weber understand by his famous postulate of subjective interpretation which has, indeed, been observed so far in the theory of all social sciences. The postulate of subjective interpretation has to be understand in the sense that all scientific explanations of the social world can, and for certain purposes must, refer to the subjective meaning of the actions of human beings from which social reality originates". (ibid.: 15)

On the other hand, Schutz agrees with Nagel's statement that the social sciences, like all empirical sciences, have to be objective in the sense that their propositions are subjected to controlled verification and must not refer to private uncontrollable experience" (ibid.: 14–15).

At this stage of analysis, we confront the question which recurrently disturbs our minds: How is it possible to reconcile these seemingly contradictory principles? Indeed, the most serious question which the methodology of the social sciences has to answer is: How is it possible to form objective concepts and an objectively verifiable theory of subjective meaning – structures? The basic insight that the concepts formed by the social scientist are constructs of the constructs formed in commonsense thinking by the actors on the social scene offers an answer to the question. The scientific constructs formed on the second level, in accordance with the procedural rules valid for all empirical sciences, are objective ideal typical constructs and, as such of a different kind from those developed on the first level of commonsense thinking which they have to supersede. They are theoretical systems embodying general hypotheses in the sense of Hempel's definition (Thomas, 1951: 81). This device has been used by social scientists concerned with theory long before this concept was formulated by Max Weber and developed by his school (Schutz, 1970: 15). Before describing a few features of these scientific constructs, we briefly consider the particular attitudes of the theoretical social scientist to the social world, in contradistinction to the actor on the social scene.

Particular Attitude of the Theoretical Social Scientist to the Social World

The theoretical scientist-*qua*-scientist, not *qua* human being—is not involved in the observed situation, which is to him not of practical but merely of cognitive interest. The system of relevances governing commonsense interpretation in daily life originates in the biographical situation of the observer. By making up his mind to become a scientist, the social scientist has replaced his personal biographical situation by what Schutz calls, following Kauffmann (1941), a scientific situation. The problems with which he has to deal might be quite unproblematic for the human being within the world and vice versa. Any scientific problem is determined by the actual state of the respective science and its solution has to be achieved in accordance with the procedural rules governing this science, which among other things warrant the control and verification of the solution offered. The scientific problem, once established, alone determines what is relevant for the scientist as well as the conceptual frame of reference to be used by him. This and nothing else, according to Schutz, is what Weber means when he postulates the objectivity of the social sciences, their detachment from value patterns which govern or might govern the behaviour of the actors on the social scene.

Schutz's analysis of the functionality of the social scientists is worth mentioning:

> "A social scientist observes certain facts and events within social reality which refer to human action and he constructs typical behaviour or course-of-action patterns from what he has observed. Thereupon he coordinates to these typical course-of-action patterns models of an ideal actor or actors, whom he imagines as being gifted with consciousness. Yet it is a consciousness restricted so as to contain nothing but the elements relevant to the performing the course of action patterns observed. He thus, describes to this

> fictitious consciousness a set of typical notions, purposes, goals, which are assumed to be invariant in the specious consciousness of the imaginary actor-model. This homunculus or puppet is supposed to be interrelated in interaction patterns to the other homunculi or puppets constructed in a similar way. Among these homunculi with which the social scientist postulates his model of the social world of everyday life, sets of motives, goals, roles in-general, systems of relevances—are distributed in such a way as the scientific problems under scrutiny require. Yet—and this is the main point—these constructs are by no means arbitrary. They are subject to the postulate of logical consistency and to the postulate of adequacy. The latter means that each term in such a scientific model of human action must be constructed in such a way that a human act performed within the real world by an individual actor as indicated by the typical construct would be understandable to the actor himself as well as to his fellow-men in terms of commonsense interpretation of everyday life". (1970: 16–17)

Thus, while compliance with the postulate of logical consistency warrants the objective validity of thought objects constructed by the social scientist, compliance with the postulate of adequacy warrants their compatibility with the constructs of everyday life.

The phenomenologist adds that the circumstances within which such a model operates may be varied, i.e., the situation which the homunculi have to meet may be imagined as changed, but not the set of motives and relevances assumed to be the sole content of their consciousness. It can easily be seen that each step involved in the construction and use of the scientific model can be verified by empirical observation, provided that we do not restrict this term to sensory perceptions of objects and events in the outer world but include the experimental form, by which commonsense thinking in everyday life understands human actions and their outcome in terms of their underlying motives and goals.

Thus, we may draw two brief conclusions from the aforesaid discussions:

1. First, a key concept of the basic philosophic position of naturalism is the so-called principle of continuity, although it is under discussion whether this principle means continuity of existence, or of analysis, or of an intellectual criterion of pertinent checks upon the methods employed (Lavine, 1953:

145–54). This principle of continuity in each of these various interpretations is fulfilled by the characterized device of the social sciences, which even establishes continuity between the practice of everyday life and conceptualization of the social sciences (Schutz, 1970: 18).

2. The second is related to the problem of the methodological unity of the empirical sciences. The phenomenologists hold the view that the principal differences between the social and natural sciences do not have to be looked for in a different logic governing each branch of knowledge. But this does not involve the admission that the social sciences have to abandon the particular devices they use for exposing social reality for the sake of an ideal unity of methods which is founded on the entirely unwarranted assumption that only methods used by the natural sciences, and especially by physics, are scientific ones. Schutz, in this context, concludes to the extent that no serious attempt has ever been made by the proponents of the 'Unity of Science' movement to answer or even to ask the question whether the methodological problem of the natural sciences in their present state is not merely a special case of the more general, still unexplored, problem how scientific knowledge is possible at all and what its logical and methodological presumptions are. It is Schutz's personal conviction that phenomenological philosophy has prepared the ground for such an investigation. Its outcome might quite possibly show that the particular methodological devices developed by the social sciences in order to grasp social reality are better suited than those of the natural sciences to lead to the discovery of the general principles which govern all human knowledge (Schutz, 1970).

Ethnomethodology: Towards Micro-sociological and Reflective Method

This part of the chapter is based on the Mennell's viewpoint on ethnomethodology (Mennell, 1976: 115–39). Ethnomethodology should not be mistaken for just one more variety of micro-sociology. It is much more; it represents a comprehensive challenge to some of sociology's most general assumptions. In the past, the ethnomethodologists' interest in small-scale interaction has led to comparisons with the work of Goffman and the symbolic interactionists (Gouldner, 1971; Denzin 1971; Gidlow, 1972) but ethnomethodologists' have vehemently rejected such parallels (Douglas, 1971; Zimmerman and Wieder, 1971). The emergence of ethnomethodology as both Bauman (1973) and Goldthorpe (1973) recognize, represents a renewal of the *Methodenstreit* that rose to prominence in German sociology around the turn of the century. The ethnomethodologists reject deductive explanation of the 'covering law' kind in social science, emphasize the necessity of grasping the 'meanings' that social interaction has for those participating in it, and are preoccupied with the uniqueness of every social situation. Though recast in subtle forms, the old arguments for a rigid distinction between the natural and social science are easily recognizable.

The philosophical roots of ethnomethodology are two-fold. Ethnomethodologists themselves mainly claim intellectual ancestry from the social phenomenology of Alfred Schutz, despite scholars like Hindess (1972) and Bauman (1973) have cast doubt on whether Schutz's work represents an accurate interpretation of Husserl's phenomenology, yet Schutz has other sociological followers—most notably Berger and Luckman (1967)—whose work represents a much less drastic break with the interests of 'conventional sociology' and from whom ethnomethodologists are at pains to emphasize their differences. What is really more distinct of ethnomethodology is its debt to Wittgenesteinian 'ordinary language' philosophy. The nature of these twin debts are being examined below.

The foundation of ethnomethodology, as a school of thought and as a methodology within sociology, is usually attributed to Harold Garfinkel. Although ethnomethodology did not attract very wide attention among sociologists until a spate of publications by Garfinkel and his followers appeared in the mid-1960s, Garfinkel himself has traced his basic ideas back as far as 1945, when he was investigating how juries arrived at their decision. The term 'ethnomethodology' was invented much later as a conscious analogy with the terms 'ethnoscience', 'ethnobotany', 'ethnomedicine' and so on, as they are used by anthropologists. It was meant to signify that just as native classifications of plants or illnesses cannot be taken as science but as data to be analysed by the social scientists, so can the 'methods' employed by participants in social situations.

The substantive research carried out by ethnomethodologists and their critique of 'conventional' (or 'absolutist' or 'constructivist' or 'positivist') sociology are closely related, but a few points can be made about their style of research. A feature of Garfinkel's early studies was his stratagem of disrupting familiar situations in order to expose the background assumptions and expectations—the stock of knowledge and 'methods'—which participants unconsciously deploy in them.

> "Procedurely, it is my preference to start with familiar scenes and ask what can be done to make trouble. The operations that one would have to perform in order to multiply the senseless features of perceived environments; to produce the socially structured affects of anxiety, shame, guilt and indignation, and to produce disorganized interaction, should tell us something about how the structures of every day activities are ordinarily and routinely produced and maintained ... my studies are not properly speaking experimental. They are demonstrations, designed ... as 'aids to a sluggish imagination'. I have found that they produce reflections through which the strangeness of an obstinately familiar world can be detected". (Garfinkel, 1967: 37–38)

A famous example was that in which students were asked to behave as lodgers in their homes (ibid.: 41–44), to the bewilderment and often anger of the rest of the family. Sudnow's 'Passing on the Social Organization of Dying' (1968) is an example of a large-scale study entailing the analysis (but not in this case the disruption) of the minutiae of interaction in hospital wards.

More recently, two fairly distinct (though not mutually exclusive) trends have appeared in ethnomethodological investigations. One is the study of behaviour within organizational settings, especially in organizations dealing with people—as patients, as delinquents, as recipients of welfare payments and so on—focusing particularly on the way in which the clients are categorized and official records manipulated for 'good organizational reasons'. The second trend, in which Harvey Sacks is the outstanding figure, has been towards the development of a new kind of sociolinguistics—the analysis of actual tape-recorded conversations. The rationale for these two tendencies is apparent in the light of the ethnomethodologists' critique of 'conventional sociology'.

The Ethnomethodological Critique of Conventional Sociology

In his, *Method and Measurement in Sociology* (1964), Aaron Cicourel launched a thoroughgoing critique of the whole paraphernalia of sociological research methods. On the first page, he wrote:

> "My basic assumption is that the classification of sociological language is important because linguistic structure and use affects the way people interpret and describe the world. Since sociologists have evolved their own theoretical terminologies and frequently discuss, on the one hand, in these varying terms the language and substance of each other's theories and on the other hand the language of persons in every day life whose behaviour they are interested in explaining and predicting, it is quite likely that the syntax and meaning of these languages will become entangled."

For their view of what would constitute acceptable sociological theorizing, the ethnomethodologists rely on Schutz's distinction between first and second degree constructs. Schutz contended that we experience the external world of things, people and events as typifications, classifications and categorizations. The corpus of everyday knowledge handed down to us also includes an armoury of practical actions, "efficient recipes for the use of typical means for bringing about typical ends in typical situations" (Schutz, 1964: 14). But any individual's stock of everyday knowledge taken as a whole is to a greater or lesser degree incoherent, inconsistent and fragmentary. Perfect clarity is neither attainable nor necessary, for his knowledge serves essentially practical purposes. The sheer diversity of practical actions is an obstacle to coherence and, moreover, while the practical recipes 'work', producing the desired and expected results, there is little incentive for conscious pursuit of clarity (Mennell, 1974). For the social scientist, this poses a paradox. He has to give clear and consistent explanations of a subject matter that is itself often unclear and inconsistent. Schutz suggested that this is achieved by the construction, for scientific purposes, of typifications of the typifications subjects make for their practical purposes—by building constructs of the second degree.

The ethnomethodologists however argue that conventional sociology generally fails to carry out this procedure. As they put it, it tends to use commonsense knowledge of social structures as both a topic and resource of enquiry (Garfinkel, 1967: 31). Many of the 'facts' that sociologists tend to accept as data have been created in everyday situations for practical purposes. They are not facts but 'accomplishments'. As Zimmerman and Pollner express this argument:

> "Sociology's acceptance of lay member's formulation of the formal and substantive features of sociology's topical concerns makes sociology into an eminently folk discipline ... . In so far as the social structures are treated as a given rather than as an accomplishment, one is subscribing to a lay inquirer's version of those structures". (1971: 82)

To this extent, it is argued, conventional sociology is merely on a par with any person's understanding of his everyday situation—'a first degree' corpus of knowledge 'competitive' with everyday practical knowledge.

The thrust of this view can be seen in repeated criticisms of the use of official statistics in sociology (Cicourel, 1968; Kituse and Cicourel, 1963; Douglas, 1967). Douglas takes a case of classic concern to sociology that of suicide rates, and argues that they reflect the interpretation of deaths by coroners. Their judgements cannot be reduced merely to a formal rule of categorizations—the rules are always interpreted, and Douglas purports to show that the interpretations of different coroners are inconsistent with each other. Cicourel extends similar reasoning to the field of delinquency, showing how the unconscious background assumptions of probation officers and police lead them to find delinquency where they expect to find it and to be more ready to categorize acts by certain types of people than others as delinquent. The conclusions are similar: aggregate statistics are meaningless, or at most reflect only the operation of the official bureaucracy, because identical 'real world events' may be placed in different categories, while quite different events may be placed in one and the same category.

Sociologists have no doubt frequently used official statistics too uncritically. As Hindess (1973) argues, it is disastrous to impose alien categories and then to reify the resulting statistics, as he shows happened dramatically in the classification of the agrarian population in the Indian census of 1951. Categories are theoretical constructs, whose choice must be justified as appropriate. Given this, however, a great deal can be done by the framing of detailed instructions and training of enumerators, interviewers and officials to minimize the inconsistent application of categories. But, as Hindess points out, the ethnomethodologists do not show much interest in the possibility of estimating the degree of error present in statistics of substantially improving them.

Why these possibilities do not interest them may become a little clearer in the light of Pollner's critique (1974) of Becker's version of the labelling theory of social deviance. The theory is summed up in Becker's statement that the deviant is one to whom that label has successfully been applied; deviant behaviour is behaviour that people so label (Becker, 1964: 9). Pollner, however, accuses Becker of not following this principle consistently, and thereby confusing the commonsense actor's model of deviance with a sociological one. For the commonsense actor deviance is an objective quality of another's action that causes and justifies an appropriate reaction to it by the community. On the other hand, Pollner writes, "viewed sociologically, the deviant character of the act is not intrinsic to the act but depends upon or, more emphatically, is constituted by the subsequent response of the community" (1974: 29). Becker (1963: 20) employs both these perspectives to produce his cross-classification of types of deviant as shown below:

Types of Deviant Behaviour	*Obedient Behaviour*	*Rule-breaking Behaviour*
Perceived as deviant	Falsely accused	Pure deviant
Not perceived as deviant	Conforming	Secret deviant

Pollner, on the other hand, draws on his study of an American traffic court where, as he points out, many of the convicted feel aggrieved because their commonsense knowledge tells them that the same offence is continually being committed without the offenders being apprehended:

> "not all those who violate rules are categorized as deviant and not all those who are categorized as deviant have violated a rule. Presumably (i.e. in perfect conformity with the criterion of rule violation), if all the faults of police and judicial processing were removed so as to provide for homogeneous categories, then labelling would be superfluous. Rule violation and application of the label '*deviant*' would coincide and the deviant would in effect be he who has violated a rule and only incidentally he who has been labelled deviant". (Pollner, 1974: 30)

Since this condition is not met, Pollner rejects the idea of 'real deviance' as a matter of no relevance for sociologists, as being in effect an unknowable "*Ding An Sich*". Becker's classification is just the same as that employed by judges (who for this purpose count as laymen using commonsense practical reasoning): 'conforming' and 'pure deviant' behaviour correspond to a just acquittal and a just conviction.

The deeper roots of the ethnomethodologists' critique of conventional sociology lie in their views on the nature of social interaction and the use of language within it. Underlying most sociology, they see what Wilson (1971) calls the 'normative paradigm'. This is based on two related ideas that interaction is rule-governed, and that deductive explanation is appropriate to sociology. "Deductive explanation means logically deducing the facts to be explained from a number of theoretical premises under given empirical conditions. This necessitates that each description entering into deductive explanation must be treated as having a stable meaning that is independent of the circumstances in which it is produced" (Wilson, 1971: 71). For this to be true in the explanation of social interaction, behaviour has to be seen as governed by rules, which Wilson defines as "a stable linkage between the situation of an actor and his action in that situation" (1971: 60). What this really amounts to, he contends, is that in order to treat various instances as examples of the same category of social situation, sociologists have to assume a degree of 'cognitive consensus'—to assume that actors agree in recognizing situations at different times and in different places as being instances of 'the same kind' of situation, and therefore behave similarly.

In contrast, underlying the work of phenomenological sociologists is "the principle of the contextual determination of meaning" (Douglas, 1971: 37). Of course, conventional sociologists recognize that the same idea of behaviour (a lie, for instance) can have different meanings in different contexts. Ethnomethodologists, however, take an unusually radical view of the interpretative nature of the process of social interaction. They see actors as continually groping towards a definition of the situation at hand, and situations as being subject to continuous redefinition. In particular, all conversations contain numerous expressions that are not explicitly defined in a particular situation and, participants have to achieve 'operational' or working definitions of all such 'indexical' expressions, which are valid only in the situation at hand.

'Indexicality' is a key term in ethnomethodology. It is taken from the work of the logician Bar-Hillel (1954) who defines an indexical expression as one that depends for its meaning on the context in which it is produced (cited in Wilson, 1971). Bar-Hillel gives as examples of indexical expressions the statements like 'It is raining' and 'I am hungry' as contrasted with a non-indexical statement such as 'Ice floats on water' which has universal validity. Abercrombie (1974) has pointed out that Bar-Hillel argues only that indexical expressions depend for their reference, not their general meaning, on the context in which they are produced, and that this argument does not justify the much stronger principle of the contextual determination of meaning. The meaning immediately becomes clear when the reference is made evident. Garfinkel (1967: 25–26), on the other hand, illustrates his view of indexicality with an excerpt from a highly elliptical conversation between a husband and a wife, together with the much longer expansion needed to make it intelligible to an outside observer. Yet conventional sociologists remain unconvinced that this is a matter of vast importance. They take it as a common place that people in close relationships anticipate a large stock of relevant knowledge on the part of the other, making possible elliptical conversation, but that participants could explain the reference of their conversation to an outside observer if necessary and thereby make its meaning manifest, and that this is sufficient for purposes of sociology.

Nonetheless, the ethnomethodologists stand by their view that meaning is utterly dependent on unique situational contexts:

> "It is apparent that in the interpretative view of social interaction, in contrast with the normative paradigm, definitions of situations and actions are not explicitly or implicitly assumed to be settled once and for all by literal application of a pre-existing culturally established system of symbols. Rather, the meanings of situations and actions are interpretations formulated on particular occasions by the participants in the interaction and are subject to reformulation on subsequent occasions". (Wilson, 1971: 69)

Similarly, Zimmerman and Pollner (1971: 97) argue that the "features of social situations are unique to the particular settings and therefore may not be generalized by the analyst to other settings". That the new Methodenstreit is but the old reborn is here very evident. Bauman (1973: 34) succinctly comments that those who argue for the uniqueness of socio-cultural events are "convinced that the uniqueness of what they see and describe is an attribute of the phenomenon described and not of the very low level of particularity they have deliberately chosen or unknowingly inherited". But given their insistence on the 'irremediability' of indexicality, the ethnomethodologists consider the interpretative view of social interaction incompatible with the logic of deductive explanation. McHugh (1974: 3) goes so far as to say that "speech never solves this problem, if by solve is meant to remedy, because any imaginable solution (any new speech) is itself a new version of the same old problem". It is difficult to see how some extreme position is compatible with Schutz's views on the use of second degree constructs.

Ethnomethodology and Schutz

Since ethnomethodology stands in opposition not only to conventional sociology but also to the work of other sociological followers of Alfred Schutz, we would draw attention to an ambiguity in Schutz's work (referred earlier) and to the ethnomethodologists' interpretation of it.

In a generally very clear statement of his position. Schutz (1962: 48–66) spelled out the points elaborated earlier in this chapter on which he was in agreement with Ernest Nagel who may be taken as representative of all that ethnomethodologists dislike in the logical positivist philosophy of science.

Schutz, then, clearly embraces the deductive mode of explanation for the social sciences. Of course, he goes on to argue that Nagel misunderstands the nature of 'Verstehen'. He explains that it has nothing to do with introspection but, just like commonsense experience of the everyday world, is a result of processes of learning and acculturation. And, 'Verstehen' is "by no means a private affair of the observer which cannot be controlled by the experience of other observers" (ibid.: 56). So, Schutz here endorses the assumption of a degree of cognitive consensus rejected by Wilson.

In the same paper, Schutz proceeds to reiterate his familiar points that because social reality already has meaning for people living within it, the social scientist must work with constructs founded upon the everyday constructs of the daily world. This notion of constructs of the second degree is the source of great difficulty. For one thing, it is not entirely clear whether Schutz thought that all or only some of our sociological constructs must be of second order. The ethnomethodologists certainly believe that all of them must be. On the other hand, Schutz remarks at one point that "all scientific explanations of the social world can, for certain purposes, must refer to the subjective meaning of the action of human beings from which social reality originates" (ibid.: 62). This seems to imply that Schutz would agree with Gellner (1960) that for example, to understand the class structure of a society, one must not only know what rank, etc., mean in it, but also how many people occupy each grade, and this is a matter of counting, not understanding.

More importantly, Schutz repeatedly argued that 'constructs of the second degree' must conform not only to the 'postulate of logical consistency' but also the 'postulate of adequacy'. By this he meant:

> "that each term in such a scientific model of human action must be constructed in such a way that a human act performed within the real world by an individual actor as indicated by the typical construct would be understandable to the actor himself as well as to his fellow men in terms of commonsense interpretation of every day life". (1962: 64)

But this statement is deeply ambiguous. If Schutz means only that social scientists' theories must be able logically to subsume the practical 'recipies' of commonsense, and so to relate generalizing propositions to descriptions of how actual people behave in actual situations, thus this is nothing exceptionable. On the other hand, "if what he means entails that the commonsense view of the social world must be immune from correction and modification by the discoveries of social science, then what he asserts is not only false but deprives the social sciences of part of their genuine importance. Our commonsense beliefs about society are not only often false, but are also incorrigible at the level of commonsense" (Emmett and MacIntyre, 1970; Lassmann, 1974, quoted from Thorns, 1976).

The ethnomethodologists seem fairly clearly to opt for the second degree of these two interpretations. This is the burden of their criticisms that conventional sociology is merely a first degree or 'folk' sociology, and that its vocabularies and theories seek to remedy the indexical properties of members' talk and conduct (Garfinkel, 1967: 11). On the other hand, there is evidence that Schutz intended his remarks in the contrary sense. First, he often referred to 'sets of motives, goals and roles' (1962: 64) as examples of valid second degree constructs—and these are precisely the kinds of concept distrusted by ethnomethodologists (Mennell, 1974; McHugh, 1974; Cicourel, 1973). Second, in both his early and late work (1962: 64–65; 1972: 244–46) he spoke appreciatively of the progress of economic theory—for example, models of perfect and monopolistic competition—which claims great generality and its poles apart from the ethnomethodological style of investigation. Third, in his comments on Nagel at least he makes it clear that his quibble is not so much with how social scientists have in the main done their social science (though of course he had specific criticisms), but with Nagel's way of representing that procedure (Mennell, 1974: 150).

It is true that Schutz at times appears to give more support to the ethnomethodological position. For instance, in a paper taken by Garfinkel (1967) as the basis for the influential last chapter of *Studies in Ethnomethodology*, Schutz (1964: 64–68) was at pains to emphasize that we should not speak simply of a concept or ideal type, but must specify the problem for which it has been constructed. Here, Schutz is essentially criticizing what Wagner (1964) was later to call the 'fallacy of the displacement of scope' (of concepts and theories from their micro- or macro-level of origin to the other), but rather broadens the issue. He says, "To be sure, it must be admitted that the term 'level' applies strictly only to whole systems of problems; nevertheless, the consequences are, in principle, the same". However, Schutz's conclusions are broadly the same as previously mentioned. He admits that a great part of social science can be performed "at a level which legitimately abstracts from all that happens in the individual actor" (1964: 84–85), though he regards it as a kind of intellectual shorthand. Where 'real scientific work' is done, however, the scientist will always have the option of shifting to the level of the individual actor. This condition is clearly met in even so apparently 'abstract' and generalizing a branch of social science as macro-economic theory, and it is all that is required to meet the postulate of adequacy.

On the whole, although Schutz undoubtedly presents problems of interpretation, it seems that writers like Berger and Luckmann follow him more clearly than do the ethnomethodologists. In practice, the ethnomethodologists' criticisms of conventional sociology seem to be supported by appeals to certain arguments of Wittgensteinian philosophers.

Ethnomethodology and the Wittgensteinians

In its modern form, the case against generalizing deductive explanation in social science has repeatedly been stated by Wittgensteinian philosophers, and the ethnomethodologists often appeal to the writings of philosophers such as Winch (1958, 1964), Louch (1966) and Austin (1961, 1965) to support their own arguments.

Winch's basic argument is that the reasons people give for their actions, their explanations of their motivation, cannot be taken as the causes of those actions, because the relation between a reason and an action is internal and logical, not external and contingent. Reasons are not therefore anything distinct from their supposed effects. This view is echoed loudly in the work of McHugh and others (1974: 27–28). They see 'motive' as a commonsense formulation, the acceptance of which by the sociologists contributes to sociology's status as a 'folk discipline'. They claim that the conventional sociologist still conceives of motive as a practical actor's concrete report of his state of mind: he only shifts his focus from the state of mind to the talk, by treating the talk as sort of public indicator of the mind (ibid.: 3). They conceive of reasons as the "ad hoc reconstruction of the concrete practice of following a rule" (ibid.: 86). Again, this rests on the view that rules, always having to be reinterpreted in every new situation, cannot give any clear guidance to action. Reasons, in fact, are seen as post facto justification for actions, and bear no relation to what brought them about. "It is something like a logician who wants to do a formal proof. The rules of logic do not provide a correct answer, they provide a guide to how answers should be defended. Reasons should be seen in a similar way" (ibid.: 88).

This position seems, however, inevitably to lead some ethnomethodologists to try to get at meetings entirely through what is extremely available so that paradoxically they end up in virtually a behaviourist position. The distinguished behaviourist Skinner has written:

> "What is said by a sentence is something more than what the words in it mean. The impulse to explicate a meaning is easily understood. We ask 'what do you mean?' because the answer is frequently helpful. Clarifications in this sense have an important place in every sort of intellectual endeavour. For the purposes of effective discourse, the method of paraphrase usually suffices; we may not need extra-verbal referents. But, the replication of verbal behaviour

> should not be allowed to generate a sense of scientific achievement. One has not accounted for a rework by paraphrasing 'what it means'". (1957: 8–10)

The resemblance to ethnomethodological views on indexically and the unacceptability of reasons as causes of actions is striking.

Of course, conventional sociology rejects this position by assuming, along with Schutz, that it is possible to interpret motivation through a process of 'Verstehen'. This essentially the same as the commonsense process of ascription of motives, though an attempt is made to systematize and clarify sets of motives for sociological purposes—a procedure again sanctioned by Schutz. The ethnomethodologists, however, seem sceptical about the possibility of attaining such clarity because they consider polymorphism to be inevitable and all-pervasive both in the concepts of everyday life and within the sociological realm.

What is meant by polymorphism? Gellner (1968) sees it as one of the main pillars of the 'linguistic philosophy' of the Wittgensteinian. The principle is perhaps most easily explained by means of the distinction between a concept and a homonym. An example of a very obvious homonym is the word 'racket' which can either refer to a kind of criminal activity, to an implement used in the game of tennis, or to a medieval musical instrument. In this case, there is no connection between the three meanings, but in the case of polymorphism which Wittgensteinians see as such more pervasive than simple homonymity in the ordinary use of language, a word has a variety of related though far from identical meanings. As Gellner (1968: 50–51) pointed out, traditional, pre-Wittgensteinian philosophy assumed that "a concept, if clear, has one criterion (which may of course contain a number of conditions in conjunction or even as alternatives), and that if on the other hand there is a multiplicity of sets of criteria, we are already dealing with homonyms".

But this clarity is precisely what is denied by 'linguistic' philosophers, who strenuously emphasize complexity, variegation, blurred boundaries and transitions between concepts. More precisely:

> "The 'polymorphous' diagnosis offered of this situation by Linguistic Philosophy runs as follows: a term may very well apply to

> a whole class of objects A, B, C, etc., in such a way that A does have something in common with B, and B with C, but not necessarily A with C. There may, as it is put, be a 'family likeness' such as occurs when a member of a family is recognizably one of it, yet no two members need have any features in common". (Gellner, 1968: 48)

This is the classic Wittgensteinian idea of 'family likeness' and something very close to the principle of polymorphism is clearly a key part of the ethnomethodologists' case. Apparently, only Coulter (1973) has actually used the word 'polymorphism', but the principle is perfectly evident in ethnomethodological criticisms of official statistics and discussions of indexicality. Obviously, it would be futile to deny that there are imperfections both in social statistics and in sociological vocabulary (consider the term 'role' or the Minoan labyrinth of terminology used in the study of social stratification). Sociologists need not deny it, so long as they remain convinced, as the ethnomethodologists are not, that in social science just as in natural science, progress is always possible through the process of criticism towards greater consistency, coherence and clarity.

But a second pillar of 'linguistic' philosophy identified by Gellner is the 'Argument from the Paradigm Case' (APC for short). This is the argument that words mean what they are used to mean. If we deny that a word means what it is customarily said to mean, we must either be ignorant of the language or be intent upon reforming on correcting it. Both the 'linguistic' philosophers and the ethnomethodologists claim this is absurd (Mennell, 1976: 154). The ethnomethodological variant of the APC can be seen in the following passage from Garfinkel:

> "Characteristically, formal investigations have been concerned either with devising normative theories of symbolic usages, or while seeking descriptive theories, have settled for normative ones. In either case, it is necessary to instruct the construing member to act in accordance with the investigator's instructions in order to guarantee that the investigator will be able to study their usages as instances of the usages the investigator has in mind. But, following Wittgenstein, person's actual usages are rational usages in some *'language game'*. What is their game? As long as this programmatic question is neglected, it is inevitable that person's usages will fall short. The more will this be so the more subject's interests in usages dicted by different practical considerations from those of investigators". (1967: 70)

Plausible as the APC may appear, Gellner (1968: 37) argues that it is basically silly; it confuses connotation and enotation. The fact that people in a given society have a use or a range of uses for a term (such as 'miracle') in no way establishes that their suppositions about the workings of the world are correct. The APC is a manifestation of an ancient philosophical tendency, against which Popper (1972: 24) argues:

> "When Kant said our intellect imposes its laws upon nature, he was right—except that he did not notice how often our intellect fails in the attempt: the regularities we try to impose are psychologically a priori, but there is not the slightest reason to assume that they are a priori valid, as Kant thought".

Science can and must seek to correct commonsense (Mennell, 1976).

Thus, while Mennell argues the superiority of Popper's realism over phenomenology logical positivism and Wittgensteinianlism as an epistemological basis for social science, Popper's remark (1972) does point towards some general conclusions that can be drawn from the foregoing discussions of ethnomethodology.

The fundamental flaw in the ethnomethodologists' position is their two-level conception of knowledge, for which they draw support both from Schutz and the Wittgensteinian, and which entails the view that there is a 'commonsense world' that sociology cannot and must not attempt to correct or 'remedy' but only to analyse. In consequence, as raw material for analysis, they call for 'literal descriptions' of social interaction and talk (Wilson, 1971: 7; Filmer, 1971: 107, 115; Mennell, 1976: 155). Along with logical positivists like Carnap, they accept the possibility of pre-theoretic 'observation language' (Hindess, 1973: 54–58). Popper, on the other hand, argues that all observation, both laymen's everyday observation and scientific observation, is theory impregnated. It is not possible to know or describe anything without employing some general concept. There is no sharp discontinuity between everyday and scientific knowledge; propositions from commonsense are the starting point of all science, and scientific knowledge evolves only by these being systematically exposed to the process of criticism. In this limited sense, the ethnomethodologists' charge that sociology is a 'folk discipline' is correct. To admit this, however, they allege,

> "… assumes sociology to be a disciplined investigation that is fully competitive with members' relaxed investigation … . Such an assumption leaves unexplicated members' methods for analyzing, accounting, fact finding, and so on, which produce for sociology its field of data". (Zimmerman and Pollner, 1971: 83)

According to Mennell (1976: 156), the latter conclusion is untrue. There seems little reason why the new interests in linguistic behaviour and what might be called the 'ultra-micro-analysis' of social interaction cannot be handled within other epistemologies, and indeed Sacks and his colleagues (Sacks, 1972; Schegloff and Sacks, 1973) have already produced generalizations from conversational analysis that seem quite capable of being absorbed into orthodox sociology.

Ethnomethodologists often approvingly quote W.I. Thomas' famous dictum that "if men define situations as real, they are real in their consequences", but they have a strong tendency to abbreviate it in effect to "if men define situations as real, they are real" (1951: 81). That social reality must remain akin to the shadows of the prisoners in Plato's cave seems to be the drift, for example, of Pollner's criticism of Becker, mentioned above. Such a view seems to stand in the way of asking the questions of most interest to both sociologists and laymen, for Thomas' dictum in its untruncated vision leads to the study of the unintended consequences of social actions, which is the very basis of sociological theories combining propositions about participants' perceptions of the situation with propositions contributed by sociologists about the dynamics of the wider structures in which participants are enmeshed but can only partially or inaccurately perceive from their individual vantage points. Merton (1968) takes Thomas' dictum as the point of departure for his classic discussions of the self-fulfilling and self-contradictory prophecy. But, the idea of unintended consequences of social action can be interpreted much more broadly (Mennell, 1974), so that investigating them is arguably sociology's very raison d'etre.

Hence, ethnomethodologists are violently opposed to the view that there is no fundamental difference between the phenomena of the natural and social sciences. For them, the natural world is an object world that 'exists' out there, independent of a knowing human subject. Because of the externality of this world, it can be validly apprehended by the methods now employed in the natural sciences. The social world, on the other hand, is most fundamentally a product of human actors. It is not a reality sui-generis. It has no existence apart from its member's definitions of it. Societal members, in the process of going about their everyday activities, 'make' social reality. Thus members learn to produce appropriate verbal accounts that other members consider to be acceptable explanations of behaviour in routine societal situations. It is in this manner that the notion of an external social order comes to be constructed. That is, in the process of going about their everyday behaviour and in their 'commonsense' accounts of it members externalize and objectify to the extent that a social reality emerges.

To the extent that social reality is therefore an emergent phenomenon that is continually being produced, sustained and changed by actors, it is ludicrous to take this reality as an external 'given' that can be called upon as a resource to 'explain' social phenomena within a cause-effect framework. According to the phenomenological sociologists, this is what positivists do and in doing this their stance to the data is no less naive than that of 'lay' as opposed to 'scientific' members of these societies. Since the positivist problematic is of the same order as that of layman, and since they draw upon the same pool of commonsense to formulate their problems and reach their decisions, the knowledge they produce is of no higher order than that of the layman. Every man, in this sense, is a sociologist, "the scientific rhetoric of the professional notwithstanding".

The task to which sociology should be addressing itself is the study of those processes by which members assemble social structure. In order to do this, the sociologist must deliberately suspend his belief in the existence of an external objective social world—a belief he will undoubtedly carry as a consequence of the fact that he is indeed a member of the social milieu which has constructed that world. He must forsake this natural commonsense towards the world and replace it with the theoretic stance (Douglas, 1971). In the theoretic attitude, he becomes anthropologically strange and is in a position to step outside the 'Lebenswelt' and to reflect upon it—and its construction—from a perspective akin to phenomenological epoch. In this manner, the everyday world of commonsense becomes a topic for examination. For the ethnomethodologists this is as close as a sociologist can come to disinterestedness.

From this perspective meaning is always problematic, both for members of society and for the researcher attempting to apprehend their actions. The so-called 'shared' meanings of the symbolic interactionists are most directly accomplishments of members' glossing practices. Thus symbolic interactionists, no less than most other sociologists, presuppose that a shared symbolic world exists and forms the social order. To this extent they retain the mundane commonsense stance, and are similarly fettered by it.

Kuhn's account (1970) of the way in which facts are shaped according to the conceptual framework from which they are viewed, describes the way in which ethnomethodologists perceive the actualities of positivist research. The latter is seen to be essentially a self-validating procedure in which the operant paradigm precludes the collection of any data that might serve to undermine the paradigm itself. Partly as a result of this and partly as a result of the intrusion of the individual researcher's own commonsense knowledge and background assumption, positivist sociology is said to be notorious for producing conflicting accounts of what is supposedly the same phenomenon.

For the ethnomethodologists, the researcher in the theoretic stance attempts to cleanse his mind of presuppositions before setting out to describe in straightforward 'observation' language the behaviour of individuals in social situations. The aim is to build up a storehouse of this simple accurate description to such an extent that the 'awesome indexicality' of behaviour can be overcome. Then and only then, will sociology be in a position to trans-situationalize knowledge. This is the point at which meaningful theory construction can occur. Theory has to be built up from the bottom by a process of induction. Current attempts at theory construction in positivist sociology are deemed to be not only premature but also doomed to failure as a direct result of its adherents' mundane stance to the data.

From the above discussion, it becomes obvious that there are several points at which the ethnomethodologists and phenomenologists claim to diverge from positivist's sociology. Chief among these would seem to be the following:

1. Denial of the proposition that there are no fundamental differences between the natural and social sciences.
2. Denial of the proposition that the methods of the natural sciences are directly applicable to the social sciences.
3. Denial of the proposition that an objective social reality exists independent of a knowing human subject.

4. Denial of the possibility of producing and/or testing deduction theory.
5. Affirmation of the proposition that social reality is an emergent phenomenon.
6. Affirmation of the proposition that "social structure remains an accountable illusion of the sociologists' commonsense knowledge unless we can reveal a connection between the cognition processes that contribute to the emergence of contextual activities, and the normative accounting schemes we use for claiming knowledge as laymen and researchers" (Cicourel, 1973: 7).

References

Abercrombie, N., 1974, Sociological Indexicality, *Journal for the Theory of Social Behaviour.*

Austin, J.L., 1961, *Philosophical Papers*, London: Oxford University Press.

——, 1965, *How to do Things with Words*, London: Oxford University Press.

Bar-Hillel, Y., 1954, Indexical Expressions, *Mind*, 63, pp. 359–79.

Bauman, Z., 1973, On the Philosophical Status of Ethnomethodology, *Sociological Review*, 21.

Becker, H., 1963, *The Outsiders*, New York: The Free Press.

Berger, P. and Luckman, T. 1967, *The Social Construction of Reality*, London: Allen Lane.

Cicourel, A.V., 1973, *Cognitive Sociology*, Harmondsworth: Penguin Books.

——, 1964, *Methods and Measurement in Sociology*, New York: The Free Press.

——, 1968, *The Social Organization of Juvenile Justice*, New York: Wiley.

Coulter, J., 1973, Language and the Conceptualization of Meaning, *Sociology*, 7 (2).

Denzin, N.K., 1971, The Logic of Naturalistic Enquiry, *Social Forces*, 50.

Dewey, John, 1910, *How We Think*, Boston: Heath.

——, 1934, *A Common Faith*, London: Oxford University Press.

——, 1965, *The Influence of Darwin on Philosophy*, Bloomington: Indiana University Press.

Douglas, J.D., 1967, *The Social Meanings of Suicide*, Princeton N.J.: Princeton University Press.

——, 1971, *The Relevance of Sociology*, New York: The Free Press.

Emmett, Dorothy and MacIntyre, A. (eds.), 1970, *Sociological Theory and Philosophical Analysis*, London: Macmillan.

Filmer, P. et al., 1972, *New Direction in Sociological Theory*, London: Collier-Macmillan.

Garfinkel, Harold, 1967, *Studies in Ethnomethodology*, Englewood Cliffs, N.J.: Prentice-Hall.

——, 1968, "The Origins of the Term Ethnomethodology", in R.J. Hill and R.S. Crittendon (eds.), Proceedings of the Purdue Symposium on Ethnomethodology, Institute Monograph Series No. 1, Purdue University.

Gellner, E., 1960, Review of P. Winch: The Idea of Social Science, *British Journal of Sociology*, 11.

——, 1968, *Works and Things*, Harmondsworth: Penguin Books.

Gidlow, B., 1972, Ethnomethodology: New Name of Old Practices, *British Journal of Sociology*, 23 (4).

Goldthorpe, J.H., 1973, A Revolution in Sociology, *Sociology*, 7, 3.

Gouldner, A.W., 1971, *The Coming Crisis in Western Sociology*, London: Heinemann.

Hempel, C.G., 1952, "Symposium: Problem of Concepts and Theory Formation in the Social Sciences", in Ernest Nagel and C.G. Hempel (eds.), *Science, Language and Human Rights*, American Philosophical Association, Eastern Division, Philadelphia, pp. 43–64.

Hindess, B., 1972, The Phenomenological Sociology of Alfred Schutz, *Economy and Society*, 1 (1).

——, 1973, *The Use of Official Statistics in Sociology*, London: Macmillan.

Kauffmann, Felix, 1941, *Methodology of the Social Sciences*, New York: Oxford University Press, p. 126.

Kituse, J. and Cicourel, A.V., 1963, A Note on the Use of Official Statistics, *Social Problems*, 11.

Kuhn, T.S., 1970, *The Structure of Scientific Revolutions*, Chicago: University of Chicago Press.

Lassman, Peter, 1974, "Phenomenological Perspectives in Sociology", in John Rex, *Approaches to Sociology*, London: Routledge and Kegan Paul.

Lavine, Thelma Z. 1933, Note to Naturalists on the Human Spirit, *Journal of Philosophy*, pp.145–54.

Louch, A.R. 1966, *Explanation and Human Action*, Oxford: Basil Blackwell.

McHugh, P. et al., 1970, "On the Failure of Positivism", in J.D. Douglas (ed.), 1970, *Understanding Everyday Life*, Chicago: Aldine.

——. et al., 1974, *On Beginnings of Social Inquiry*, London: Routledge and Kegan Paul.

Mennell, Stephen J., 1974, *Sociological Theory: Uses and Unities*, New York and Washington: Praeger Publishers.

Mennell, Stephen J., 1976, "Ethnomethodology and the New Methodenstreit", in David C. Thorns (ed.), *New Directions in Sociology*, Newton Abbot, London: David and Charles.

Merton, R.K., 1968, *Social Theory and Social Structure*, New York: The Free Press.

Nagel, Ernest, 1952, *Science, Language and Human Rights*, American Philosophical Association, Eastern Division, Philadelphia, pp. 43–64.

——, 1961, *The Structure of Science*, London: Routledge and Kegan Paul.

Pollner, M., 1974, "Sociological and Common Sense Models: Models of the Labelling Process", in R. Turner (ed.), *Ethnomethodology*, Harmondsworth: Penguin Books.

Popper, Karl R., 1972, *Objective Knowledge*, New York: Harper and Row.

Sacks, H. ,1972 (a), "An Initial Investigation of the Usability of Conversational Data for Doing Sociology" in Sudnow, D. (ed), *Studies in Social Interactions*, New York: Free Press.

——, 1972 (b), "On the Analysability of Stories by Children", in Gumpery, J.J. and Hymes D. (eds), *Directions in Socio Linguistics: The Ethnography of Communications*, New York: Holt.

Schegloff, E. and Sacks, H., 1973, Opening of Closings, *Semiotica*, 8.

Schutz, A., 1962, Collected Papers I, *The Problems of Social Reality*, The Hague: Martinus Nijhoff.

——, 1964, Collected Papers, *Studies in Social Theories*, The Hague: Martinus Nijhoff.

——, 1966, Collected Papers II, *Studies in Phenomenological Philosophy*, The Hague: Martinus Nijhoff.

——, 1970, "Concept and Theory Formation in Social Sciences", in D. Emmett and A. MacIntyre (eds.), *et al.*

——, 1972, *The Phenomenology of the Social World*, tr. by G. Walsh and F. Lehnert, London: Heinemann.

Skinner, B.F., 1957, *Verbal Behavior*, New York: Appleton-Century-Crafts.

Thomas, W.I., 1951, *Social Behavior and Personality*, E.H. Volkart (ed.), New York: Social Science Research Council, p. 81.

Thorns, D., 1976, *New Directions in Sociology*, Newton Abbot, London: David and Charles.

Wagner, Helmut R., 1964, "Displacement of Scope: A Problem of the Relationship between Small-Scale and Large-Scale Theories", *American Journal of Sociology*, 69 (5).

Wilson, T.P., 1971, "Normative and Interpretative Paradigms in Sociology", in J.D. Douglas (ed.), *et al.*

Winch, Peter, 1958, *The Idea of Social Science*, London: Routledge and Kegan Paul.

——, 1964, Understanding a Primitive Society, *American Philosophical Quarterly*, 1 (4).

Zimmerman, D.H. and Pollner, M., 1971, "Everyday World as a Phenomenon", in J.D. Douglas (ed.), *et al.*

Zimmerman, D.H. and Wieder, D.L., 1971, "Ethnomethodology and the Problem of Order", in J.D. Douglas (ed.), *et al.*

4

Positioning the Positivistic Dispute in Frankfurt Tradition

In the previous chapter, we have analysed the emergence of phenomenological critique of positivism, which has presented a radical empirical or idealistic alternative to positivism. This has reached its most advanced form in the writings of ethnomethodologists (Cicourel, 1964; McHugh, 1970). Further renewed interest in Marx's critique of political economy has given some way to restoring Marx to the realm of credibility. Only now, however, has Marx's methodology begun to be examined. This late examination may partly be accounted for by the lack of availability of some of Marx's key works and more significantly, by the difficulty of incorporating Marx's methodology into an empiricist or neo-positivist framework (Althusser and Balibar, 1971; Marx, 1971).

These developments do not, however, essentially amount to a systematic challenge to the dominant methodological reflection of neo-positivism. Indeed, some writers appear not to see the issue as central. Gouldner, for example, in his attack on Western sociology views Parsons as the ghost in the sociological machine from whom sociologists appear to have great difficulty in escaping. However justified Gouldner's obsession may be, it remains true that in more general terms Mill's critique was perhaps more to the point with his suggestion that grand theory constituted one tradition amongst others which were then dominant. The positivist tradition would appear to be of more significance both in the US and in Britain (Frisby, 1974).

This predominance of a neo-positivist paradigm for social research requires explanation. One significant factor must be the requirements of that legitimation process in which sociology had to undergo from its inception. There were apparently contradictory trends within sociology: on the one hand, the need for empirical research to support social reform and on the other hand, the unsystematic reflection on social theory. Both traditions have little difficulty in achieving some form of coexistence. With the late expansion of sociology after the Second World War in Britain, the former tradition proved the stronger within a situation in which the legitimation of sociology as a social science was conceived in terms of a model of the prestigious natural sciences. Since the older tradition of reflection on social theory could no longer attract prestige and it had not been supported by a strong philosophical tradition, it is hardly surprising that its defeat, though not total, occurred. Support from American sociology was essential for the new positivist tradition in Britain. In the USA, sociology had achieved its struggle for acceptance through the provision of marketable data as well as ideologically supportive theory. In Britain, however, the methods of research were seldom able to match the rigour of their American counterparts. However, as in the USA, the neo-positivist orientation was able to socialize its future practitioners and ensure its continued existence. The existing division of labour in the social sciences had to be reformed in order to incorporate sociology. However, the scientific division of labour does not arise as a matter of course out of its subject matter but is a social and historical creation (Frisby, 1974: 207). Within this discipline, an elaborate socialization process may take place which has stultifying effects. As Feyeraband argues, scientific education proceeds in the following manner:

> "First, a domain of research is defined. Next, the domain is separated from the remainder of the history (physics, for example, is separated from metaphysics and from theology) and receives a logic of its own. A thorough training in such a logic then conditions those working in the domain so that they may not unwittingly disturb the purity that has already been achieved. An essential part of the training is the inhibition of institutions that might lead to a blurring of boundaries". (1970: 76)

> In the process of scientific education, the procedures, rules and orientations which are deemed 'methodology' are most often taken as given, as self-evident truths; an understanding of them within their social and historical context is discouraged, indeed such a context is not even deemed to exist. A further implication of Feyeraband's characterization is that the manner in which the boundaries have been drawn with respect to sociology will condition the methodology which is deemed to be most appropriate for that discipline. At its simplest level, this reveals itself as the problem of the location of sociology within two possible models of scientific procedures—natural or cultural scientific. (Frisby, 1974: 208)

However, to suggest that the neo-positivist orientation assumed a monopoly of the world view of methodology is not to impute perfect success to that enterprise. In Britain, the apparent sophistication of much positivist methodology has seldom been attained in research practice. Rather, neo-positivism has provided the ideological justification for those practices which, in no way, being identical to them. This has been possible because the alternatives to versions of positivism have been so weak. Challenges to its presuppositions and prescriptions have never attained the persuasive power of methodological disputes in other traditions of sociology. Attacks on aspects of positivist methodology have usually taken the form of piecemeal criticism of particular theses, whilst the overall positivist account of sociological practice has remained unchallenged. This is in striking contrast to developments in sociology in Germany in recent decades. There, at least since the original "Methodenstreit in political economy and the Werturteilsstreit, the positivist standpoint has seldom remained unchallenged" (Menger, 1963: 31; Ritzel, 1950). This has taken the form of a critique of positivism by writers within the Frankfurt tradition which is worthy of careful examination as a tradition which runs counter to a dominant trends in sociology today (Frisby, 1972). Frisby has resorted too often to unexamined positivist prescriptions in order to support both its theoretical orientation and its research practice. A thoroughgoing critique of the positivist orientation in sociology must take account not merely of the methodological issues involved in social research but also of the theoretical and practical domains within which positivism exists. For this task, the work of the Frankfurt School provides one of the most comprehensive critiques of positivism in the social sciences. Though the works which develop this critique are scattered we will make an attempt to bring them together within the framework of a paradigm which contrasts positivism with critical theory. The designation of positivism and critical theory certainly hides important differences within these positions. For example, Popper has been critical of many aspects of the positivists tradition, even though, as Habermas (1971) argues, he remains within that camp. If Habermas is included within the critical theory tradition of the Frankfurt School, then his work suggests quite different orientations in some respects from that of suggests quite different orientations in some respects from that of Adorno and Horkheimer. This opposition of positivism and critical theory has its historical antecedents in the social sciences and philosophy. Habermas (1973) has drawn attention to the critical and conservative intentions of sociology for its inception in the works of Scottish economists. Marcuse (1941) highlighted the two contrary traditions in social thought deriving from Hegel and Comte. Horkheimer (1982) posed a distinction between traditional and critical theory in terms of academic science since Descartes and Marx's critique of political economy. One of Lukacs' concerns in 'Geschichte and Klassenbewusstsein' was to illuminate the positivist and critical tradition within Marxism itself (Lukacs, 1922). The other development of the opposition will be presented in terms of their general orientation to social theory, their methodological prescriptions and some implications of their diverse approaches. Finally, some problems which face critical theory itself will also be examined.

Any critique of the positivist standpoint must immediately render problematic areas of social science experience which have been excluded by fiat from discussion. Habermas has suggested that positivistic self-understanding has restrictive consequences; methodological self-reflection is confined to limited areas of experience designated as scientific. What constitutes methodological reflection is circumscribed by a scientific presupposition. This scienticism constitutes 'science's belief in itself', i.e., the conviction that we can no longer understand science as one form of possible knowledge, but rather must identify knowledge with science (Habermas, 1971: 4). Included in any methodological reflection must be some understanding of what Horkheimer, in posing an opposition between traditional and critical theory addressed himself to this in his support for the critical intention of social science established by Marx's critique of political economy.

> "Theory in the traditional sense organizes experience on the basis of statements of a problem in a manner which devotes itself to the reproduction of life within contemporary society. The social genesis of the problems, the real situations in which the science is used, the ends to which it will be applied, validate themselves externally. The critical theory of society on the contrary, has its object men as the producers of their total historical forms of life. The conditions of reality from which the science commences, appear to it not as givens (Gegebenheiten) to be established and calculated purely on the basis of the laws of probability. What in each case is given depends not solely upon nature but also upon what men wish to make of it. The objects and the manner of prescription, the statement of the problem and the interpretation of the answer are created from human activity and the degree of its power". (Horkheimer, 1982)

The controversy in German sociology between Popper and Albert on the one hand and Adorno and Habermas, on the other, has again questioned the goal of sociology. Bair (1969) has suggested that this is manifested in three areas of dispute. The first of these is whether the role of sociology is the repetition or reproduction of existing social reality or rather whether it is to be concerned with the transformation of that reality. The positivist orientation perceives reality as a reservoir of protocol areas of relevance such that the question of the truth of a theory becomes a question of the replicability of facts. In more general terms, Habermas has argued that the cognitive interest of positivism is technical:

> "Empirical analytical sciences disclose reality in so far as it appears within the behavioural system of instrumental action. In accordance with their immanent meaning, nomological statements about this subject domain are thus designed for a specific context in which they can be applied—i.e., they grasp reality with regards to technical control that, under specified conditions, is possible everywhere and at all times". (1971: 195)

In contrast, Habermas argues that a dialectical sociology is motivated by an emancipatory interest whose intent is the liberation of individual from alien structures and definitions which arise out of system of domination. Whilst positivism attempts to increase the calculability of social systems, a dialectical sociology should attempt to liberate men from such systems. The two other areas are closely related to the first: the relation of sociology to history and to historical explanation. For a positivist sociology there can be no historical transformation, whereas a dialectical sociology directs research towards the objective context of social events and the possible direction of historical development. As Habermas states it:

> "Sociology is indifferent to its relation to history. It processes its data without respect for a specific context; from the very beginning the historical value position of data is neutralized. Sociology transforms history to the present—admittedly not in the sense of reflexive representation of an irreversible and unrepeatable process. Rather history is projected to the level of universal contemporaneity and thus robbed of its real spirit". (1988: 91)

This difference points to the third area, i.e., generalized or individualized tendencies in sociology. Positivism does not examine the question of which concrete subject is able to conceive of global theory or which subjective interest will contribute to the promotion of objective progress (Frisby, 1974: 211). The restricted methodological self-reflection of positivism either ignores these problems or is indifferent to them. The latter response can arise from "the basic thesis of the absolute independence of science, of its constitutive character for all knowledge. What becomes questionable is whether a precise disjunction exists between knowledge and the real life process; whether on the contrary knowledge is mediated through it" (Adorno, 1969: 10).

Even within science itself, with respect to the organization of disciplines, positivism had a restrictive effect. The existing division of labour has not often been maintained through demarcation disputes, the most general, of course, being the demarcation between science and metaphysics. All problems demoted to the latter sphere can easily be ignored as non-scientific, non-sociological. Popper argues that "a so-called scientific discipline is only a circumscribed and constructed conglomeration of problems and attempted solutions" (1969: 108).

Such a definition does not provide us with the means of criticizing the existing division of labour as artificial. Feyeraband's characterization of the stultifying effects of such process has already been alluded to (Frisby, 1974: 211).

More specifically, Adorno has suggested that the existing division of labour with respect to sociology is problematic:

> "Sociology has been compelled to emancipate itself from philosophy in order to match that conception of science to which, since inception, it has been attached: positivism. Insistently, sociology has sought to distinguish itself from the neighbouring sciences, above all from psychology and political economy, and this with a zeal itself hardly rational-derived from the predominance of methodological interests over those in content". (1959: 35–36)

Further, some research would suggest that fundamental advances in science occur through cross-fertilization even where the existing division of labour is not overcome (Mulkay, 1969). However, not merely discipline boundaries have been circumscribed by positivist methodology, but also the appropriate model of science has been imposed upon sociology. This has been accompanied by the rewriting of the sociological past so that a positivist present is the culmination of a positivist past. Whilst the most extreme versions of positivism had little difficulty in deciding upon physics as a model for the natural science, the choice in the social science has been more difficult, since many disciplines have been deemed unscientific. However, where a choice has been made, this has often fallen upon economics as the appropriate model of a nomological social science. Earlier versions of critical theory have commenced from a critique of that discipline, i.e., Marx's critique of political economy. Habermas has attempted to introduce the hermeneutic model, though in a critical manner (Habermas, 1971; Frisby, 1974: 212).

The origins of the positivist models in the social sciences lie in the work of Comte. Habermas (1971: 4) has argued that Comte defines science in terms of methodological rules of procedure and elucidates these rules. Knowledge is verified by the recourse to the 'sense certainty' of systematic observation that secures 'inter-subjectivity' and by methodical certainty or the unity of method. Further, "the exactitude of our knowledge is guaranteed only by the formally cogent construction of theories that allows the deduction of law like hypotheses". This knowledge is technically utilizable, since it facilitates "technical control over process of both nature and society", and can be expanded through "the development and unification of theories". A corollary is that our knowledge is in principle unfinished and relative, in accordance with the "relative nature of the positivist spirit". Finally, Habermas argues that Comte's critique of ideology which is a critic of metaphysics 'assumes the form of the presumption of meaninglessness', with the consequence that metaphysical statements fall into disuse even when they are essential to the very intelligibility of positivism. Frisby (1974: 212) adds that these rules bear a striking resemblance to more recent methodological rules often asserted in the social sciences. However, it might be objected that the opposition between Comte and critical theory would represent a false opposition, since not every version of positivism appears as inflexible as that of Comte. One alternative is to examine the formulation of the sophisticated methodologist such as Popper, since it is possible to examine widely held tenets of positivism through a contrast between Popper's thesis on the logic of the social sciences and their critique by Adorno. This critique can be extended to Habermas' exchange with Albert, a supporter of Popper (Albert, 1968, 1971; Popper, 1970; Rodnitsky, 1970).

In what follows the central areas of opposition will be set out in order to classify the methodological issues.

Popper vs Adorno: A Debate in Positivistic Methodology

Popper's position may be summarized in terms of the central thesis which he has put forward on the logic of the social science. Scientific knowledge commences from a problem either theoretical or practical. The methods of research consist in the way in which we search for a solution to our problems. Solutions are proposed and criticized, that is, the tentative search for solution is restrained by the sharpest possible critique. If a solution does not withstand rigorous attempts at refutation, then it is considered unscientific; if it does withstand refutation, then we may accept it though only provisionally, since it may be refuted in the future. The objectivity of scientific knowledge rests upon the objectivity of critical method and tradition, a tradition which does not rest upon individuals but upon social processes. As Popper suggests:

> "The theory of scientific objectivity can only be clarified through social categories as, for example, competition (both of individual scientists and of different schools); tradition (namely the critical

> tradition); social institutions (such as, for example, publications in different competing journals and through different competing publishers; discussions in congresses); power of the state (namely, political tolerance of free discussion)". (1969: 113)

The methods by which this objectivity is achieved in the research process are subsumed under the critical method.

At the centre of the Popper's critical method is the falsification criterion—a theory is falsified with the assistance of basic propositions which state the existence of some phenomena. These basic statements must be inter-subjectively verifiable. They can be falsified only through other statements. The theory or set of propositions can be free from criticism—a criticism whose means are logical. Thus, Popper states, "the most important function of pure deductive logic is that of an organon on critique" (ibid.: 115). This logic enables us to transfer the truth of premises to their conclusions such that "if the premises of valid conclusion are true, then so must the conclusion also be true" (ibid.).

Popper not merely establishes falsificationism as a demarcation criterion of scientific knowledge, he further introduces what Habermas has termed 'decisionism'. Popper establishes two realms of knowledge: in the one, we enquire as to the relevance of propositions and hypotheses to the problems under consideration within the scientific process itself; in the other, we question the relevance of these propositions relative to the diverse extra-scientific problems. The former are informed by scientific values, whereas the latter by extra-scientific values. The latter are largely a matter of decision; they lie outside the bounds of scientific enquiry.

Adorno criticized the central concept of Popper's methodology from the standpoint of critical theory. For Popper problems are located in our knowledge, in our statements, about reality. Adorno argues to the contrary that "a problem is for Popper something basically epistemological and for me rather something practical, in the final instance entirely a problematic condition of the world" (1969: 129).

Problems, Adorno continues, are not created through our discovery that some aspect of our knowledge is not in order. It is society itself which is problematic. Popper's methodological individualism leads him to attest that the social sciences should concern themselves solely with the specific problems. However, to accept restricted, circumscribed problems as the only real scientific problems instals simplicity as an evaluative criterion of knowledge in sociology. The prescription that sociology should concern itself only with those areas of social reality translatable into statements about individual problems leads to a situation in which the complexity of the object studied is ignored. If it is argued that social reality is permeated with contradictions, then, these contradictions are in no way removed by a clearer formulation of statements about reality; these lie in the facts of sociology themselves.

Popper's insistence on methodological ideals as the guide to research, once a specific problem has been chosen for study, leads him to assume that research practice actually operates on the basis of these ideals. Adorno argued that our approach to an object rests upon the object itself rather than upon methodological ideals, whilst at the same time recognizing that the selection of much sociological research is circumscribed by existing methodological procedures. A problem of study having been selected, solutions are proposed and criticized on the basis of existing empirical evidence. It is often assumed that this evidence is somehow independent of the society from which it has been selected and independent of the cognitive interests of the investigators. Adorno argues that the contrary holds true in that:

> "Facts are not in society ... the resting points on which knowledge is founded because they themselves are mediated through society. Not all theories are hypotheses; theory is the telos not the instrument of sociology". (1969: 132–33)

In other words, Adorno denies empirical evidence of the status of finality on which all knowledge is presumed to test. That independence for empirical evidence is not possible, since the object of sociology—society—is structured. To assume that it is not is to leave its present structure unquestioned (Frisby, 1974: 214–15).

There are other aspects of critical tradition which Adorno questions. Central to the refutation process is the role of tests in research procedures. Adorno argues that if the notion of discrete individual facts is rejected and replaced by facts existing in a dialectical relationship with societal totalities, then no experimental procedure can be instituted which examines the dependence of some phenomenon upon a societal totality, since this very totality itself could never exist in an experimental research procedure. Here, Frisby's comments deserve quote:

> "Though Popper designates his approach as critical rationalism, the concept of critique differs markedly from that employed in critical theory Popper would limit the critical activity of sociology to self-criticism, to reflection upon its own statements, theories and methods, whereas Adorno insists that it must be a critique of its object. In other words, criticism cannot remain confined to the level of immanent critique but must at the same time be a material critique, a critique of society. This must be the case once the assumption is removed that some how societal facts are given in an unmediated manner". (1974: 215)

Thus criticism cannot be confined to the reformulation of contradictory statements, since "'such logicity can become false through the displacement of the real import" (Adorno, 1969: 136). An acceptance of an immediate conception of social facts would lead to the displacement of actual societal relations in favour of their externalizations. A purely cognitive or subjective concept of critique evaluates the unanimity of knowledge and not the legitimation of known things (Horkheimer, 1947).

Popper takes the logical means of assistance of critique, the process of logical contradiction, as objective, yet Adorno suggests that this is to neglect the relation between this critique of facts themselves, since the two realms cannot remain isolated. The strict division between the realm of science and the realm of social reality then ceases to be absolute. This is based upon contrasting conceptions of reality. As Lundz has argued:

> "Logical empiricism recognizes only one reality which is, so to speak, composed cummulatively from diverse individual phenomena and their grasping. The critical theory of society however, conceives more strata of this reality according to the character of the heterogeneous continuum of societal reality which is conceptualized as totality, as merely a dialectical unfolded relation of subject and object, particular and general, concrete and abstract". (1963: 418)

This distinction has further implications:

> "In logical empiricism, knowledge should be independent of the subject whilst in critical theory the subject-object relation is given through the mode of recognition". (ibid.: 423)

Some of these aspects are taken up by Habermas and are being considered below:

Habermas' Methodology: The critical method is closely linked with Popper notion of objectivity. That scientific method follows a series of conventions implies for Adorno that social conformism is introduced as a criterion of meaning in the social sciences under the guide of conventionalism. Popper's idealized version of the social factors responsible for scientific objectivity such as competition, tradition, social institutions and state power have been countered by Adorno (Merton, 1957; Mulkay, 1969). Competition may be interpreted as implying that market forces condition both the quality of facts and intellectual constructs (Frisby, 1974: 216; Veblen, 1918: 4); tradition may be constrained by productive forces; and the scientific apparatus and its institutionalization are already moulded by society.

Many of the above issues as well as new ones have been raised since the original Popper-Adorno dispute in 1961, some of which we will now consider. Habermas (1970) has distinguished a number of differences between dialectical and analytical-empirical theory, which restate the issues already raised:

(i) *The relation of the theory to its object:* Habermas argues that in so far as the empirical social sciences conceive of themselves as analogous to the natural sciences in their intention, they remain indifferent to their object. Theories are conceived as "ordering schemata which we construe at will in syntactic bounded realms". These theories, however, ignore our interest in society. In so far as the natural science interest in knowledge for the domination of nature is accepted, we hereby falsify the object of research in the social sciences. Such an interest in theory surrenders any self-reflections that the theory itself remains a moment in the objective context which it is attempting to analyse. Further,

> "the scientific apparatus circumscribes an object of whose structure I must certainly have previously had some understanding if the chosen categories are not to remain external to it. The circle is not to be broken by a priori or empirical immediacy of access but only in connection with dialectical thinking through the natural hermeneutic of the social life-world". (ibid.: 158)

The categories and theories which we use are not independent of the social world in which we exist.

(ii) *Nature of experience in empirical-analytical science:* The second distinction which Habermas draws is related to the nature of experience in empirical science:

> "With the relation of the theory to its object, there is also transformed that of theory and experience. The analytical-empirical modes of behaviour permit only a type of experience which they themselves define. Empirical sciences in the strict sense insist upon the fact all discussable statements can be controlled at least indirectly through that very narrowly channeled experience". (ibid.: 159)

In contrast, a dialectical theory of society insists that the coherence of theoretical statements rests upon the very societal process to which sociological research itself belongs. It must be related to the societal totality of which it is a moment. Not all theorems of dialectical theory can be resolved by experimental means, since they are mediated through the societal totality and may be directed in its claims to a future or transformative aim. This reinforces Habermas' claim that where theory takes on an emancipatory interest, the restricted experience which validates theory oriented to technical control is inappropriate.

The relation of theory to history is also determined by that of theory and experience. There exists no historical laws for empirical analytical sociology, and any discipline which excludes history from the realm of theory deprives it of any possibility of questioning the meaning of history. Such an orientation assembles individual historical appearances without integrating them as moments of a societal totality. Critical theory directs its research towards both the objective context of events and the possible direction of historical development. In so far as this is the case, such a theory must be not merely dialectical but hermeneutic (Frisby, 1974: 217).

The relation of theory to history in turn transforms that of science or theory to practice. A sociology which restricts itself to definite prognoses and causal explanations remains confined to the technical interest in the acquisition of knowledge. This technical interest confines sociology to the questioning of the appropriate means for system in which the ends are given. It does not reflect upon the emergence of this technical system; rather, it remains at the level of reification. Critical theory highlights the discrepancy between practical questions and established roles, on the one hand, and on the other hand, practice as the emancipation of acting individuals. Habermas had alluded to this contradiction within the development of sociology itself in terms of a conception of sociology as both what Brinkmann termed as 'oppositional science' and a science of stabilization.

(iii) *The problem of value freedom:* Finally, Habermas raised this issue central to methodological reflection in sociology, and institutionalized in the Werturteilsstreit—The problem of value—freedom. Adorno in his debate with Popper had already questioned the latter's statement of the problem. Adorno argued that value and value freedom are not exclusive concepts—each concept viewed on its own as a thing-in-itself is false—rather, they are contained in and must be subsumed in each other. Adorno continues:

> "The separation of evaluative and value-free conduct is false in so far as value and thereby value-freedom are reifications; correct in so far as the conduct of mind is not able to withdraw itself from the position of reification out of discretion. What has become known as the value problem became constituted primarily in a phase in which means and ends work torn asunder in order to dominate nature without difficulty in which rationality of means progressed by unreduced or, where possible, increasing irrationality of ends". (Adorno, 1969)

Adorno argues that the present value concept is not abstract but structured by the relations of exchange, i.e., it exists as value for others. Indeed, the overemphasis upon value freedom to the neglect of facts has the same results as a sociology which is based on more or less arbitrary values. Adorno sees the problem of value freedom as having been presented in a manner which has consistently neglected all insights into ideology and socially necessary illusion.

Habermas, too, through a historical analysis of exchange relations, encapsulates the concepts of value and value freedom as a product of reification. His critic, Albert, has suggested that the sociologist is not responsible for the rationality of goals. The question of which theoretical system should be transformed technologically in positivism does not rest upon the application of value premises but is excluded as a meta-scientific problem. An economy which favours choice of means can also leave its central goals to an arbitrary decisionism. Yet it is plausible to argue that science can raise the question of its own nature scientifically. As Hofmann maintains:

> "The question of the authority of science, expressed by virtue of particular value statements, possesses not only an epistemological but also a sociological scientific meaning. The function of science and with it the position of the scientist himself, the double relationship of a thinker to the society as his object and at the same time in the society as the general bearer of science becomes thematic". (1961: 12)

However, it has been a central assumption of much sociology that the discipline would progress to the extent to which it either adopted a value free perspective or totally ignored the problem (Frisby, 1974: 218). In its relation to theory and practice, the problem is perhaps highlighted by Popper's apparently contradictory affirmation that "my own social theory which favours gradual and piecemeal reform strongly contrasts with my theory of method which happens to be a theory of scientific and intellectual revolution" (Popper, 1969: 255).

Here, Frisby rightly comments:

> "On the one hand, Popper supports a theory which accounts for scientific progress in logical terms, i.e. he gives an account of its development in purely theoretical terms, while on the other hand, the assumptions which lie behind his social theory have seldom been examined". (Frisby, 1974: 219)

Wellmer (1967) has suggested that not even Popper's theory of scientific progress is satisfactory, since there exists no small tension between progress through greater verisimilitude and an extreme formulation of the falsificationism thesis.

The value-free controversy presents one level of a duality between theory and practice, theory and methodology and, like the oppositions to which it is related, it is often stated falsely. For critical theory, and for Marx and Weber, the separation of methodology from theory falsifies the actual situation in which the two are dialectically related. Methodological disputes confined merely to reflections on method are meaningless; such disputes cannot help but raise issues concerning theory, the goals of science, and the relationship between research and society. Indeed, a purely methodological dispute would presuppose that the division of scientific labour was so advanced that certain people were concerned only with methodology even to the extent that it becomes a distinctive discipline (Frisby, 1974). Much philosophy of science appears to have taken this course to such an extent that Feyerabend (1969) has suggested that there now exists a close parallel between the development of the philosophy of science and ecclesiastical history.

Concepts of Society and Totality

Since the distinction between theory and methodology remains only analytically useful, it is in order to examine some specific aspects of the Frankfurt School's theoretical standpoint. The concepts of society and totality and critique of ideology will provide some central illustrations of their sociological theory.

Concept of Society

The concept of society is not a neutral category as in positivist sociology; it is bound to the notions of totality and contradiction. Society conceived as a totality is not an affirmative but rather a critical category. As Adorno maintains:

> "Society is not consensual, not simple, also not neutrally left to the discretion of categorical forms, but on the contrary awaits already the system of categories of the discursive logic of its objects. Society is full of contradictions and thereby determinate; at once rational and irrational, system and fragile, mediated through blind nature and through consciousnesses". (1969: 138)

Analysis of society must commence from these contradictions, which cannot be overcome through their assimilation in an arbitrary categorical system. For example, antagonisms which exist in society are often transformed into a classificatory model which assumes a harmonious whole. Adorno cites as an example Parsons' attempt to construct a unified science of man through a system of categories retaining individuals and society, psychology and sociology, as if they existed on a continuum. Yet, the concept of society itself, specifically bourgeoise and anti-feudal, implies a conception of an association of free and independent subjects. Even though that conception was contradicted by social reality, nonetheless it was originally a critique of existing social relations. Critical theory attempts to break down its object—society—into the existent and the possible, the actuality and the potentiality, both of which as moments of a totality in a dialectical relationship (Frisby, 1974).

Concept of Totality

The concept of totality is not an affirmative one. Adorno distinguishes it from a positive conception of the whole society in the following manner:

> "The difference between the dialectical views of totality and the positivist one rests primarily on the fact that in the dialectical concept of totality 'objective' is intended actually to produce an understanding of each and everyone of its individual manifestations whilst the positivistic system of theories would like, solely by choosing categories which are as general as possible, to include determinations in as uncontradictory a manner as possible in a single logical continuum without recognizing the highest concepts of structure as a precondition of the facts which are subsumed under them". (Adorno, 1969: 21)

Such a conception of totality, opposed as it is to methodological individualism, does not culminate in some abstract totality. Rather, society as totality produces and reproduces its rational and irrational elements through its individual moments such that each element is understood only in terms of the totality which has its basis in the development of the individual elements themselves (Frisby, 1974).

Habermas recognizes that analytical empirical versions of sociology also have some conception of the societal whole but its theories are theories of systems, quite often the functionalist concept of system (Popper, 1970). Habermas suggests that it is an important distinction which can easily be obscured.

> "The distinction between system and totality in the recognizable sense may not be directly characterized, for in the language of formal logic it is destroyed, in the language of the dialectic it must be transcended". (cited in Adorno, 1969: 156)

The weakness of the concept of system is characterized by Habermas in the following way:

> "In the realm of a strict empirical scientific theory, the concept of system can only formally describe the interdependent connection of functions which on their part are interpreted as connections between variables of social behaviour. The concept of a system itself remains as external to the analyzed sphere of experience as the theoretical statement which it explicates". (cited in Adorno, 1969: 156–57; Habermas/Luhmann, 1971)

The implication of this distinction may be drawn from an examination of sociological understanding of contemporary society. Adorno has pointed to some of consequences of discussion of capitalist or industrial society. The characterization of contemporary society as industrial or capitalist has important consequences for its analysis. As Adorno argues, "Contemporary society is through and through an industrial society at the level of its productive forces. In contrast, society is capitalist in its productive relations" (1969: 18).

To emphasize the former at the expense of the latter is, in Habermas' terms, to remain at the level of technical interest orientation. In the analysis of industrial societies is often found a particular conception of social class. Whereas the criteria of class relations are often reduced to indices of income, living standards and education and to that extent rests upon individual findings, the older concept of class was developed independently of indices.

> "A dialectical theory of society rests upon laws of structure which condition facts in which they are manifested and through which they are modified. Under laws of structure is to be understood tendencies which more or less follow stringently from the historical constituents of the total system. Marx's models for this were the law of values, the law of accumulation, the law of crisis". (ibid., 1970: 13–14)

Here, then, the class relations are related to the dialectical forces and relations of production. If sociological analysis sets out from a conception of industrial society, then it emphasizes the technocratic moments of Marx's work without taking into account its societal mediation through productive relations. Such an emphasis leads to an ideological formulation of the concept of contemporary society.

> "That productive forces and productive relations can today become one and that one can thereby construe society unceremoniously

> from productive forces is the real form of socially necessary illusion". (ibid.: 25)

This raises the problem of how a critique of ideology is to be undertaken.

Critique of Ideology

The critique of ideology was a central aspect of Marx's critique of political economy and remains central to the methodology of the Frankfurt School, particularly since at least their earlier writings were concerned with, and may have been most successful in, engaging in critiques of aspects of the superstructure. The critique of ideology does not accept the facts as they are immediately presented to us not as they may be mediated by formal categories (Frisby, 1974: 222). Adorno gives the example of exchange relations in our society which invest the society with a mechanistic character. A positivist sociology will reproduce this mechanistic character in its theoretical formulations. Critical theory must commence its analysis with an examination of existing contradictions. To remain with Adorno's example, exchange relations must be understood in conjunction with real relations, just as Marx examined the relationship between exchange and use values with regard to commodity fetishism. Such contradictions as exist between the two must be made manifest.

> "The experience of the contradictory character of social reality is no arbitrary starting point, rather the motive which above all else first constitutes the possibility of sociology". (Adorno, 1969: 142)

Ideology and Sociology of Knowledge: An Appraisal

The critique of ideology can be understood in relation to its counterpart in academic sociology which has often taken up a positivist stance—the sociology of knowledge. Many versions of the sociology of knowledge, in so far as they do to introduce the concept of ideology, do so in a positivistic manner (Geiger, 1953; Frisby, 1974). In so far as it merely develops the apparently simple proposition that social existence determines social consciousness without thereby introducing the critical notions of socially necessary illusion and false consciousness, it remains limited.

Horkheimer (1968) has argued that in the sociology of knowledge, ideology is related to a social group in such a simple manner that the position of a social group corresponds to a definite content of thought. What it ignores is a notion of ideology which examines the process in terms of a definite form of knowing, evaluation and action. The study of ideology becomes a value-free study in much sociology of knowledge (Frisby, 1974: 222–23).

Adorno (1969), in a critique of Mannheim's later work *Man and Society in an Age of Reconstruction* argues that he adopts a positivist standpoint in his study of ideology. The analysis of the dynamic of ideology creation is reduced to a static relation between ideology and society through the psychologising of ideology, the fetishism of truth and the disappearance of economic relations. The critique of ideology has been associated with a historical orientation in sociology in so far as it has been present at all. Habermas speaks of a situation in which "sociology has primarily—and by no means in an unproblematic manner—assisted the self-reflection of social groups in given historical situations" (Habermas, 1963: 261) and asks what would happen to a sociology which abandoned this aim,

> "how would it be if a successful positivistic scientific policy were able to completely reject this task and banish it to the vestibules of scientific discussion? For the critique of ideology in the hands of the positivists has this purpose. It concerns itself with purging the practical consciousness of social groups of those theories which cannot be reduced to technically utilizable knowledge and which nevertheless make a theoretical claim". (ibid.: 262)

The task of the critique of ideology would certainly be negated and replaced by a positivistic intellectual spring-clearing. The position of critical theory is not immune from critique. It contains within itself diverse and sometimes contradictory moments which are often difficult to reconcile. The critique of positivism has meant an aversion to empirical studies as such (Frisby, 1974: 223). As Adorno (1969) remarked:

> "Empirical investigations are not only legitimate but essential even in the realm of cultural phenomena, but one must not confer autonomy upon them or regard them as universal key. Above all, they must terminate in theoretical knowledge. Theory is no mere vehicle that becomes superfluous as soon as the data are in hand"...

Frisby comments:

> "In the original formulation of critical theory by Horkheimer, other problems were raised. Horkheimer did not intend to criticize traditional theory in the hope that it would somehow become critical of itself, but rather he started out from untranscendable theoretical differences which he felt must remain as long as discussion remained solely in the academic medium" (Horkheimer, 1968; Wellmer, 1969). In its original statement, the critique of political economy stood not only as a model but remained a central part of critical theory. This critique was asserted in opposition both to positivism and to orthodox Marxism, to the extent that the latter had adopted a mechanistic standpoint. Critical theory reflected an intellectual isolation and developed a strong theme of cultural pessimism which Lukacs later characterized as the 'Grand Hotel Abyss'. Perhaps one of its greatest successes may have been ironically in its application to the study of cultural phenomena". (Frisby, 1974: 224)

One apparent dilemma may be seen as one which affects much neo-Marxist sociology. As Kruger has remarked:

> "Current dialectical sociology engages in so-called critique of ideology, i.e., it provides critical analyses of social phenomena with reference to the totality of a given society. A precondition for any critique of ideology, however, is a substantive theory of society. A theory of advanced industrial society, from the viewpoint of dialectical society, is still unwritten. Consequently, contemporary critiques of ideology are without concrete reference points". (1969: 160)

However, in terms of British sociology, the problem has hardly advanced this far, since the tradition established by Marx's critique of political economy has only begun to penetrate sociological consciousness.

The aforesaid discussion enables us to conclude that there exists at least one significant tradition which is able to offer an alternative to positivist methodology. The critical nature of the Frankfurt School tradition enables it to go beyond the theoretical problems of sociology and pose the alternatives in its practice which have long been ignored. The emancipatory interest in the acquisition of knowledge must, however, be continually reasserted and striven for (Frisby, 1974: 224).

The principal thrust of this school is towards a reuniting of theory and praxis in a manner modelled on Plato's *Republic*. Plato fused his theory of society with the nucleus of his metaphysics in a classic attempt to unify knowledge and action, and with the specific aim of alleviating human misery.

For the Frankfurt School the positivism founded by Comte, and still dominant in various forms in sociology, was most fundamentally a reactionary response to the turbulent social milieu. Positive philosophy was to employ the methods of the natural sciences to discover the natural laws by which the societies operated. Inherent in this was the assumption that social phenomena were to be merely observed and described as precisely as possible. The sociologist as scientist was expected to adopt an objective neutral stance to the phenomena.

In the course of this development of positivist sociology the demand for a scientific (objective) stance led directly to a separation of theory from practice. More to the point, it specifically proscribed serious intervention in societal affairs. Interference with the natural laws could only be disruptive and, if persisted, would lead to the destruction of society. Obviously, these tenets of positivism are, in part at least, aimed at 'negative philosophies', such as Marxism, which specifically advocated the overthrow of the existing social order. The positivists' policy of objectivism and non-interference functions to maintain status-quo. Intervention could only be tolerated when it is kept within the scope of the existing natural laws. This, of course, seems to prohibit the advocacy of any kind of action until such time as these natural laws are discovered—in the contemporary approach, until we know the 'facts'.

It is in this sense that the Frankfurt School has come to look upon positivist sociology as the guardian of the status quo. From the Frankfurt perspective, so long as society is allowed to develop haphazardly (naturally), it is naive in the extreme to expect that laws that will allow of precise prediction can be induced. Thus, the positivist prohibition against meaningful invention discredits every attempt that would no longer leave the institutions of society to the blind conflict of forces, but would consciously and rationally take them in hand. With the cult of the 'positive', reason surrenders to irrationality (Frankfurt Institute, 1973: 6).

The basis of the Frankfurt objection to positivism lies in the latter's continued determination to separate theory from praxis and the success it claims in separating knowledge from interests. The phenomenological philosopher Husserl had shown that objectivism is an illusion. In other words, the positivist attempt to separate knowledge and interests, through the objectivist stance to phenomena, was not successful. Husserl sought to remedy this by proposing his phenomenology as a way of finally separating sciences from interests. Habermas agrees with the Husserl that objectivism, as practised in the sciences, does not succeed in separating the two. For Habermas, however, the core of objectivism has more sinister underpinnings. Objectivism constitutes a concerted effort to create the impression that separation between knowledge and interests has been effected.

> "Even though phenomenological description would effectively dispel the illusion of objectivism, objectivism in no way prevents science from influencing practice; what was needed was not to restore the practical significance of the sciences by making them finally break with interest, but rather to reveal the true relationship of knowledge and interest which the objectivist attitude conceals". (Habermas, 1970: 36)

The key to understanding the distinctiveness of the Frankfurt School's orientation—and correlatively its stance against positivism—lies in grasping the way in which it has come to fuse a Hegelian-Marxist theoretical perspective with a phenomenological methodology. As Wellmer (1969) has shown, the early formulation of theory within the Frankfurt School was based on what has come to be seen as a dogmatic and positivist Marxism. This latter, now viewed by the Frankfurt theorists as the core of historical (as opposed to dialectical) materialism, placed the centre of Marxist theory at the level of the critique of political economy. The upshot of this was that the supposedly 'critical' theory of the early Frankfurt School simply railed against the existing class structure and warned of the impending revolution which the unfolding of the idea would eventually make manifest. Thus, the adoption of a linear temporality and eventism (D'Amico, 1973) is now seen as a form of historicism. It came to be seen as a mechanical Marxism which, in a sense, supported the essentially bourgeoise and positivist perception of history as a natural process—natural laws, waiting for the process of autogenesis in the dialectical process to bear fruit, etc. This led, logically, to a policy of allowing the 'objective conditions' free flow and to a de-emphasis on the role to be played, in revolution, by the subjective consciousness of individuals. It led, too, to an implicit endorsement of the kind of 'bureaucratic socialism' that had begun to emerge.

Frankfurt theorists such as Horkheimer and Adorno became aware of the paradoxical situation that had arisen in the school's brand of Marxism, and it has been their efforts to resolve this that have given the school its contemporary raison d'etre. Thus, the objectivist illusion under which scientists' (particularly positivist social scientists) laboured became the bete noire. This was so since it led to

> "... a misrepresentation of the object under scrutiny and to an accommodating conformism on the part of the scientists. Because they no longer see exactly how 'in every act of perception' (Habermas) they remain imprisoned in and take their bearings from the process of social life, they misrepresent human history as a natural process and willingly act out the role assigned to them by the capitalist system as useful and 'irresponsible' experts whose knowledge can be smoothly integrated in the system's utility structures." (Wellmer, 1969: 12)

Positivist social science, in its neutral stance, gleans knowledge that is subsequently used for mediating objective social conflict under the objectivist illusion perpetuated by positivist social science. The members of society are locked into a closed universe of false consciousness in which reified relationships and technical rationality play key roles. Inherent in this is a prevailing instrumental concept of reason that justifies the means-end rationality of the capitalist mode of production. What was needed was a critical theory that could raise consciousness in a meaningful way, employing a reflective materialist epistemology. This entailed a return to Marx's critique of Hegel's "*Phenomenology of Mind* in an effort to understand how Marx had confused the unique critical character of a science of man with neutral science" (Schroyer, 1971).

Positivist sociology, the handmaiden of powerful interest groups (David, 1976), keeps up a steady flow of information about society to these groups. To this extent, and in spite of its 'hands off' policy, positivism is seen to be most directly an agent of social control. To the deep concern of the Frankfurt theorists such sociology seems to have lost any meaningful sense of critical consciousness. For them, what is needed in a return to a concept of theory that outlines an ideal state, one in which the humanity of mankind is no longer a subordinate consideration. The implication is that man should not be placed under the onus to adapt himself to the social conditions, but that social conditions should be designed to make for the best possible kind of human existence. As Horkheimer has phrased it:

> "The more social life loses the character of the blind processes of nature and society sets about constituting itself as a rational subject, the more social processes too can be predicted with precision". (1973: 14)

Theory, then, is to operate as a blueprint for society and not, as is now the case in positivist sociology, as a kind of inductive storehouse for the 'IS'. Crucial too, to the Frankfurt conception of theory, is that the research done to check the progress of the 'IS' towards the 'Ought' must be thoroughly and consciously soaked in theory. Thus, for example, strict probability sampling will not always be appropriate in social survey. Rather,

> "the social researcher must bear in mind that the social tendencies, say, the political developments, frequently do not correspond to the statistical cross section of the total population, but to the most powerful interests and to those who 'make public opinion'. He must conduct his surveys according to the concrete differences rather than always orienting himself by statistical means. Such problems clearly show the necessity for a theory of society, even for the empirical reliability of the findings. What constitutes a valid sample cannot be learned from statistical theory as such, but only from reflections about the actual distribution of power within society". (Frankfurt Institute, 1973: 122)

Clearly, the sociological enterprise at Frankfurt is aimed not simply at building an image of social reality, but of first blueprinting and then continually going through the cycle of researching, consciousness—raising, intervening and re-researching, with the 'explicit' intention of pushing the reality progressively closer to the blueprint.

In terms of the premises that we have taken to be constitutive of the central characteristics of positivist sociology, the main criticisms of the Frankfurt School would seem to come down to the following conclusions:

1. Denial of the proposition that positivist sociology is value-neutral.
2. Denial of the proposition that sociology ought to be value-neutral.
3. Denial of the positivist conception of theory.
4. Affirmation of the need and to reunite theory and practice.
5. Affirmation of the need to revive both a meaningful critical spirit in sociology and a mood of self-reflection among its practitioners.

References

Adorno, T.W., 1959, "Contemporary German Sociology", in *Transactions of the Third World Congress of Sociology*, Vol. 1, Washington.

——, 1969, "Einleitung", in T.W. Adorno et al., (Eds.) *Der Positivismustreit in Deutschen Soziologie*, Neuwied/Berlin: Luchterhand.

——, 1969, "Einleitungsvortrag Zum 16. Deutschen Soziologentag", in *Spatkapitalismus Oder Industriegesellschaft?*, Stuttgart: Enke.

Albert, H., 1968, *Traktat uber Kritische Vernunft*, Tubingen: Mohr Siebeck.

——, 1971, *Pladoyer fur Kritischen Rationalismus*, Munich: Piper.

Althusser, L. and Balibar, E. 1971, *Reading Capital*, London: New Left Books.

Bair, 1969, "Soziale Technologie Order Soziale Emanzipation? Zum Streit Zwischen Positivism and Dialektikern Uber die Aufgabe der Soziologie", in B. Schafers (ed.), *Thesen Zur Kritik der Soziologie*, Frankfurt: Suhrkamp.

Cicourel, A.V., 1964, *Method and Measurement in Sociology*, New York: The Free Press.

D' Amico, 1973, 'The Contours and Compures of Structuralist Theory', Telos.

Frankfurt Institute for Social Research, 1973, 'Aspects of Sociology'.

Feyeraband, P.F. 1962, "Explanation, Reduction and Empiricism", in H. Fegi and G. Maxwell (eds.), *Minnesota Studies in the Philosophy of Science*, Minneapolis: University of Minnesota Press.

——, 1969, "Classical Empiricism", in R.E. Butts and J.W. Davis (eds.), *The Methodological Heritage of Newton*, Toronto: University of Toronto Press.

——, 1970, "Against Method", in M. Radner and S. Winokur (eds.), *Minnesota Studies in the Philosophy of Science*, Vol. 4, Minneapolis: University of Minnesota Press.

Frisby, David, 1972, The Popper-Adorno Controversy: The Methodological Dispute in German Sociology, *Philosophy of the Social Sciences*, Vol. 2, No. 2.

——, 1974, "The Frankfurt School: Critical Theory and Positivism", in John Rex (ed.), 1974, *Approaches to Sociology: An Introduction to Major Trends in British Sociology*, London: Routledge.

Geiger, T. 1953, *Ideologie Und Wahrheit*, Stuttgart: Wien: Humboldt.

——, 1973, *Aspects of Sociology*, Frankfurt: Suhrkamp.

Gouldner, A. 1971, *The Coming Crisis in Western Sociology*, London: Heinemann Educational Books Ltd.

Habermas, J., 1963, *Theory and Practice*, Neuwied/Berlin: Luchterhand.

——, 1970, "Knowledge and Human Interest", in D. Emmett and A. McIntyre (eds.), *Sociological Theory and Philosophical Analysis*, London: Macmillan.

——, *Zur Logik de Sozialwissenschaften*, Materialen, Frankfurt: Suhrkamp.

——, 1971, "Science and Technology as Ideology", in J. Habermas (ed.), *Towards a Rational Society*, London: Heinemann.

——, 1971, *Kritische Und Konseruative Aufgaben der Soziologie*, Frankfurt: Suhrkamp.

Habermas, J. et al., 1969, *Student and Politik*, Neuwied/Berlin: Luchterhand.

——, 1971, *Hermeneutic Und Ideologie Kritik*, Frankfurt: Suhrkamp.

Hofmann, W., 1961, *Gesellschaftslehre als Ordnungsmacht: Die Werturteilsfrage heute*, Berlin: Duncker and Humbolt.

Horkheimer, M., 1947, *The Eclipse of Reason*, New York: Seabury Press.

——, 1968, *Kritische Theorie der Gesellschaft*, 2 Vols., Frankfurt: Suhrkamp.

——, 1973, "On Problems of Prediction in the Social Sciences", in Frankfurt Institute for Social Research.

Kruger, M., 1969, Sociology of Knowledge and Social Theory, *Berkeley Journal of Sociology*.

Lukacs, G., 1971, *Geschichte Und Klassenbewusstsein*, London: Merlin Press.

Lundz, C., 1963, 'Zur Frage mach den Bedingungen der moglichkeit einer Kritische Gesellschafttstheorie', Archiv fur Rechts-Und Sozialphilosophie'.

Marcuse, H., 1941, *Reason and Revolution*, New York: Oxford University Press.

Marx, K., 1971, *A Contribution to the Critique of Political Economy*, London: Lawrence and Wishart.

McHugh, P., 1970, "On the Failure of Positivism", in J.D. Douglas (ed.), *Understanding Everyday Life*, Chicago: Aldine.

Menger, Carl, 1963, *Problems of Economics and Sociology*, trans. F. Nock, ed. intro. L. Schneider, Urbana.

Merton, R.K., 1957, "Science and the Social Order", in *Social Theory and Social Structure*, Chicago: University of Chicago Press.

Mulkay, M., 1969, Some Aspects of Cultural Growth in the Natural Sciences, *Social Research*.

Popper, K.R., 1969, "Die Logic der Sozialwissenschaften", in T.W. Adorno (ed.), 1969, *Der Positivismustreit in Deutschen Sociology*, Neuwid/ Berlin: Luchterhand.

——, 1970, "Reason or Revolution", *European Journal of Sociology*, XI.

Ritzel, G., 1950, *Schmoller versus Menger*, Frankfurt: Suhrkamp.

Rodnitsky, G., 1970, *Contemporary Schools of Metascience*, Goteborg.

Schroyer, T., 1971, "Review of Albrecht Wellmer", in *Kritische Gesellschaftstheorie Und Positivismus*, Telos.

Veblen, T., 1918, *The Higher Learning in America*, New York: B.W. Huebsch.

Wellmer, A., 1967, *Methodologie als Erkenntnistheorie, Zur Wissenschaftslehre Karl R. Popper*, Frankfurt: Suhrkamp.

——, 1969, "Empirisch-analytische Und Kritische Sozialwissenschaft", in *Kritische Gesellschafts Theorie Und Positivismus*, Frankfurt: Suhrkamp.

5

Structural Approach and the Ideology of Positivism

Structuralism arrived in Britain in the late 1960s through a number of routes: through social anthropology, particularly the work of Léach and Needham, through trendy culture critics, and through the generation of students, mainly in sociology, who had taken part in the student movement. Structuralism seemed to us to provide answers to some of the questions that academic sociology did not even raise. It provided rigorous and systematic theory and method and offered an indisciplinary outlook, which did not carve up the social world into pre-conceived areas and corresponding academic disciplines or hypostatize the 'social' as an autonomous and reified level of reality. More important, it was anti-capitalist and anti-imperialist, challenged bourgeoise justification of capitalism and imperialism, and seemed to provide a potential link between theory and practice—which structural-functionalism certainly did not—by enabling a strategy for transforming society to be based on a scientific analysis of the ongoing social formation (Glucksmann, 1975: 230).

This chapter is mainly concerned with C. Levi-Strauss, the anthropologist, and Louis Althusser, the Marxist political economist and epistemologist, and their structuralist methods. I shall argue that the most distinctive features of approaches that have been called structuralist is their epistemology and methodology, the approach they propose for the analysis of social and cultural phenomena. Most of the discussions of structuralism that have appeared in Britain have a quite different interpretation from the one proposed here. They tend to see it as the application of the method of structural linguistics to cultural products, other than language, and to social phenomena. This means that the Marxists are usually left out of the discussion, as is epistemology (Lane, 1970; Leach, 1970).

Here, we will confine ourselves to Levi-Strauss and Althusser partly because they are the most apparently divergent and incomparable of the group; the most significant similarities between their respective thought structures are to be found at the epistemological level, and it is by examining this aspect, too, that one can pinpoint the radical departure of modern structuralism from 'structural' thought in anthropology and sociology. Finally, the significance of structuralism as a distinctive approach within the social sciences is also to be seen in terms of its epistemology and methodology.

Structuralism as an Analytical Approach

Structuralism cannot be understood as a coherent intellectual movement with clear-cut boundaries and conscious adherents or as a fully articulated approach to the study of social life (Glucksmann, 1975: 231). Many theorists working in different discipline have been called structuralist, e.g., Saussure and Jakobson in linguistics, Barthes in semiology, Popper in the study of folklore, Lacan and Lagache in psychoanalysis, Foucault in the history of ideas, Godelier in anthropology (Saussure, 1959; Jakobson, 1962; Jakobson and Halle, 1956; Barthes, 1967; Propp, 1958; Lacan, 1966; Foucault, 1967, 1971; Godelier, 1966, 1967). All of them use the concept of structure to give meaning to the raw material they study; all examine such phenomena in terms of the interrelationship of its constituent elements; and all reacted against the orthodox methodology of their disciplines. But, apart from this, there is nothing very obvious about the similarities between them, and none has an explicit epistemology. To discover the ways in which they converge and this is particularly crucial with Althusser and Strauss, requires a method which works through their writings and substantive propositions to find its internal structure. In other words, the latent structure of their work has to be drawn out and made explicit. For Levi-Strauss and Althusser, there are five important elements of their thought structures to examine (Glucksmann, 1975: 231–32).

(i)	Epistemology	Theory of acquisition of knowledge
(ii)	Philosophy	Substantive world-view
(iii)	Theory	Substantive hypotheses to account for their object of study
(iv)	Methodology	Lower level prescriptions as to method, e.g., thought experiment or hypothetic-deductive method
(v)	Field of study	Actual object of study, e.g., myth or kinship

By comparing the theorists along these dimensions, it becomes possible to assess the similarities and differences between them systematically. There is no avoiding the fact that Althusser is materialist and Levi-Strauss is an idealist or psychological reductionist, a difference which has important political implication, since Althusser believes that it is possible for men to challenge the world consciously and that philosophy is an auxiliary revolutionary weapon, whereas Levi-Strauss believes that men possess certain inbuilt innate categories and that they always have a mystified conception of social reality, and this inevitably imposes severe restraints on the possibility of conscious social change (ibid.: 232). But, despite this, they have a very similar epistemological approach opposed to that of positivism.

Levi-Strauss and Structuralist Anthropology

To gauge the distinctiveness of structuralist anthropology is to look at the way the term 'social structure' has been differently used by C. Levi-Strauss and A.R. Radcliffe-Brown. For Radcliffe-Brown (1948, 1952), the units of social structure were individual persons in roles, and structure was the arrangement of persons in institutionally defined positions. In this way, he made no radical distinction between social relations and social structure, as structure appeared to be the abstract framework of social relations.

Radcliffe-Brown's conception of social structure was naturalist, empiricist and allied to a particular type of comparative method. The first two of these aspects are connected, since for him, the term 'structure' had a naturalist derivation and was allied with his aim to produce a 'natural science of society'. Spencer introduced the term 'structure' into sociology from biology in the 19th century, and the original analogy between organic and social structure remained in Radcliffe-Brown and Durkheim for that matter. The analogy implied that, in both the natural and social world, structure is the organization of the observable parts of a whole, and that there is an intimate and natural connection between structure and function, and that structure in the social world has the same kind of empirical existence as physiology. This positivism entailed for Radcliffe-Brown a particularly empiricist methodology in which the analysis of social life was to be based on direct observation, and social structure related to actually existing social relations observable to the field worker.

The following quotes from Radcliffe-Brown's book *Structure and Function in Primitive Society* (1952) will illustrate this:

> "My view of natural science is that it is the systematic investigation of the universe as it is revealed to us through the senses. Social phenomena constitute a distinct class of natural phenomena. Social structures are just as real as individual organisms' ... direct observation does reveal to us that human beings are connected by a complex network of social relations. I use the term 'social structure' to denote this framework of actually existing relations". (190)

> "In the study of social structure the concrete reality with which we are concerned is the set of actually existing relations, at a given moment of time, which link together certain human beings. It is in this sense that we can make direct observations". (ibid.: 192)

In addition to this naturalistic empiricism, the theoretical part of anthropology was to depend, in Radcliffe-Brown's conception, on abstract propositions derived from comparing social structures. The unit for comparison was either societies as a whole or selected social institutions or social relations in different empirically existing societies.

Levi-Strauss' conception of social structure breaks with all three of these characteristics. For him, structure is also a part of reality, but at a much higher level of abstraction, and because of this, the isolation of the structural features of society depends on a completely different theoretical and methodological approach. Structure means, for Levi-Strauss, the syntax of transformations which pass from one variant to another (Levi-Strauss, 1969). He is less concerned than

Radcliffe-Brown with the actual organization of society, and more with the formal manner of arrangement of the parts. He emphasizes the possibility of several modes of arrangement of the same phenomena or structural elements, and opposes the atomism of the comparative method by seeking relations that give to the elements they unite a position in an organized whole. Thus phenomena that were previously thought to be completely different, or incomparable, such as totemism and caste, or the medieval European custom of Charivari and Bororo myths, can be seen to be intimately related on a formal and structural level, and structural possibilities can be visualized even if they do not exist empirically.

(i) First, Levi-Strauss is apparently anti-naturalistic in the sense that he believes that no social or cultural phenomena can be explained by reference to a biological base. (Even so his cultural universalism leads to a naturalism of different order, emanating from psychology and particularly the cognitive faculty of the brain, rather than biology). He dislikes the evolutionist overtones of such naturalism and the assumption that certain social arrangements, such as kinship organization, are natural or linked with some abstract human nature and apply to different stages of social development.

(ii) Second, the anti-empiricism of Levi-Strauss' concept of structure. For him, structure is not observable and cannot be perceived or discovered by the senses. It has a real existence but cannot be reached by fact collection. From Levi-Strauss' point of view, the most important task of anthropology and sociology is to develop concepts adequate to account for and describe the phenomena under investigation, and not rely on analogies from other disciplines. The need is for theoretical work, for producing concepts by mental work, and the end-result will be a one-to-one relationship between the concepts and the reality they conceptualize (Levi-Strauss, 1969). Levi-Strauss argues here that the myths 'speak' through him and that he is only making explicit their internal structure, rather than adding anything to them. There is thus no practical distinction between the concepts he uses and what he applies to, or between theory and the object of the theory (Glucksmann, 1975, 234).

(iii) The type of comparison that Levi-Strauss believes relevant to the subject matter is best expressed in the method outlined in *Totemism* (1964). The method we adopt in this case, as in others, consists in the following operations:

(a) define the phenomenon under study as a relation between two or more terms, real or supposed;

(b) construct a table of possible permutations between these terms; and

(c) take this table as the general object of analysis which, at this level only, can yield necessary connections, the empirical phenomenon considered at the beginning being only one possible combination among others, the complete system of which must be reconstructed beforehand (Levi-Strauss, 1964: 84).

Here, the emphasis is on discovering the fundamental relations between the constituent elements of the phenomena in question. Structure does not reside in the content of any individual object, but in the relation between series of objects. The units of comparison may be the themes of myth, types of cross-cousin marriage, and phenomena which are not related to each other in an empirical, historical or geographical way. An example of this type of comparison is Levi-Strauss' analysis of the structural relationship between totemism and caste in the *Savage Mind* (1966). For him, totemism is one specialized variety of a universal human activity, the classification of social phenomena by non-social categories. Primitive men have an intimate knowledge of their natural environment and order all objects in the natural world by verbal categories which serve as codes capable of assimilating any kind of content. These also impose order on human society: the differences between animal species are also applied to social groups, and the difference between one social group and another is felt to be of the same order as the difference between one animal species and another. Totems are often accompanied by rules of conduct with regard to totemic emblems: the differences between animals which man abstract from nature and transfers to culture are adopted as emblems by groups of men to reduce their own resemblances (Glucksmann, 1975: 235). Levi-Strauss goes on to argue that castes can be seen as logical inversions of totemic groups. Totemic groups are based on the postulates of homology between the relation of natural and social groups, so that clan I is to clan II as bear is to eagle. Caste societies apply the homology to the terms rather than to the relations, so clan I is bear and clan II is eagle. In the first case, social groups are distinct but parts of a whole, in the second, the diversity between social groups is all important and it becomes difficult to maintain links with other groups, particularly exogamic relations. Totemic groups exchange women who are naturally produced by other biological individuals; castes exchange goods and services which are socially produced. So, there is an individual symmetry between totemic groups and occupational castes. The analysis reveals the structural relations between the two types of social system (ibid.).

Thus, for Levi-Strauss, comparative data are treated as variations on a theme, where not all possible themes may exist, where the theme itself never has a pure empirical existence, and structure comprises the overall theme and its variations. It is in this sense that structure is syntax. For Levi-Strauss, social organization must be seen as one amongst others. As the determinant relations which constitute the structure cannot be observed, structure can only be reached by abstract conceptualization and theoretical work.

Glucksmann (1975: 235) summarizes the main points about Levi-Strauss' approach:

(a) His central theoretical concept is that of structure or 'combinatory' which expresses the possibility of various permutations between structural elements.

(b) His analysis is 'geological' (his term). It is concerned with internal construction of phenomena, with their layers, levels and elements, and the many possible relationships between them. This is the reason for his attention to formal relations such as homology, symmetry, inversion, opposition, binary discrimination and so on.

(c) His approach is anti-historicist. He believes that the explanation of the sort of anthropological data that he is interested in, can be synchronic, that they can be explained in terms of the present and non-developmentally, and that causes are to be sought within the phenomenon. Explanation thus consists in demonstrating how things work, in revealing their basic principles of operation rather than referring them to something external or to their historical origins. This is a particular and very delimited conception of cause, which owes much to phonetics. For example, the cause of myth is its internal logic, and this is the structure of relations between the terms which remains invariant through the different versions of the myth. Structure is meaning and semantics is somewhat ignored. This is the reason for the criticisms that Levi-Strauss' analysis of myth is non-sociological. Because of his overriding concern with structure, he overlooks the social origins and functions of the myths and more important, neglects the differing relations between thought and society, and science and society, in different social formations.

Althusser and Structuralist Marxism

One of the more theoretically controversial critiques of positivism to emerge in recent years is the structuralist Marxism. This position is best represented in the writings of Louis Althusser.

In a well-known thesis Althusser claims to have established that a clear qualitative break exists in Marx's work thereby justifying the drawing of a distinction between the 'young' and the 'mature' Marx. Althusser basing his argument on a critical reading of *Capital* insists that the crux of the 'epistemological break' centres on Marx's so-called 'inversion' of Hegel. For Althusser, Hegel is locked into an idealist/empiricist problematic that confuses thought with 'real'. The Hegelian conceptual scheme is simply an inversion of the empiricist. That is, whereas the empiricists assume thought to be a part of the reality known, Hegel reduces the 'real' to thought by conceiving of all the phenomena (philosophy, economy, law and so on) of an era as simply the externalization of a particular moment in the unfolding of the idea. In the Hegelian scheme, such phenomena are imbued with an omnipresent spiritual essence, which manifests itself in them. Since all these phenomena are merely an expression of this underlying essence, it is possible to reduce all of them to it. Thus, the abstract universal produces itself in concrete phenomena by means of a 'dialectical movement'. In the Hegelian conception, this constitutes the autogenesis of the concept, whose 'dialectic' is such that the final product is qualitatively no different from the original essence—simply the development of the '*in-itself*' into the '*for-itself*'. From within this framework, scientific practice—the movement from the abstract to the concrete—is seen as:

> "the autogenesis of the concept, that is, as a simple development via the very forms alienation of the original in-itself in the emergence of its end-result an end result which is no more than its beginning". (Althusser, 1969: 189)

For Althusser, Hegel has not grasped the essential qualitative differences and transformations, the fundamental discontinuities that are an integral part of actual theoretical practice. Empiricism makes essentially the same mistake, and is therefore an ideological rather than a scientific practice. This is so since empiricism simply postulates the existence of a given objective reality (a concrete) on which a human subject must perform an operation of abstraction to obtain knowledge of that reality. In this way, it is presumed that the subject is able to abstract the real essence from this given reality. For Althusser, however, empiricism thus "confuses thought with real by reducing thought about the real to the real itself" (Althusser and Balibar, 1970: 87). Three interrelated themes of Althusser's work are relevant to a consideration of his structuralism:

(i) the concept proposed for a historical materialist analysis of modes of production;
(ii) his interpretation of Marx; and
(iii) his epistemology.

The highly abstract and meta-theoretical nature of following exposition is a reflection of Althusser's work, which contains little concrete illustration.

One of the main features of the structuralist or Althusserian analysis of Marxism is anti-humanism: it has no notion of human essence or human nature and the unit of analysis is the social formation as a whole rather than the individual (Althusser, 1969). The Marxist totality is conceived as a complex internally structured totality of various layers and levels related to each other in all sorts of relations of determination and interdependence. It is not a simple dialectic of essence and phenomena (economic base and superstructure) but a complex unity of separate and specific levels of practice which may be relatively autonomous of each other within a given social formation. The totality may be dominated by one of its elements and this Althusser calls a 'structure in domination'. The autonomy and interdependence of the various layers and levels is expressed in terms of 'overdetermination' (a concept borrowed from Freud), and a key distinction is made between determinance in the last instance by the economy, and the dominant role which may be taken by any level in the social formation. There are four distinct practices in any social formation: economic, political, ideological and theoretical, and although the economy is determinant in the last instance, the dominant role is taken by politics, or ideology, or by kinship in primitive societies. Each must be examined as a specific practice with a relative autonomy of its own. Whereas the Hegelian 'expressive totality' is characterized by one single, central contradiction between essence and phenomena, which is taken over in what Althusser calls 'historicist-humanist' version of Marxism (Althusser and Balibar, 1970). As one central contradiction between the forces and relations of production, or between labour and capital, with all other contradictions emanating from this one, in the 'structural' totality, there is the possibility of the multiplicity of contradictions which may be related to each other in a number of complex ways. Althusser's category of historicists is very wide, including, curiously, Sartre and Gramsci, as well as Lukacs and Korsch. They do not share exactly the same notions of structure and history, nor conception of relationships between structure and history, and it is rather unclear why they are lumped together (Althusser and Balibar, 1970; Glucksmann, 1975: 245). Althusser draws heavily on Lenin and Mao, as well as Marx, to demonstrate the difference between the Marxist structuralist and historicist concepts of structure and contradiction.

Althusser and Balibar (1970) argue that modes of productions are to be analysed in terms of a 'combination' of five elements which co-exist and define each other reciprocally, and that different modes of production are defined by different types of relationship between these elements. The elements are:

(i) the direct producer-labour power;
(ii) the means of production-objects and instruments;
(iii) the non-worker, appropriating the surplus product.
These are combined by two relations:
(iv) property connection: relations of production; and
(v) real or material appropriation connection: productive forces.

These provide the possibility of conducting analyses of the structure of modes of production in terms of the different possible combinations and contents of these elements (Althusser and Balibar, 1970, Section 2).

The key concepts of Althusserian historical materialism are thus overdetermination, relative autonomy, and the distinction between determinancy and dominance. Social formations are conceived as composed of elements which are relatively autonomous of each other but interrelated in a complex way which is not predetermined. Each element, contradiction or revolutionary rupture, is 'overdetermined', i.e., is caused several times over and has more than one raison d'etre. The term was originally used by Freud to denote how single dream image expresses several dream thoughts or unconscious desires, but Althusser uses it to express the complexity of contradictions. Revolutionary ruptures depend not on one single contradiction but on the fusion of several contradictions. For example, the revolutionary situation in Russia, in 1917, depended not on one contradiction between the forces and relations of production, but on an accumulation of contradictions, on the fact that Russia was simultaneously a hundred years behind the imperialist world, and at the highest point of its feudal development. The contradictions could not be overcome by the ruling class, and Lenin saw in them the objective conditions for revolution (Althusser and Balibar, 1970: 237). So, a revolutionary situation can exist only when many contradictions fuse.

Linked with this is the distinction between determinance and dominance. The social formation is determined in the last instance by the economy, but the economy is never active in a pure state, and the last instance may never come. So, at any given time, the social formation may be dominated by another of its levels: ideology or politics. These levels are relatively autonomous of the economy, and are not strictly determined by it. In the structure in domination, there is the possibility of a hierarchy of levels and contradictions which may be relatively autonomous practices, dominant in the short run or determinant in the long run. Dominance consists in setting limits to the independence of other levels, and defining the looseness of the degree of fit between the elements of the structure (Althusser, op. cit.).

The orientation takes the focus away from the economy and class as the sole locus of contradiction. There may be contradictions internal to particular levels of the social formation (e.g., the educational system, the structure of sexual relations), or between the levels. Class contradictions are only one of these, and the development of a revolutionary situation depends on the compatibility of the contradictions and their all working in the same direction (Glucksmann, 1975: 238).

There are several similarities between this conception of the social formation and Levi-Strauss' structural anthropology. It conceives of a finite number of elements which can be combined in a finite number of ways to produce different modes of production, though not all the combinations have necessarily been realized in practice.

It also pays attention to the internal construction of the social formation or mode of production, looks for different types of determination and relations of subordination, domination and independence of the elements, pays attention to the different time trajectories of different elements in a way that entails a conception of causation which is very similar to Levi-Strauss' and very different from traditional conceptions of cause. Causation is to be sought within the process and consists in showing how the social formation works and hangs together, and what its strong and weak links are. Althusser describes this type of cause operating in the combination as an 'immense machine' or 'play without an author', or 'the presence of an absence' (Althusser, 1969; Althusser and Balibar, 1970), since the internal articulation of the social formation does not rest on the activity of men as individuals or groups. Relations of production constitute the unit for analysis, not men, and rather than looking for external causes of structures, it is more pertinent to think in terms of an absent cause or the 'existence of structure through its effects'. This Althusser calls 'metonymic' causality.

Althusserian Marxism is explicitly anti-historicist: modes of production are not thought of as evolving through stages from one to next in an evolutionary way. Althusser replaces the idea of the gradual unfolding of innate properties by that of a genealogy of the elements of social formation. Each element of the combination has its own history. For example, the transformation between feudalism and capitalism depended on the emergence of two elements, viz., the free worker and capital. These had different histories and their relationships can only be studied retrospectively from the point of view of the capitalist system where they are combined. So, rather than focusing on the gradual unfolding from one system to another or on origins, Althusserian history concentrates on a genealogy of the different elements, and in this way history represents the discontinuous succession of modes of production (Glucksmann, 1975: 239).

To summarize, in Althusserian terms, the Marxist totality is constructed from four specific and relatively autonomous practices, and modes of production are to be analysed in terms of the interrelation between their elements. This involves a synchronic approach which concentrates on internal construction, internal causation, and implies that the main task for political economy is to establish the concepts appropriate to each mode of production and each practice. This view of the Marxist totality is fused with a particular interpretation of Marx and with Althusser's attempt to develop a Marxist epistemology.

The main point emerging from Althusser's reading of Marx is that there was an epistemological rupture between Marx's humanist writings up to 1845 and his later scientific work after 1845. The break occurred at the time of the 'German Ideology', when Marx rejected the concept of human essence, and abandoned all forms of humanism and idealism. Instead, he founded a new theory of history and politics based on entirely new concepts which owed nothing to Hegel or Feuerbach: social formation, productive forces, and relations of production, superstructures, and ideology. According to Althusser, this rupture with anthropological humanism was inseparable from the birth of historical materialism as a science: these concepts could not have been thought in the old problematic. The old problematic, before 1845, had assumed that there is a universal essence of man and that this is an attribute of each individual man, and rested philosophically on an empiricism of the subject (individual men) and an idealism of the essence (human essence). In rejecting this, Marx also rejected a whole set of postulates in political economy, history and philosophy, and the foundation of historical materialism was correspondingly accompanied by a new philosophy which replaced the subject/essence coupled by a dialectical materialism of practice, i.e., a theory of the different specific levels of human practice (Glucksmann, 1975: 239).

Finally, there is Althusser's epistemology and here is the key concept is production. Althusser is adamant that knowledge must be produced through systematic and rigorous theoretical activity, or 'theoretical practice' like all other forms of production. In his view, theoretical activity forms one of the levels of the social formation and has its own internal organization and relative autonomy from all other levels. He maintains that theoretical practice is specific one and that its products and their validity are independent of their embeddedness in the social structure, and that theory is a form of production.

Theoretical practice is one of the four levels of the social formation, with its own specific forms of combination of productive means, labour and material. In his theory of theoretical production, Althusser distinguishes between raw material, means of production and resultant product or knowledge, and he calls these Generalities I, II and III (Althusser, 1969). Generality I represents the first matter which science transforms into specific concepts and concrete knowledge, and these constitute Generality III. Generality II is the means of production of this transformation. This conception of scientific development contrasts with the sort of empiricism that assumes that science works from something given whose essence constitutes knowledge and is reached by abstraction. Althusser rejects the distinction often made between concrete real and abstract science as based on idealism and empiricism in the following ways:

> "any view of science as abstraction from the concrete observable rests on empiricism of the object, i.e., the view that the correct object can be empirically perceived, and on an idealism of the essence or the belief that the empirical object contains its own truth within itself which can be extracted by an abstraction. Althusser, on the other hand, sees knowledge as concrete and science as proceeding from abstract to concrete rather than the reverse. This is because, for him, theory works not on empirical objects but already existing general concepts which it transforms or refines. They thus have theoretical object. For example, he argues that Marx took as the basis for his study of Capital not empirical facts about capitalist society, but general concepts such as production, work, and exchange which had been used by the classical economists but which he transformed. In this way, theory proceeds by a critique of past knowledge, and there is an absolute distinction between reality and the scientific description of reality, or between the orders of reality and thought". (Glucksmann, 1975: 240)

The logical consequence of this epistemology presents a serious challenge of positivist conceptions of how science is done. The positivist approach to survey research, for example, assumes that 'true' knowledge of social reality can be captured independent of problematic. In other words, 'true' knowledge is 'out there' to be discovered by the diligent social scientist. In this view, to the extent that knowledge is discovered and not produced, human experience and not a theoretical framework becomes the basis of knowledge. The Marxist-structuralists, however, would argue that the knowledge obtained in a survey would vary according to the theoretical framework employed, since the way the problem was posed would depend on this. The kind of problem posed would, in turn, affect the concepts used and research categories considered relevant. Different categories could produce radically different sets of knowledge from the same 'objective reality'. At the same time, the set of 'real', 'objective' (atheoretical) categories for some specific set of phenomena does not exist. That this explains many of the contradictory 'findings' about allegedly the same social phenomena seems very plausible. In other words, the major problem may not be one of measurement—the 'measurement-error' scapegoat runs rampant in positivist explanations of 'what went wrong'—but essentially conceptual.

The Marxist-structuralist perspective seems to present serious challenges to positivist sociology on the following issues:

1. Denial of the validity of the empiricist epistemology.
2. Denial of the validity of theory testing in the positivist mode.
3. Affirmation of the proposition that knowledge is produced and determined by a structure of theory.

A Comparison

In terms of the levels of their thought structures outlined above, there are differences as well as similarities. Starting with the least abstract, the field of study, they are fairly incomparable, both in nature (Levi-Strauss' analysis of the empirical data of kinship and myth, as opposed to Althusser's textual analysis of Marx) and in depth. In terms of methodology, however, there are substantial similarities. Both aim at the elaboration of concepts appropriate to the area under investigation, and most of their methods proposed are the same: apart from emphasizing the importance of analysing past ideology, both stress that the correct units of study are the relationships between structural elements, not individuals, and that structural elements are not necessarily observable. Both warn against the danger of analogy, especially as regards the construction of theory. And, both consider the criterion of validity of their theory to be intelligibility rather than verification/falsification.

At the theoretical level, the concept of structure is central to both Althusser and Levi-Strauss, and the combination and combinatory are very similar. Both believe that structures are based on a limited number of elements which may combine in a finite number of ways to produce different but related empirical social realities. In both cases, the elements are given, though their content may change according to the particular combination, and the particular mode of articulation between the elements gives the resultant structure its unique character.

The main differences are to be found at the level of philosophy. For Althusser, structures which are social formations or modes of production are materially based. The basic premise of his framework is that man's characteristic activity is production, in which a raw matter is transformed into a finished product, and this is so whether the sphere in question is economics, politics, ideology or theory. Levi-Strauss' structures are not bounded in this way; and are more ideal or psychological than real. For example, in *Elementary Structures of Kinship*, Levi-Strauss (1968) reduces a vast amount of data about kinship to its structural skeleton. He shows in a very skilful way that all the diverse practices can be seen as resting on two relatively simple types of exchange of women—one narrower and one wider. The function of this exchange, and of marriage and exogamy in general, is to produce and maintain social alliances and ultimately social solidarity. But, in thinking about the causes of this, he runs into the difficulties: in the last analysis he sees kinship as based on a universal incest taboo or exogamy (he does not distinguish clearly between them), which in turn reflects a universal principle of reciprocity. There is no explanation of such reciprocity other than as existing at a psychological level—an innate cultural characteristic that the human species possesses as such. The same problem exists in his analysis of myth. He looks for common themes and concepts, differently expressed in different cultures (for example, incest and riddles in Oedipus and Holy Grail myths), and for the ways in which abstract concepts are expressed in simple empirical terms (like raw and cooked) in primitive thought. But his four-volume study of South American mythology is based on the premise that the themes and structure of myths are to be explained as based on man's conceptual apparatus which is innate and universal, as deriving from the logical faculty of the brain.

In the field of epistemology, both Strauss and Althusser uphold an anti-empiricist conception of reality and stress the need for elaborating adequate and appropriate concepts; for both, structure has primacy over history and their theories are based on an explicit anti-historicism. There is one apparently important difference between them in this respect: for Levi-Strauss, there is no distinction between his theory and the object it theorizes, between reality and the scientific understanding of reality, for example, in his myth analysis; for Althusser, on the other hand, there is an absolute distinction between the orders of the thought and reality, and between theory and the reality it theorizes. However, at analytical level, this difference is not an absolute one: both conflate theory and its object, but in opposite directions. Levi-Strauss assimilates theory into concrete reality, while Althusser assimilates reality into theory, with his conception of the 'theoretical object'. For him, theory is theory of a theoretical object and does not work directly on empirical data. Structurally, then, their position on the relation between theory and the object of theory is identical, though their terminology differs; theory and its object are both subsumed into the object in the one case, and into theory in the other (Glucksmann, 1975: 245).

So, there are great similarities between Levi-Strauss and Althusser's theory, epistemology and methodology, even though their philosophies and fields of study are different. Both look for structures as combinations of elements, concentrate on internal causation, and proceed in their analyses in a similar way, but what they tie the structures to once they have isolated them is different in two cases. Still, the similarities between the two are sufficient to be able to conclude that there is a distinctive structuralist approach to social and cultural phenomena.

Thus, a distinction can be made between structural and structuralist thought. Both use the term 'structure', but as part of different systems of idea. Both presuppose that social life cannot be explained in terms of individuals. But, in one case, structural thought, the approach derives from the analogy with biology, and involves an empirical investigation of the structure of social relations, while the other takes this level of analysis for granted and tries to discover more abstract principles of organization governing social relations. Structure refers to quite different levels of reality in the two cases.

From a sociological point of view, the most significant features of structuralism are its distinctive concept of structure and its critiques of empiricism and historicism, which entail many practical implications. But the most easily assimilable aspect of structuralism is its attention to the internal construction of social and cultural phenomena. In all fields—linguistics, and semiology as well as anthropology and political economy—the structuralist orientation is defined by its attention to finding the concepts and ways to describe how elements are related to each other—what the various weightings of the relationship are, for those specific phenomena, that is, its attention to analysis and synthesis which is not based on analogies, and with structural causality. This should lead to sociology reviewing its conceptions of explanation and causation, and the relationship between sociology and history, or synchrony and diachrony. The geological approach to social reality enables comparison of phenomena which were previously thought to be at different stages of development and hence incomparable and also breaks down barriers between intellectual disciplines. Whether structuralism has lived up its political promise, however, is quite a different matter (Glucksmann, 1975: 243).

References

Althusser, L., 1969, *For Marx*, London: Allen Lane.

Althusser, L. and Balibar, E., 1970, *Reading Capital*, London: New Left Books.

Barthes, R., 1967, *Elements of Semiology*, London: Cape.

Foucault, M., 1967, *Madness and Civilization*, London: Tavistock

——, 1971, *The Archaeology of Knowledge*, London: Tavistock.

Glucksmann, Miriam, 1975, "The Structuralism of Levi-Strauss and Althusser", in John Rex (ed.), 1975, *Approaches to Sociology*, Boston, Mass, USA: Pearson Education.

Godelier, M. 1966, *Rationalite et irrationalite en economie*, Paris: Seuil.

——, 1967, "System, Structure and Contradiction in Capital", in R. Miliband and J. Savile (eds.), *Socialist Register*, London: Merlin Press.

Jakobson, R., 1962, *Selected Writings*, The Hague: Mouton.

Jakobson, R. and Halle, M. 1956, *Fundamentals of Language*, The Hague: Mouton.

Lacan, Jacques, 1966, *Ecrits*, Paris: Seuil.

Lane, M. (ed.), 1970, *Structuralism: A Reader*, London: Cape.

Leach, E., 1970, *Levi-Strauss*, London: Fontana.

Levi-Strauss, C., 1964, *Totemism*, London: Penguin.

——, 1966, *The Savage Mind*, London: Weidenfeld and Nicolson.

——, 1968, *Elementary Structures of Kinship*, London: Penguin.

——, 1969, *The Raw and Cooked*, London: Cape.

Propp, V. 1958, Morphology of the Folktale, *American International Journal of Linguistics*, Vol. 24.

Radcliff-Brown, A.R., 1948, *A Natural Science of Society*, New York: The Free Press.

——, 1952, *Structure and Function in Primitive Society*, London: Cohen and West.

Saussure, F. de 1959, *Course in General Linguistics*, New York: The Philosophical Library.

6

Postmodernism

New Conversions in Theory and Research Methodology

The social sciences have never had the luxury of feeling secure in their identity or social role. Since their inception, the meaning of the social sciences has been contested. Questions about the epistemological, methodological, political and moral status of the social sciences have persisted to this day. Are the social sciences really scientific or are they part of the humanities? Is social science different from natural science in its concept formation, explanations and methodology? Is social science necessarily ideological or its moral and political character indicative of its underdeveloped state? These questions not only raise serious concerns about the intellectual and institutional legitimacy of the social sciences but also have the implications for methodology in social sciences (Seidman and Wagner, 1993).

The 1960s and 1970s were a crucial period in the debate over the meaning and method of the social sciences. The dominant positivism of the social sciences was subject to a barrage of criticism. A series of philosophical movements, most notably hermeneutics, ordinary language philosophy of science, ethnomethodology, critical school and post-structuralism, converged in assailing the dominant positivist orthodoxy. The critics who espoused these positions argued that the natural and social sciences involve an interpretative ordering of empirical reality; that philosophical, aesthetic and moral considerations play a role in all empirical inquiry; and that in its resistance to empirical verification science resembles literary interpretation. Although these critics agreed on certain basic points, there was disagreement on other equally fundamental issues. For example, hermeneutically inclined social scientists favoured a more contextual and descriptive approach to the generalizing analytical explanations of post-empiricists.

Out of these polemics between positivism and its critics there developed a shift in the centre of debate. On the one hand, the discussion now centred on arguments over the respective merits and defects of interpretive, post-empiricist and critical-normative paradigms of social sciences. In other words, while a positivist model of social science was rejected in these theoretical debates, the epistemic privileging of science went unchallenged. Thus, social scientists advanced hermeneutics or post-positivism or critical method and theory as alternative foundations for social science. On the other hand, the critique of positivism, especially by post-structuralists and some feminists, challenged the scientism of positivists and their critics. Many began to emphasize the social and historical embeddedness of an inquiry, its essentially moral and political nature, and the failure and indeed undesirability of all efforts to provide a unifying social scientific paradigm. A new division was drawn between those social scientists who defended the possibility and desirability of achieving secure analytical foundations—modernists—and critics of this project. In the social sciences, postmodernism describes the critique of the modernist project to ground and unify the social sciences. In its critique of modernist social science, postmodernists consider the relationship between scientific knowledge, power and society as well as the relation between science, critique and normative.

Enlightenment and the Modernist Quest for Scientific Knowledge and Social Progress

Despite their critique of metaphysics and religion, the philosophes never abandoned the notion that true knowledge must be universal and grounded in some metadiscourse. Appeals to theological dogma were replaced by science as the medium of truth. Initially developed in the context of the study of nature; the scientific paradigm was extended to human nature and society. By the end of the 18th century, there was a proliferation of proposals for a social science. They all shared two basic assumptions: First, the aim of social science was thought to be to discover general principles and to evolve its own method. The ideal was to achieve a conceptual and analytical unity by reducing the human and social domain to a limited number of general principles or laws. Scientific knowledge would be grounded in a metadiscourse that, in France and England, typically took the form of an empiricist epistemology. Second, the philosophes agreed that social science would function as an instrument of social progress. It would abolish longstanding prejudices and ignorance by revealing truths about human nature, society and history. Scientific enlightenment would enable humankind to fashion a social order in accordance with the true principles of nature and society. Science would make possible humankind's rational self-creation.

From the founding years of social science to its classical age, the modernist project was sustained. The major classical figures—Comte, Marx, Durkheim, Spencer, Weber, Pareto, Albion Small and Lester Ward—endorsed, indeed propagated, the epistemological privileging of science, its quest for intellectual unit based upon discovering general principles, and its beneficial practical role. For example, although Comte and Marx disagreed on the conceptual structure and explanatory principles of a social science, they both contrasted their own scientific efforts with the pre-scientific or merely "ideological" standpoint of their predecessors and contemporary rivals. Moreover, these classic figures viewed science as contributing to social progress. Comte anticipated that his 'positive philosophy' and 'positive polity' would be a guide to social reconstruction in post-revolutionary France. Marx saw his critique of political economy as contributing to human emancipation by becoming a material force in transforming the working class into a revolutionary political agent.

This is, however, one way in which classical figures departed from their predecessors. Whereas the former grounded social science in a philosophical metadiscourse, the latter looked increasingly to social theory to provide foundations. We can detect the beginnings of a concept of social theory and method as a foundational discourse in the 19th century. Its aim is to set out the basic premises, concepts and problems of social science, to provide standards in terms of which empirical and analytical disputes can be resolved; to elaborate an overarching conceptual framework that would unify inquiry. This definition of the role of theory as a grounding discourse is apparent, for example, in Marx's 'German Ideology' or in his 'Introduction to the Critique of Political Economy', which purports to advance epistemic reasons defending the proposition that labour or the mode of production can serve as the foundational category of a science of society and history. No less foundational in their aims are Durkheim's 'Division of Labour in Society' and 'Rules of Sociological Method', Tonnies' 'Gemeinschaft and Gesellschaft', Weber's 'Economy and Society', and Simmel's 'Sociology'.

In the 20th century, social science underwent a process of institutionalization and cultural legitimation. This has shaped social science in distinctive ways. The academization of social science has meant the heightening of its scientific claims. In their effort to achieve institutional legitimacy and material resources, contemporary social scientists have often felt compelled to suppress the practical-moral or political role of science. Logical positivism provided the initial intellectual rationale. As the social sciences have sought institutional autonomy, they have developed their own analytical and research agendas. Intellectual disputes have tended to be handled as purely discipline-bound analytical or methodological problems. Accordingly, the role of social theory as a metadiscourse whose aim is to adjudicate disciplinary disputes, has expanded. Today, theory especially sociological theory, is typically defined as distinct specialty or field of expertise concerned with its own 'autonomous' epistemological, analytical and methodological problems. For example, theorists are expected to take positions on the relation between concepts and the social world, the logical structure of sociological explanation, the nature of social action, order and change, the linkage between agency and social structure or micro and macro levels of analysis and so on. Theory has assumed the role of safeguarding the rationality of social science by holding that current disagreements are, at bottom, resolvable analytical or methodological problems. In its role as a grounding discourse social theory has become increasingly metatheoretical.

The Postmodern Critique

Ironically, the very institutional success of social sciences may have inadvertently contributed to the critique of the modernist project. For example, the increased dependence of social sciences on private and public funding agencies which inevitably shapes social research, raises doubts about its claims to be value-neutral. Similarly, the effort to establish a disciplinary consensus through analytical means has met with little success. Stephen Turner's (1992) essay documents the absences and inconsistencies in the various foundationalist projects pursued by sociologists in the 20th century:

> "Richards Rorty's 'Philosophy and Mirror of Nature' (1979) showed that Heidegger, Dewey, and Wittgenstein had each been groping towards a rejection of 'foundationalism', the attempt to find some sort of grounding for our ultimate presuppositions. Modern social theorists from Hobbes to the present have employed foundationalist appeals. Paradigmatically, these have been appeals to criteria of cognitive validity: behaviourist attempts to exclude explanations with mental predicates, neo-Marxian charges that given theories are 'unhistorical' and Alexander's claims that various formulations of Durkheim or Weber are insufficiently 'multi-dimensional' may all be given instances. But all these arguments have been inconclusive. Each step in the argument proceeds on though, by raising the matter in theoretical dispute to the next level of abstraction to the level of criteria for theory choice, we will arrive at an unequivocal victory for one of the solutions to the problem under dispute. But what occurs in something different: at each level there prove to be a variety of possible criteria. And when we try to resolve the conflict between them by going to the next level of abstraction, i.e. to construct criteria of adequacy for these answers, we find the same thing" (1992: 101).

However, whereas Stephen Turner argues that these projects often lead to fruitful programmes, they have also generated metatheoretical discourses whose sole reference point seems, at times, to be other texts and discourses on texts. This has encouraged a heightened skepticism towards the foundational aims of modernist social science. Moreover, the effort to reconfigure social inquiry into a purely analytical mode, purging it of practical, moral and political intent, has reinforced a public perception of the obscurity of social science. This is particularly true with respect to social theory which, in its effort to ground social inquiry, has often become wired in a web of metatheoretical tangles. Postmodernism seems, in part, to be responding to this condition and to the contradictory pulls of social science towards an aimless empiricism and an equally aimless theoreticism. Postmodernism, at one level, can be characterized as a movement of intellectual revitalization.

Postmodernism is not, of course, the first effort of intellectual renewal through critique and reconstruction. The history of social science reads almost like a continuous effort at revitalization. From Comte's critique of the philosophes or Marx's critique of Comte, to Durkheim's and Weber's critique of Marx, to the Parsonian quest to synthesize the classical tradition and the subsequent efforts to supersede structural-functionalism by neo-Marxism, exchange theory, or structural sociology, the wish to revitalize social analysis through critique and reconstruction is an abiding motif.

The postmodern critique is perhaps unique in that it challenges a project of social science shared by virtually all rival schools or paradigms. Postmodernism criticizes the modernist notion that science itself, not this or that theory or paradigm, is a privileged form of research or the medium of truth. It disputes the scientistic claim that only scientific knowledge can be securely grounded. It takes issue with the unifying consensus-building agenda of science. It contests the modernist idea that social theory has as its chief role the securing of conceptual grounds for social research. And, postmodernism criticizes the modernist notion that science is or should be value-neutral. Postmodernism underlines the practical and moral meaning of science (Seidman and Wagner, 1992: 6).

Central to postmodernism is its critique of the claim that scientific knowledge is universal and can be justified in a non-contextual way. Postmodernists contend that standards of truth are context-dependent. In "On the Postmodern Barricades", Linda Nicholson (1992) argues that social theories derive their coherence and compelling power because they are part of socially effective cultural traditions. The standards of European and Anglo-American social science knowledge are said to be inextricably bound up with culturally specific presuppositions of Western modernity. For example, the separation of cognitive truths from moral and aesthetic knowledge and indeed the prioritization of cognitive truths, the emphasis upon propositional knowledge, or the rationales for what counts as evidence or facts get their coherence from Western cultural traditions. Within the social scientific disciplines, moreover, there are conflicting evaluative criteria regarding what counts as valid research or theory. For some social scientists, predictability, conceptual economy or quantifiability are the chief standards. Others emphasize explanatory comprehensiveness, descriptive richness, discursive cogency, or moral political or aesthetic criteria. These heterogeneous criteria seem immune to reasoned consensus.

The postmodern critique goes beyond a general historical contextualizing of science. Seidman (1992) has argued for a radical decentering of science. The explanation he wishes to offer regarding the state of sociological theory and method focuses on certain assumptions that theorists have held about sociology as a science and about the role assigned to theory.

> "Many sociological theorists believe that science is an epistemologically privileged type of knowledge. Its defense is necessary, moreover in order to preserve rationality and a society that guarantees freedom and social progress. They assume that the defense of sociology as a science must take the form of theory providing foundations or grounds for sociological analysis. Providing foundations entails explaining why sociology should adopt a specific set of premises, concepts and explanatory models. In a word, theorists assume that the task of resolving disciplinary disputes or paradigm conflicts requires proposing general criteria and ideals for a correct or valid sociology. Sociological theorists step forward as virtual police of the sociological mind, creating order and disciplinary coherence in the name of rationality and progress. They have not been successful. Their efforts have yielded not a defense of reason but a bewildering proliferation of text discourses and disputes that render sociological theory intellectually obscure and make it irrelevant to broader public concerns. Ironically, this effort also has elicited a suspicion of the non rational character of sociology. This quest for foundations, for providing proofs or principles of justification, causes much of the malaise of sociological theory and research" (Seidman, 1992: 47–48).

Seidman further adds, "In the past, these assumptions about science and theory have been challenged by a discursive clamouring that frequently goes under the name of postmodernism (Kellner, 1988; Foster, 1983; Lash, 1985). The postmodern intervention is not merely another reshaping of debates between scientific and humanistic sociologists. Indeed, these seemingly endless discussions may be taken as symptomatic of the current impasse of sociological theory and of its stultifying insularity. Postmodernism raises questions about this very configuration of debate. The postmodern intercession aims to revitalize sociology by reforming its disciplinary code" (ibid.: 48).

Accordingly, under the banner of postmodernism, Seidman has offered a series of reservations about sociological theory. He has urged a shift in the role of theorists from building general theory or providing epistemic warrants for sociology to serving as moral and political analysts, narrators of stories of social development, producers of genealogies, and social critics. He advocates a change from a discipline-centred inquiry whose reference point is debates in specialty areas to contextualized local narratives that address public conflicts. He proposes that social scientific knowledge bears the imprint not only of the broad civilizational and national culture of which it is a part but typically of the more specific class, race, gender, or sexual orientation of its producers. Every attempt to advance a general theoretical standpoint is deconstructed or shown to reveal, in its basic concepts and explanations, the particular social standpoint and interests of its author. For example, Seidman criticizes Marxism by showing that it not only incorporates the scientism, utilitarianism and millenialism of the liberal bourgeoise society it criticizes but that its basic conceptual framework exhibits the standpoint and bias of a white European, middle-class heterosexual male. A general theory of society and history that is centred on economically based class dynamics neglects and marginalizes social and political dynamics that revolve around gender, ethnicity, race, sexuality, or age.

A decentred view of social science underscores its practical-moral and political significance. Lemert (1992) suggests that the politics of social science is inextricably tied to its epistemology. The categories and explanations of social science, he contends, unavoidably construct social reality in a way that emphasizes certain social processes and privileges specific groups and social agendas. Indeed, postmodernists view social scientific knowledge as implicated in practical projects. It is not a matter of science providing knowledge which has practical utility. Rather, social scientific knowledge is seen as a strategy by which individuals and groups promote their interests, pursue a social agenda, or struggle for power. The link between science and power goes beyond ideological politics. The social sciences are a major social power in modern societies. As Nicholson (1992) says, their practical character is fully exhibited only when we realize that science is often implicated in the institutional power of hospitals, psychiatric clinics, mental asylums, prisons, and in bureaucratic administrative strategies to regulate our behaviour and shape our body images, identities, and daily conventions. From a postmodern perspective, science stands alongside the economy, state, family, or church as a major social and political force.

Postmodernists tend to favour forms of social inquiry which incorporate an explicitly practical and moral intent, that are contextual and restricted in their focus (local stories are preferred over general ones), and that are narratively structured rather than articulating a general theory. Thus, Seidman (1992) argues for transfiguring general theory into social narratives that incorporate a moral pragmatic interest. Lemert recommends a deconstructionist mode of social inquiry that would reveal false conceptual closures and force us to attend to the socially constitutive aspects of discourse. Yet Nicholson defends a postmodern theorizing that would permit cross-cultural, generalizing conceptual categories. Postmodernism does not necessarily reject methodologically sophisticated and analytically informed social analysis but rather invokes a suspicion regarding claims that social inquiry can be grounded in someway that gives it a privileged epistemological status. Likewise, postmodernism does not necessarily repudiate generalizing analytical moves but rejects the modernist one of a totalizing general theory or the quest for a unified social scientific paradigm. Postmodernists are more likely to theorize in deconstructionist mode, to substitute genealogical analysis for the theory-building efforts, to reintroduce moral and political concerns as central discursive topics (Seidman, 1992: 8).

Reproaching Postmodernism in Defence of Scientific Theory

The postmodern challenge to the discipline has generated its own critics. Many modernists do not concede impossibility of foundations in social science. Renewed efforts to frame theory as a foundational discourse have appeared, most notably in the writings of Habermas and Giddens. Others have raised practical and moral doubts about the consequences of the postmodern critique. Does postmodernism end in relativism and nihilism? Does its radical decentering call into question any rational standards of discourse? Questions have been raised about whether repudiating the project of a general theory means the abandonment of a strong programme of analytical and critical theorizing. Does postmodernism's radical deconstructionism mean that all general categories become problematic or illegitimate? Does its radical historicist critique lead to a descriptivism that lacks the deep critical impulse of analytical theorizing?

One of the most basic failings of postmodernism the critiques identify is its failure to distinguish the relativism of the frameworks within which sociological theorizing must proceed from the knowledge generated by employing those frameworks. The choice of a framework for investigating social phenomena is accepted as an inherently particularistic choice, subject rather directly to the deconstruction that postmodernism encourages. However, the actual investigation of social phenomena, given the adoption of a frame of reference, need to be particularistic. Deconstruction at this level does not lead directly to solipsism, the critics argue. Thus, Randall Collins, in *The Confusion of the Modes of Sociology* (1992) imagines a 21st century review of a physics text, given success of the postmodernist critique throughout science. He parallels this fantasy with the analysis provided by Michael Mulkay in *The Word and the World* (1985). In his deconstruction of Mulkay's postmodern 'deconstruction' sociological analysis, Collins playfully suggests that Erving Goffman must have been the book's author; authorship is simply a matter of interpretation and presentation any way. In Collin's view, postmodernism provides no means of disputing such claims.

As a consequence, the critics claim that postmodernism too readily dismisses the possibility of scientific theorizing in sociology. Most sociological critics of postmodernism argue that some sort of general or generalizing theory is both possible to attain and desirable to pursue. Some even argue that cumulative knowledge of fundamental social processes has already been generated in a number of areas.

This is certainly Collin's view. He believes that we should focus on the investigation of fundamental social processes at an abstract level. A great deal of knowledge of this sort has been cumulated, he claims, but this success has been obscured by the confusion of practical and ideological (i.e., evaluative) frames with the scientific frame. The practical frame is applicable only within physically closed systems. The ideological frame, when treated imperially, allows us only to see what we want to see. The scientific frame, by contrast, can encompass and articulate both of the other frames; at the same time, it goes beyond them to create general knowledge. Thus, despite the postmodern critique, Collins sees grounds for optimism in sociological theorizing and methodology.

> "One of the discoveries that has emerged from the whole sweep of subjectivist and interpretative thought in the 20th century is the multi-leveled character of human symbol systems. Erving Goffman put the point very usefully in his Frame Analysis (1974), showing how meaning on one level is typically built by putting a contextual frame around some other level of social action. The result is the hierarchy of frames in which we think; the frames are not free-floating, but are built up link by link from one another in sequence. I submit that this conception, whether in Goffman's version, or Godel's, or Garfinkel's, is a scientific one, not an ideology. It tells us how the world is, not what is desirable or undesirable about it". (1992: 196)

> "Science, practicality and ideology are all frames through which we see the social world. The proponents of different frames can fight with one another, reformulate each other in their own terms, and attempt to negate or destroy each other. But they are not in equivalent structural positions in the hierarchy of frames. In so far as they are all part of the intellectual world, the scientific frame is the largest frame for interpreting the others. We know that the ideological frame, by its moralizing, reduces the focus; it allows us to see only what it wants to see (either as good or evil) ; that which does not fit its grid of categories it must assimilate to evil. The practical frame, too, is a limited one for intellectual purpose. It operates well only in one part of the world, the part that consists of physically closed systems; when it tries to deal with the open-system part of the world, it leaves us locked in particularistic descriptions, never rising to the generality of explanations". (ibid.: 196–97)

He goes on to emphasize:

> "The scientific frame, taken in its broadest sense, is the encompassing frame. The scientific frame can understand the practical

frame, both when practicality works and when it does not. And science can both understand and empathize with the ideological frames, at whatever degree of nuance one wishes to pursue. The advantage of the scientific frame is that, by its detachment, it is able to encompass and analyze whatever it focuses upon, while relating it to the overall sphere of explanatory conception that is the storehouse of its knowledge. Science alone can turn back on itself without undermining itself; this is what the sociology of science does. Science is the one sphere that can operate without blinders; and for that reason, it is the one sphere in which we can expect to make progress as sociology". (ibid.: 197)

Others make similar arguments, although there are some significant differences in their images of the nature of the project involved. D' Amico (1992) briefly analyses Carnap's notion of 'framework relativism' and then more extensively considers Popper's division between the objects of World I (i.e., the world of physical objects and states), World II (i.e., the world of mental states and behavioural dispositions), and World III (i.e., the world of objective contents of thought). Using these ideas, he proposes how a generalizing social science might absorb much of the postmodern critique without yielding to its particularism.

"The social sciences would have to consider an alternative model of explanation if it could be shown that certain theoretical categories in the natural sciences converged on a standard of truth or replication in the external, realist sense. But if those expectations or standards are illicit, then we change frameworks in just the same way as we change from a pocketknife to a table saw, to use Carnap's analogy, when our standards of cutting change. But there is no single standard of 'cutting' and thus, no need for social science to counter its failure to live up to this standard. Beyond cultural and practical preferences, there is no correct tool of all enquiries". (D' Amico, 1992: 146–47)

D'Amico's (1992) following comments on Habermas' account of human interests at the base of knowledge are worth mentioning:

"The natural and social sciences are 'transcendently constituted' by different interests; the interest for technical control in the case of the physical sciences and the interest for communicative understanding in the case of the social sciences. These contrastive constitutive frameworks bring about correspondingly different object-domains, modes of inquiry, and cognitive standards. There is a good deal of questionable philosophical baggage in this account that social scientists need not immediately concern themselves with, except to realize that even Habermas is now doubtful about feasibility of this version of transcendentalism. Also one should note that it bears some similarity to Carnap's framework model but with a more mysterious guarantee about the 'Correctness' of specific frameworks for specific types of inquiry". (1992: 151–52)

He further speaks:

"The point is that for purposes of determining the character of social science research Habermas's more sophisticated account of a distinctive status for those sciences is rather innocuous. Habermas does not clarify why 'empirical analytic' inquiry is exclusive to the natural sciences. Since the framework supervenes over what is defined as the domain of empirical evidence, this allows for a shift in the object-domains and empirical procedures. Habermas (1971) seems to adopt an instrumentalist view that constrains research in the physical sciences to what is operationally defined and useful. But the domain of empirical research can be more broadly conceived and need not be tied so closely to instrumental criteria. In effect, the methodological heuristics that emerge from seeking communicative understanding in the social sciences allow for claims that are empirical. Of course, this weaker argument does not demonstrate which framework's empirical domain is correct but Habermas' transcendental arguments does not seem likely to supply such a proof either". (ibid.)

He concludes:

"The most interesting problem is whether the social theories themselves enter into inquiry in the social sciences in a way that they do not in the natural sciences. Does this self-reflexivity constitute the crucial and purely conceptual difference between these sciences? In this view, the point is that theoretical change in the natural sciences leaves the object of inquiry, such as a chemical reaction, indifferent and unaffected by the new theoretical categories. But in the social sciences different theories and methods literally change the reality of social life. The notion is that by successfully studying criminals with 'labeling theory' one is doing more than describing

> pre-existing natural kinds, called 'criminals', but changing our conception of that social reality. Though I think this is an important insight, again I think Carnap (1956, 1963) allows us to handle this point. We should distinguish the constituting of the domain of 'objects' from the descriptive success, utility or applicability of the theoretical framework. What a social scientist is noting with this point is the need to defend labeling theory against alternative accounts of criminality. That will often involve pedagogical, rhetorical, and practical appeals, but we should not think in having the flexibility, to change such fundamental categories we change our reality, such that it means the social sciences study a unique and mysterious ontological instability". (ibid.: 152–53)

One attempt to develop an understanding of the nature of these frameworks and their role in sociological theorizing has been pursued by David Wagner (1992). Drawing on previous largely unsuccessful attempts to bridge the gap between theoretical and empirical work in sociology (especially by Robert Merton and by advocates of theory construction), he identifies several lessons to be learned from these attempts. For example, it is possible to proceed theoretically without an articulated general framework or theory. Nevertheless, general theory does serve an integrative and directive purpose we would do well to investigate in detail.

In 'Daring Modesty: On Metatheory, Observation and Theory Growth', Wagner proposes that we view general theory in terms of 'orienting strategies' (i.e., metatheoretical entities somewhat similar to Kuhnian paradigms or Lakatosian 'hard cores'). He argues that the adoption of such strategies is necessary to do any sociological work. The truth of such strategies is not directly testable; instead, their utility is determined largely by their ability to generate more specific theories to account for social phenomena in particular explanatory domains. The success of a strategy therefore is evaluated largely on grounds internal to the strategy and is always provisional. Consequently, a single overarching general theory and method of society is not possible; general theories and therefore methods are necessary and important elements of sociological research. These arguments suggest that we ought to be more modest about our claims regarding the ontological and epistemological status of general theories and more daring in our willingness to actually implement the directive of general theories. Wagner writes:

> "It is evident from arguments, that I regard justificationism as irrelevant to the growth of our knowledge. Indeed in many ways, I see it as a hindrance to that growth. There is no epistemological privilege, no method we can use to guarantee sociological truth. Furthermore, no epistemological privilege is needed; we can and do proceed without it. To assume that it is both feasible and necessary is to perpetuate the imperial tendencies and unbridgeable divisions between theoretical and empirical sociology". (1992: 218)

Wagner further argues:

> "If there is no ultimate basis for justifying our theoretical claims (either foundationally or observationally), rather greater modesty in our ontological and epistemological claims is called for. If we cannot avoid making metatheoretical assumptions about social reality, that does not mean these assumptions must constitute the only plausible reality. Several different positions may have something legitimate to say about the social world. We might benefit from a periodic substitution of the lens of another perspective for the one we prefer, simply to see how different the world looks from that point of view. But modesty is not enough. The problem is that the lack of a firm foundation leads many to refrain from specific theorizing about social phenomena altogether. The lack of a firm foundation does not mean we cannot theorize. More than a little daring is called for. We can never be certain of the truth of our ideas, but we can conjecture and hypothesize. What if the social world operated in this particular way or that particular way? How would that affect other assumptions we make about the world? Moreover, we can learn from these conjectures and hypotheses. Our knowledge can improve in the sense that it is less prone too error than our previous conjectures were. We simply cannot be sure that we are approaching sociological truth as an endpoint. In Kuhn's (1970) terms, progress is better described as 'evolution from what we do know' (i.e., from the less articulated and more specialized theories of the past) than as 'evolution towards what we wish to know' (i.e., towards much sort of ultimate truth)". (ibid.: 218–19)

Jonathan Turner articulates á position perhaps closer to modernism than any of the other critics, although he does introduce some significant modification to that position. In 'The Promise of Positivism' (1992), Turner defends the importance of deductive rigour, prediction and falsification as criteria for evaluating theory.

However, he relaxes the application of these criteria somewhat: deductive theorizing need not be axiomatic; precise prediction is seldom possible; definitive tests are unlikely. Moreover, he thoroughly rejects the notion of theory assessment as an inductive process from neutral observations. With Collins, Jonathan Turner challenges many of the criticisms of this form of positivist sociology as flowing from phenomenological solipsism and historical particularism. He suggests that these criticisms are based on a naïve view of the nature of science and are in no way obstacles to a positive theory of society.

> "Theory should, first of all, be abstract and not tied to the particulars of a historical/empirical case. Hence, empirical modeling and empirical propositional schemes are not theory, but regularities in the data that require a theory to explain them. They are an *explanandum* in search of an *explanans*. Second, positivism emphasizes that theories must be tested against the facts, and thus metatheoretical schemes and elaborate naturalistic analytic schemes are not theory proper. Sensitizing analytical schemes, however, can be used as starting-points for building testable theory. If the anti-positivist tenets among some practioners can be ignored, such sensitizing analytical schemes provide a sound place to begin conceptualizing basic classes of variables that can be incorporated into testable propositions and analytical models. This could also be possible with naturalistic analytical schemes, but more difficult in actual practice because scheme tend to become excessively concerned with their own architectural majesty, thereby making it awkward to transform them into more precise models and propositions. Finally, in contrast to Comte's early advocacy, theory must involve more than abstract statements of regularities; it must also stress the issue of casuality, but not the simple casuality of empirical models. My view is that analytical models provide an important supplement to abstract propositions because they map the complex causal connections—direct and indirect effects, feedback loops, reciprocal effects etc.—among the concepts in propositions. Without such models, it is difficult to know what processes and mechanisms are involved in creating the relations that are specified in a proposition". (Turner, 1992: 172)

He concludes,

"In light of these considerations, then, positivist theory must be abstract; it must denote generic properties of the universe; it must be testable or capable of generating testable propositions; and it cannot ignore casuality, process, and operative mechanisms. The best approach to theory-building in sociology is thus a combination of sensitizing analytical schemes, abstract formal proposition, and analytical models (Turner, 1986). This is where the most creative synergy is; and while various theorists tend to emphasize one over the other; it is the simultaneous use of all three approaches that offers the most potential for developing a 'natural science of society'. Such would be the nature of positivism that I advocate and that I have sought to develop". (Jonathan Turner, 1984, 1987, 1988)

The following figure portrays Jonathan Turner's position in schematic form (Turner, 1992: 73).

Figure 1
Strategies for Building Theory

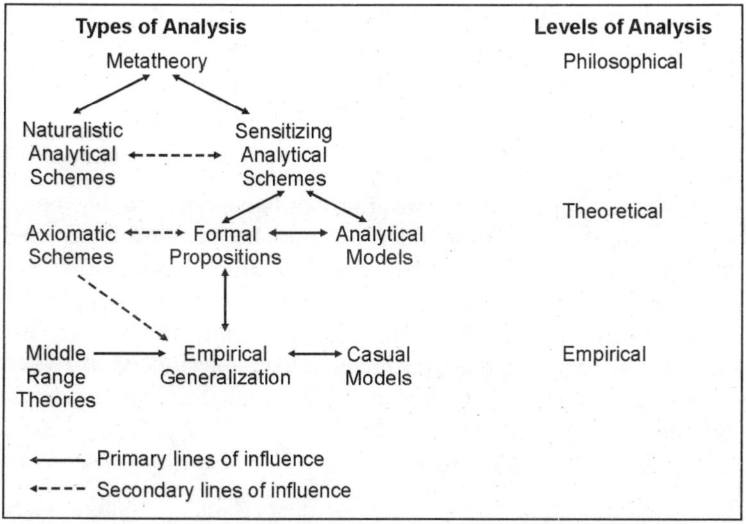

Jonathan Turner holds the view that one way to begin theorizing is by constructing sensitizing analytical schemes that denote in a provisional manner key properties of the social universe. By itself such activity is unproductive, since the scheme cannot be tested. Rather, it can only be used to denote classes of important processes, and, at best, to interpret specific empirical events. In his view, this is inadequate, it is also necessary to generate abstract and testable propositions and, at the same time, to model the processes that operate to connect the concepts in the propositions. This exercise itself, regardless of empirical tests, can force revision of sensitizing scheme. Or, construction of an analytical model can encourage rethinking of a proposition. As in the diagram, the critical point here is that these three activities are mutually reinforcing; this is what Jonathan Turner (1992: 174) means by 'creative synergy' (ibid.: 174).

In contrast, naturalistic analytical schemes and metatheorizing tend to be too philosophical and detached from the actual workings of the world. They become overly reified and either concerned with their architecture or obsessed with their scholistic capacity to resolve philosophical issues. Yet, Jonathan Turner does not consider these to be unimportant activities but rather as being useful only after we have developed laws and models in which we have confidence. Then, more philosophical discussion is useful and can force re-examination of laws and propositions. But without these laws and propositions naturalistic analytical schemes and metatheorizing become self-sustaining philosophical treatises. The vehicle for connecting propositions and models to more formal analytical schemes and metatheory is the sensitizing analytical scheme. These sensitizing schemes, when used to stimulate the formulation of propositions and when reassessed in light of tests of propositions, can provide empirically informed propositions for more complex naturalistic schemes and for metatheorizing. In turn, when metatheory and naturalistic schemes have been built from a propositional base, they can provide useful insights that force assessment of existing propositions and models. Yet, without this attachment to testable theory, analytical schemes and metatheory float away into the reified and rarefied world of philosophical speculation and debate.

Jonathan Turner comments:

> "On the more empirical side of theory-building, middle range propositions are, in essence, empirical generalizations for an entire substantive area. To be useful, however, they must be converted into abstract laws (most difficult to do) or into discrete empirical generalizations (much easier to do). Empirical-causal models can explicate the temporal processes that operate to connect variables, but to be useful in building theory, they need to be incorporated

into empirical generalizations. Then they can help to assess the plausibility of abstract propositions. Without the abstract laws and models, however, these more empirical approaches will not help to build theory. For if uninformed by abstract laws and formal models, then middle range theories, causal models, and empirical generalization are constructed ad hoc, without concern for whether or not they illustrate an underlying dynamic of the social universe. Only infrequently does one make inductions from these empirical formats and create theory, for the reality of theory-building is the other way round: theory first, then assessment with data. But the data have to be arranged in a way that makes them testable with an abstract proposition". (1992.: 175)

Such is the position of Jonathan Turner on positivism:

"Start with sensitizing schemes, propositions and models, and only then move on to the formal collection of data or to metatheorizing, and scheme-building. In this way, it will be possible to generate scientific knowledge about the social universe, with the result that sociology can take its place among the natural sciences. If all this seems naive and idealized, such is no doubt the case. But my sense is most practicing scientists—that is, those who try to understand how things work—engage in a process, often implicitly, of using sensitizing schemes, analytical models, and propositions. Such should be case for sociologists, especially theorists, who start to theorize rather then merely proclaiming all of the difficulty involved, or retracing, once again, the history of ideas. In my view, the problems facing social science are no different than those in the natural sciences. Social theorists just think that they are and, as a result, rarely get around to actually theorizing". (ibid.)

Between Modernism and Postmodernism: Towards Contextualizing General Theory and Method

While postmodernism and general scientific theorizing are perhaps not polar opposites, they do reflect dramatically different images of the character and goals of sociological theorizing, especially in relation to political ideology. Some investigators attempt to find some middle ground between these two opposed images. Generally, these investigators take some portion of the postmodern move as given, but they also seek to go beyond that critique to recover some more general notion regarding social theorizing (Seidman and Wagner, 1992).

These intermediate positions between modernism and postmodernism depend on acceptance of different aspects of postmodernism, and are therefore rather idiosyncratic in characters. For example, R.H. Brown (1992) argues for multiple general theories, (although he comes at the issue from a point of view very different from Wagner's). He maintains that social scientific discourse reveals a plurality of general theories, each internally consistent with a different root metaphor, a different intellectual telos, and a different ideological interest. Thus, positivist general theory uses organic and mechanistic metaphors which focus its ideological interest on the stability and maintenance of societal order. Such a theory cannot deal adequately with the reflexive character of individual lifeworlds (ibid.: 11-12).

To deal with this character, Brown proposes an alternative to the positivist general theory and method based on the metaphor of society as a discourse or language rather than as an organism or machine. He outlines an approach and then illustrates it by discussing general theorists, such as Mary Douglas (1978, 1982, 1983), Pierre Bourdieu (1974, 1984) and F. Rossi-Landi (1975, 1983). He does not advance the discursive approach to advocate a new universal paradigm, but to relativize the positivist approach and theory invites a broader pluralism of perspectives (Ford and Klumpp, 1985).

Nonetheless, the root metaphor of society as discourse may be more adequate logically, morally and politically. Logically, this metaphor can describe both social structure and personal consciousness, both *langue* and *parole*, in an integrated and consistent fashion. Morally, this approach begins and ends in the conception of personal agency and the human authorship of the world, thereby providing a theoretical resource for any possible ethics. Politically, it serves to reveal the ideological encoding of any discourse, thereby encouraging critically an openness in public debate. Brown says that

> "at the epistemological level, having begun by disenchanting the world, sociologists have come to disenchant their own absolutist mystique, forcing upon themselves a new methodological self-consciousness as a prerequisite to any future inquiry. A sequel to the unmasking of Sociology's positivistic presuppositions has been the emergence of alternative approaches for understanding social reality. Yet each of these competing paradigms appears to be rooted in conflicting ontological and epistemological assumptions.

> Each paradigm defines social reality differently. The paradigms not only have different techniques of research but different definitions of what it is they are researching, what constitutes sociological knowledge, and what are the logical procedures by which such knowledge can be gained. Hence, though the various approaches may be complementary in their results, each in some fashion giving us a piece of a puzzle that must be assembled, they appear contradictory in their underlying methods of logic. General theory thus becomes a hodge-podge of paradigms that are ontologically and epistemologically incommensurate". (1992: 224–25)

Central to the theoretical criticisms of orthodox general theory is its unanalysed assumptions about the social world it seeks to understand. Its entire edifice rests upon the analogy that society is like an organism, a machine, or more recently, a cybernetic system. Yet to unreflectively posit such an analogy is to bring many questions that society seeks to answer. It not only prevents finding out how society is possible but also posits a determinate world inhabited by creatures largely unaware of the forces that move them. Hence, the role of human agency in the constitution or transformation of society becomes elusive as a datum of analysis. The orthodox position also assumes a *priori* the interdependence of societal parts, that is, institutions, roles, and the like, each contributing to the dynamic equilibrium of the whole. Moreover, human cooperation—a basic element to be accounted for by sociology—is presumed to be the natural outcome of socialization within a common value system; yet the nature of values and socialization remain almost as much a mystery as the explanation of their effects on human *sociation*(a term used by Brown). Since socialized individuals are assumed to be actors unwittingly manipulated by invisible social forces, the positivist puts little stock in these actors' conceptions of meaning and conduct, preferring to rely on his or her own objective observations.

Brown adds that an inverted version in this orthodoxy is that of some Marxist theorists for whom cooperation is explained in terms of ideology. In this view, *sociation* is largely a product of force or fraud. But, here again, the exact nature of these key processes is little understood, and actors are seen more as automatons than as agents. By contrast, alternative approaches such as symbolic interaction, ethnomethodology or existential sociology, assume that persons are volitional actors in the social drama, or players in the social game. These approaches describe the lifeworlds of persons as negotiated, symbolically constructed realists. But they tend to provide sociology of consciousness without a sociology of structure. Moreover, it is unclear how the root metaphors of the organism or machine could be conjoined with consistency to those of drama or game. Efforts to integrate these different paradigms have remained a congeries of fragile patchworks (1992: 225-226).

These epistemological and theoretical difficulties are matched by a third problem—the relationship of theory and practice. From its very beginnings and with few exceptions, liberal sociology in America and Marxian sociology in Europe assumed that causational knowledge leads to curative action. But there remain immense gaps between the theoretical explanation of causes, the articulation of moral purposes, and the practical politics of improvement. Indeed, the achievement of morally sensitive, self-reflective, critical, phenomenological, or dialectical knowledge would appear to preclude the establishment of predictive and prescriptive theory. To be true to itself and the nature of its subject matter, general theory in the social sciences may have to remain partial and retrospective. Conversely, to yield predictive theory, sociology may have to dehumanize its subject matter and eliminate personal agency.

> "Thus, the relationship of orthodox social theory to personal dignity and civic action remains problematic. The positivist paradigm leaves both the investigator and the objects of investigation in a state of fatalistic determinism and proposes a sterile neutrality towards values. Insofar as they adhere to their ideal of knowledge without a point of view, however, positivist thinkers remain insensitive to the historically relative and inevitably partial character of their own theoretical practices. Thus policies derived from social scientific knowledge are conceived either as technical instruments to rationally facilitate a given system, or conversely, as 'ideological' and hence scientifically unsound. Despite such difficulties, commitment to the possibility of moral agency and political responsibility seem necessary if general theory is to be made a dehumanizing resource for social structural change. But how can this be achieved without violating the canons of established methods and theories?". (Brown, 1992: 226)

We can draw some implications from these conundrums. First, it seems that we can have either no general theory or several general theories, but we cannot with consistency have only one general theory. The various dichotomies and contradictions for practice emanate from the lingering Cartesianism that pervades most efforts at general theory. Cartesian bifurcations between mind and body, consciousness and world, or reason and experience, continue to inhabit social thought. Thus efforts at a single general theory tend either to patch together basically different approaches, or to diminish a plurality of approaches to a single dominant one. The first strategy yields self-contradiction; the second is a reductive imperialism .

The alternative to these sterile choices is a plurality of general theories, each internally consistent but based on a different root metaphor; each expressing a different intellectual telos and, implicitly, representing a different ideological interest. To illustrate this possibility, Brown has outlined some dimensions and examples of a general theory and method based on the metaphor of society as communicative action.

Society as Discourse: An Alternative Metaphor for Theory and Method

Discursive analysis of society reveals that social science is itself a discursive practice like all human experience, whereas science is a conversation that takes place over time, in which accounts of what is, what has occurred, and what is true of this past and present are negotiated through symbolic interaction. The metaphor of society as discourse also suggests that social structures can be understood as structures of language and these structures are invented through acts of speech. A number of theorists have taken up the challenge of analysing structural determinism from the viewpoint of a phenomenology of language, or conversely, of understanding the intentionality of speech as engendered through language-like social structures. By conceptualizing both *langue* and *parole* as emerging from discursive practices, such theorists have sought to overcome the reification of language, on the one hand, and subjectification of speech, on the other. Basil Bernstein, for example, argued that speech performances express and embody different worlds of meaning that are ordered hierarchically in society. Such symbol systems are realizations and regulators not only of speech performances but also of the structure of social relationships. One might further say that social relations are themselves symbolic systems, in that society itself is a system of communicative action (Bernstein, 1971; Brown, 1987, 1992; Harre, 1979).

This perspective has been enlarged by Mary Douglas (1972) who has sought to link structure to meaning in a model of society as language. Douglas has elaborated empirically the assumption that symbols can symbolize only within a structural framework. Meaning depends on distinction, and distinction is an essential dimension of structure. For example, the concept of a man as a semantic unit requires a grammatical distinction between meals and other kinds of eatings. This binary structure of meal/non-meal is created by distinctions within eatings that are meals, distinctions which are absent or structured differently in non-meals. In the English-speaking world, the core of a proper meal consists of meat and two vegetables, preceded by soup and followed by desert. Douglas also observed that the structural element 'meat' in relation to 'two vegetables' is homologous to the structure of a 'proper meal' as a whole with its main course and subsidiary soup and desert. This triadic structure makes it possible to distinguish meals from other eatings and so enables us to invest meals with semantic meanings. For example, a 'meal' may mean "this is for family only" or "eating thus with us, you are now a friend". As Douglas (1972) said, "Drinks are for strangers, acquaintances, workmen, and family. Meals are for family, close friends, honoured guests. The grand operator of the system is the line between intimacy and distance". Those we know at meals we also know at drinks, but not the reverse. The semantics of the meal (closeness) is made possible by its syntactics (triadic structure) as a meal (Brown, 1992: 228).

Perhaps the most successful attempt to integrate agency and structure in largely discursive terms is the work of Pierre Bourdieu (1977: 3). Bourdieu recognized the cognitive power of structuralist theories of objective economic and political relations that provide a framework for practice. Instead of protesting against scientific objectification in the name of lived experience and withdrawing into a naive humanism, however, Bourdieu urged us to put 'structuralism' "back on its feet" (ibid.: 3–4). Structuralism is off its feet because it fails to recognize the practical mastery of members, who are able to evoke the structure and deploy it to their own needs, needs that usually involve the imposition or evasion of domination (Brown, 1992: 229). Concerning kinship structures, for example, Bourdieu qualified the formulation of Levi-Strauss: "The genealogical relationship is never strong enough on its own to provide a complete determination of the relationship between the individuals which it united, and it has such predictive value only when it goes with the shared interests, produced by the common possession of a material and symbolic patrimony" (1977: 39–40).

The genealogical charts defined by anthropologists as having law-like regularities are in practice involved strategically either to establish greater inclusion by finding a common ancestor further back in time, or to mark greater exclusion by shortening the lineage to include only more recent descendents and kin. Similarly, legal codes are 'enacted' not only in parliaments, but also through their performance, that is, through strategic invocation or selective enforcement. As Garfinkel (1967) or Bourdieu (1977) might have said with Kafka, "The verdict does not come all at once. The proceedings gradually merge into verdict" (Kafka, 1956). Those with sufficient authority and wit can solemnize an incident into a precedent. What would have been a private occurrence, say, the affront of a woman named Helen, thus can become an official insult and a cause for war. Conversely, clever underlings may manipulate the formal structure for their own ends; for example, when employees "work to rule" they may subvert the intent of these regulations. In this sense, determinism and agency or social structure and individual consciousness, both emerge from the same discursive practices (Brown, 1992: 229).

Brown generates another example of this relation of semiotic structures and hermeneutic contents by comparing structuralist and phenomenological analyses of the exchange of gifts. He quotes Marcel Mauss, and later Levi-Strauss, who insisted on a complete break with natives' experience and their theories of that experience, and urged instead that the exchange, and not the actions or intentions of the individual engaged in it, constitutes the primary object of study. But, as Bourdieu noted, counter-gifts must be deferred and different if they are not to be taken as an insult. Too hasty a discharge of one's obligations is a sign of mistrust and ingratitude, for it retrospectively redefines the initial gift as intended to put one under obligation. Similarly, a counter-gift that is identical to the initial gift retrospectively redefines the relationship as one of swapping or lending. Contrary to structuralists, then, the constitution of gift exchanges requires strategy and style, timing and tact. Gift exchanges are never simply a blind grammar that operates independently of the will or consciousness of members. At the same time, and contrary to a naive hermeneutics, this subjective dimension is not identical to the self-perceptions of members nor to their own vocabularies of motive. Bourdieu (1977: 6) said, "If the system is to work, the agents must not be entirely unaware of the truth of their exchanges, which is made explicit in the anthropologist's model while at the same time they must refuse to know and above all to recognize it".

Brown (1992) has also cast the net of a linguistic approach to general theory over the big fish of economics. One way to this, he suggests, would be to expand "Saussure's theory of linguistic value to include value in general. Stated slightly differently, he creates a Marxian semiotics that subsumed the political economy of the commodities under a political economy of signs. To see how this might be done, he suggests first to distinguish theories of language as a system of signification from theories of language as a system of communication. The discursive approach presupposes a conception of language as a system of signification rather than as a system of communication. In the view of language as a system of communication, objects, ideas, relationships, selves, or institutions exist independently from the language that is used to describe them. In this theory, a message is formulated to convey (or disguise) the meaning of extra-linguistic objects, intentions, or conditions. The speaker encodes this extra-linguistic reality into words and sentences and transmits it to an audience in the form of a message, which the audience then decodes" (Thomson, 1989: 7, quoted in Brown, 1992: 231).

By contrast, in the view of language as a system of signification, Brown says, the critical category is the sign. The sign is made up of two aspects—the signifier (the sound image) and the signified (the concept). In this Saussurean view of language, Brown presents the following statements of Ahonen (1989: 36, quoted in Brown, 1992: 231).

> "Linguistic values do not involve any pre-existing ideas but emanate form the very system itself. The concepts (the signified) are purely differential and defined not by their positive content but negatively by their relations with other terms of system. This means that in the

case of the sign, the concept (the signified) openly symbolizes a value determined by its relations with other similar values."

Likewise, on the material side of signification (the signifier, the sound image) only the difference between sounds is crucial, and the means by which signs are produced are therefore unimportant.

This 'economy of signs' is not so different from a monetary economy. As Saussure himself noted, in linguistics "as in political economy we are confronted with the notion of value; both sciences are concerned with a system for equating things of different orders—labour and wages in one and signified and signifier in the other" (1982: 115; 1966: 79). And it is unimportant whether the signifier of value (the money image) be coins, paper, cowrie shells, computer bits.

By pushing this conception further, Brown says:

> "The sign constructs its own adequate signified. In this formulation, the signifier dominates the signified, and our attention is thereby directed to the conditions of discourse in order to understand the origin of meaning and sense. Meaning is not something already formed prior to its articulation, for which language serves only as a mechanism of transmission. Indeed, the 'play' of meaning and sense is a consequence of the play of signification itself, as exemplified by the system of signs that make up those very means of signification, to quote Thomson (1989: 8)". (1992: 231)

If we transfer this way of thinking to the case of money, we see that both neo-classical and Marxist economics assume the communication or representational theory of language, and thus treat money as a sign of something else. Both see money as a means of representing value, though they differ as to what the value is. For neo-classical theorists, 'value' is given by the utility obtained from the use of the commodity.

> "The amount of money consumers are prepared to pay for a commodity depends upon the utility they derive from it. Of course, that utility cannot be observed directly. It is represented by money as it remains hidden. In Marxist theories, money is a phenomenal form of value, where value is determined by the abstract labour power embodied in that community". (Thomson, 1989: 8, quoted in Brown, 1992: 232)

Here again, that value can never be seen directly. It is 'transformed' into money and prices. In both neo-classical and Marxian conceptions, then, it is the representation of value that we observe—the realm of money and prices—and not the deeper reality of utility or labour that determines it.

This representational theory distinguishes appearance (representation) from reality (the deeper meaning, structure etc.), and then decodes the reality as it is displayed through the appearance. The absent reality becomes present through its representation. It is both absent and present at the same time. If we strictly apply positivist canons to such thinking, it would appear to be a logical contradiction, even an example of mystical thought as in the absent presence of Christ's blood and flesh in the wine and the wafer. In Marxist literature, this is called the 'transformation problem'.

By contrast, if we take seriously the view of language as signification, we understand the signifier to 'construct' the signified. Analogously, money does not represent anything in terms of an extra-linguistic domain of utility or value. Instead, money 'constructs' value, but value on the same semiotic 'surface' as money itself. Thus 'value' and 'money' are synonymous. This view of money and value as 'appearance' or 'surface' would become more plausible if it were understood in the context of a general theory of economic action as a significatory system. Such a theory is hinted at in some of the writings of Saussure and Marx. Saussure (1982: 33; 1966: 16) held that "a science that studies the life of signs within society is conceivable", and he understood economics to be part of society. In a somewhat parallel notion, Marx compared the fetishism of language to the fetishism of money:

> "It is no less false to compare money with language. It is not the case that ideas are transmuted in language in such a way that their particular nature disappears and their social character exists alongside them in language, as prices exist alongside goods. Ideas do not exist apart from language". (1971: 17)

We could extend this point and say that the world does not form speech but that speech forms the world, or gives form to the world (Roche, 1973: 79–80; Mehan and Wood, 1975: 218–24). Class, economic exchange and value take their existence and form in their linguistic enactment. In *Capital*, Marx followed the logico-empiricism of Feurebach and so he conceived of the value of goods as an expression of the labour of thôse who produced them. But he also argued in the more Hegelian Gundrisse that, under capitalism language becomes reified. Language becomes the 'agent' of 'divorce' (Marx, 1971: 71). Like virtue, love, or conviction, which men had considered inalienable, language, too becomes "an object of exchange or traffic ... (what) till then had been communicated, but never sold; acquired, but never bought ... passed into commerce" (Rossi-Landi, 1975). For Marxism, the problem was whether the language in the social totality is determined or determining, whether it is part of the base or the superstructure. In admitting that language is neither of these, Rossi-Landi also recognized that any rigid theoretical separation between base and superstructure was inadequate and that the analysis of language was not possible within this framework (Bodner, 1987 quoted in Brown, 1992: 233). Thus Rossi-Landi tried to provide a new theory of the relations between structure and superstructure. His working hypothesis is that what mediates between the two is the totality of sign systems that define any particular social formation.

Rossi-Landi described the categories of social reproduction and language as a homology between material production and linguistic production:

> "One of the most important aspects of this theory is that everything that has value and therefore everything that has meaning is always a product of human work; value is something that man has introduced and continues to introduce into the world". (1975: 6)

The central feature of all social signs is that they have meaning that is produced by human work. Rossi-Landi assumed that there are two fundamental modes of social development: the production and circulation of goods (in the form of commodities); and the production and circulation of sentences (in the form of messages). These two modes are essentially homologous. To describe their coinciding properties, Rossi-Landi transcoded into semiotic terms such basic concepts of Marxist economics as work, material production, exchange and consumption. These economic phenomena are akin to linguistic activities. Goods and works are both artifacts. The material production of goods and the linguistic production of sounds, words, or sentences are forms of human work. "We sustain then, the Vichian and Marxian thesis that the notion of artifact is in principle applicable to language" (Rossi-Landi, 1975: 33).

Following Marx's political economic theory, Rossi-Landi distinguished production, exchange and consumption, and then applied these concepts to linguistic production as well:

> "The operation of total linguistic capital, i.e. of a language as constant linguistic capital together with its speakers as variable linguistic capital, is communication: (Communication is the) production, circulation and accumulation of messages within a linguistic community, in a communicative market". (1975: 155)

Rossi-Landi also attempted to discover private ownership and exploitation of signs as a logical extension of his homology: "The major misunderstanding as regards linguistic private property is that the supra-individual, public, social character of the language is considered sufficient to exclude the possibility of the language itself being subject to private ownership" (1975: 183). For example, in advanced capitalist societies, the game of economic semiosis is staked in favour of obligopolistic owners. The capitalists' discourse may overwhelm the consumers' ability to effectively respond. Even if they do protest, as consumers they reinforce the dominant capitalist discourse. In more primal societies, there also may be an elite ownership of customary or historical discourse. Thus, Hocart's informant in Fiji (quoted in Sahlins, 1985: 49) "was said to know little because he had been brought up among the common people and not the nobles"; likewise Freely-Harnick (1978: 402-17) in Madagascar found that "History is not evenly distributed because to have it is a sign of politico-religious power and authority".

Rossi-Landi's Marxist semiotics does not have a strong hermeneutic moment. There is much more structure of language than enactment of speech. Thus, communicative agents, Brown (1992: 235) says, are not seen to have much freedom; instead, their behaviour is pre-programmed by the deep grammar of the semiotic system. "Semiotics finds its proper place, its significance, and its foundation alongside the study of modes of production and of ideologies, within the sphere of the social programming of all behaviour" (Rossi-Landi, 1975: 203).

Seen linguistically, economics becomes a subject of semiotics. As objects have become commodities and relationship have become ones of commodity exchange, the use value of things or people are subordinated to their exchange value. This exchange value is stated in terms of money, the purest of signs since it now stands for virtually anything (Marx, 1946; Simmel, 1978; Lukacs, 1971; Kelemen, 1982; Brown, 1992). As Baudrillard said, "The object is nothing ... but the different types of relation and significations that converge, contradict themselves, and twist around it" (1981: 63). This semiotic critique of the political economy of the sign parallels the earlier Marxist's critique of the political economy of the commodity. Indeed, in a Marxian semiotics, they become the same critique, since commodities are now seen as signs par excellence. The commodity combines use and exchange value whereas "the sign ... combines the signifier and the signified. A Marxian semiotics merges these two structures into a single structure that may be called the 'signified commodity' (Baudrillard, 1975, 1981; Denzin, 1987; Brown, 1992).

In such a view, Brown says, economic concepts such as 'poverty' or 'wealth' are themselves the outcome of human communicative actions that alter the horizons of experience and knowledge (1992: 235). "Goods acquire apparently necessary significances, much language seems to lose its arbitrariness, because of a social context in which those goods are read as defining one's social availability" (Herzfeld, 1985: 170, quoted in Brown, 1992). Once the semiotic properties of economic exchanges are recognized, they cease to be an isolated facet of human experience. Instead, "the meanings of goods are viewed as construed within a fluid social environment that is itself negotiated. Production and consumption are active processes in which all the social categories are being continually redefined" (Douglas and Isherwood, 1978: 68, quoted in Brown, 1992). This is true of local firms and markets as well as of national and international economic processes, since ultimately producers and consumers alike remain actors in creation of significance (Brown, 1992: 236).

Social Theory, Method and Civic Dialogue

The aforesaid reflections are intended to suggest the possibility of an alternative general theory, one based on the metaphor of society as discourse or language rather than as organism or machine. According to Brown, as a relatively new paradigm or rather a Renaissance paradigm only recently revived, the discursive approach to general theory has not been elaborated nearly as much as the normal science of positivism. But, Brown's point is not that a linguistic orientation will or should become the new, single, unifying one. On the contrary, his arguments are those of a systematic pluralist. Hence, he advances the discursive metaphor not to overthrow positivism, but only to limit its sometimes absolutist and imperious claims.

Nonetheless, Brown believes that the metaphor of society as discourse has certain logical and moral-political advantages over organistic and mechanistic ways of thinking. First, general social theory on the linguistic model can encompass micro-social phenomena such as meals, mezo-level phenomena such as gift exchanges, and macro-social phenomena such as economic structures. In the discursive approach, language is neither a natural fact of daily life nor a mere epiphenomenon of forces and relations of production. Instead it expresses a social covenant. As Saussure put it, this covenant is "the social side of language, outside the individual who can never create or modify it by himself; it exists only by virtue of a sort of contract by the members of the community. The community is necessary ... by himself the individual can not fix a single value. Each time I say a word I renew its substance" (Saussure, 1982: 14, 109, 113, quoted in Brown, 1992: 236–37).

The dichotomy of base and superstructure or structure and agency is mediated by discourse. The structure, envisioned as language, is both a constraint and resource for enactments, envisaged as speech. The semiotic moment of the linguistic metaphor deals well with structure, while its hermeneutic moment treats well of meaning and action. Both these dimensions—syntactic and grammatics, on the one hand, and semantics and pragmatics, on the other—are contained and logically consistent within the metaphor of society as discourse. In effect, this metaphor combines in linguistic terms Durkheim's conception of constraining structures with Marx's idea that the system of exchanges is the source of values (Lemert, 1990). But it also incorporates Mead's and Garfinkel's conceptions of social reality as constructed through symbolic interaction.

Second, on a moral-political level, the discursive approach is reflexive. It sees the social sciences as providing *logoi* by which members generate their own social texts. Thus, general theory on the metaphor of discourse explicitly recognizes its moral and political functions. That is, it acknowledges that its discourse about society reflects and engenders discourse within society. It thus sees social science as value-soaked civic talk about our common life (Brown, 1992: 237).

The discursive approach to social theory also abandons the distorting notion of disciplines as well as positivist and hermeneutic dichotomies within these disciplines. Instead, it enables us to slice-up modes of argumentation differently and understand 'theory construction' in terms of various linguistic and textual strategies. Such an approach highlights the presuppositions and meta-logics of all the social sciences and thus brings values back to the fore. The devices of discovery and judgement or invention and legitimation, are of course rhetorical terms; under the aegis of the language metaphor of society they now can be used to develop general social theories as discourses for reasoned civic judgment.

The following comments of Brown, here, are worth mentioning:

> "In abandoning the anti-rhetorical rhetoric of positivism, the discursive approach recovers the ancient function of social thought as a moral and political practice. In this critical rhetorical view in constructing general theory we attend not only to logical propositions and empirical contents, but also to linguistic methods and existential functions. From this perspective, the linguistic dimension of social theory is an integral part of its truth or falsity to social life. This is for two reasons, first truth and validity are themselves rhetorically constructed. Second, as rhetorical interventions, social scientific theories convey an existential as well as a propositional truth. Scientific truth about society is a truth of facts or meanings, an appeal to the telos of elegance and precision, predictability or comprehension. But seen discursively or rhetorically, such truth is also an implicit call to action. Its existential telos is self-understanding, critique and emancipation. Positivists have sought to silence this existential dimension by treating general theory as an external object that makes no personal moral claim upon us. But social theories do convey an existential truth. And, unlike propositional truth, existential truth is not merely to be cross-examined. Instead, when it speaks, we ourselves become its 'object' and we must examine ourselves, for it is we who are addressed. (1992: 237)

Thus, different approaches to general theory, according to Brown, are not merely competing or complementary language games. Instead, each of them implies a different moral affirmation. For a purely language analytic philosophy, all interpretations are equally valid within the limits of the theory that provides their given rules of reading. But each subset of rules also has its own existential function (Ricoeur, 1980: 107, quoted in Brown, 1992: 238). The telos of psychoanalysis, for example, is an archaeology of the subject, the telos of positivist social science is technical direction of society and the telos of a discursive analysis of society is the human authorship of the world.

Stanley Aronowitz's (1992) proposal for general theory and method also here deserves special mention. He argues that the Frankfurt School developed a powerful critical social theory. Its focus shifted from a critique of political economy to a critique of technical reason, mass culture and consumerism. Critical theory provided an alternative to positivism which was viewed as contributing to social domination. He argues that the critical theory is today in need of reconstruction. Its social analysis has rendered social change virtually impossible. Its standpoint has become one dimensionally negative and rhetorical. He calls for a reconstruction of critical theory that evolves general categories that both articulate social conflicts and assume a critical stance towards them.

In the first place, the leading exponents of critical social theory viz., Adorno, Horkheimer and Marcuse, were urgently concerned with history, not only that of society but also, perhaps predominantly, the break between natural and human history as regulative of relations within the social order. For the Frankfurt School, the domination of nature was a defining event in human history. With Weber, Horkheimer and Adorno understand the history of capitalism as a disruption of the relatively stable social order marked by a low level of technological development and a moral order in which nature was accorded substantial respect. An agrarian based ethic is displaced by a new ethic in which nature becomes an antagonistic 'other' to society and ethics are defined by the degree to which mankind devotes itself to exploiting its natural environment to meet historically defined human wants or needs (Horkheimer and Adorno, 1972; Marcuse, 1978).

However, while Weber privileges self-denial and work as the content of this spiritual upheaval, critical social theory focuses on the changed relationship between humans and nature made possible by science and technology. On the one hand, biological science places 'man' at the apex of natural history; on the other, science becomes a metaphor for dominion of the new capitalist social order over the natural order, the laws of which, having been discovered by experiment, become the foundation of human intervention (Horkheimer and Adorno, 1972: 3–42). Scientific ideology postulates that we are no longer bound to our biological givens. As Parsons argues, fully consonantly with this tradition, society is governed by norms, by the cultural system. The organism constitutes only a boundary condition for other systems, but does not control human destiny (Parsons, 1951, 1955: 627–33, quoted in Aronowitz, 1992: 290). In fact, after Weber, whose later investigations constitute a tacit critique of his earlier historical preoccupations, social theory loses its historical dimension as time is taken itself as merely a framework for the structural and function relations between system and subsystem of the social and cultural order (Parsons, 1951: 11). General social theory true to Durkheim's rule to treat the social as fact sui generis, generates hierarchically arranged categories of social being (Durkheim, 1966, cited in Aronowitz, 1992: 290). The lower forms are, ineluctibly, functionally linked to the higher forms and thereby retain only a relative autonomy from the system of which they are a contingent part; they owe their existence to the 'control' by the higher system. Thus, while the biological organism is a condition for the personality, social and cultural system in Parsons' theory, the cultural systems embodies the norms by which society retains equilibrium (Aronowitz, 1992: 290).

Parsons models his sociology on classical mechanics with its categories of inertia and equilibrium, and borrows from biology a systems approach according to which change results from external influences that disrupt the natural intertia of society. What has become the fundamental departure of relativity and quantum physics from the classical Newtonian framework is assiduously ignored in Parsons' scheme—the question of the space/time continuum and more profoundly, the whole scaffolding of causality in the Newtonian system (ibid.: 291):

> "The relations present what, for us, is a simpler problem. All the empirical sciences take it for inexorable fact that certain events have occurred at given time sequence. Given certain antecedent time determinations other time determinations can be deduced by

> theoretical reasoning; this is what we mean by prediction in its temporal aspect. But time is never a manipulable variable; time is a frame of reference within which one can state and interpret the assumptions about and consequences of the operations of manipulable variables ... time is one fundamental aspect of the giveness of the empirical world which provides the empirical base from which any deduction or prediction can be carried out". (Parsons, 1955: 638)

Of course, Parsons allows for exigencies between system and sub-system, but these are relegated to "deflection" in an otherwise invariate structure within which internal relations are fixed by determinations of hierarchy (ibid.: 632, quoted in Aronowitz, 1992: 291).

In the current revival of the philosophy and social theory of the Frankfurt School, two distinct modes of appraisal can be discerned. (Aronowitz: 291):

(i) By far the most prevalent is critical theory as a somewhat iconoclastic social theory that accounts for historical changes—the problem of technological domination in late capitalist societies; considerations in the cultural and political history of fascism and especially the rise of the authoritarian state; the problem of mass culture and consumer society as subversions of democracy; and the relevance of psychoanalytic theory to understanding social life. Some of these themes were taken up by others, although in a different way. For example, Parsons himself openly invokes Freud's categories of cathexis and the unconscious to explain disruptions in system maintenance. Like Horkheimer, but with a different political perspective, Arendt (1956) derives the fascist moral and political order from some aspects of the Enlightenment, refusing the liberal view of the Holocaust as an astonishing mutation from the norms of Western culture. And, Gasset (1932) sees the decline of the West as a consequence of the rise of mass culture, but from a deeply conservative standpoint, which nevertheless postulates an integrated past in which high culture flourished—a position not far from that of the Frankfurt School. Despite many political differences among these writers, they share a common bond of humanism and, Parsons excepted, a penchant for negative philosophical assumptions. That is, their concern is to account for disruption as more than contingent, but rather as the mode of being of contemporary life. In this mode such categories as equilibrium and inertia are exceptional, rather than regulative of social relations, at least in the 20th century.

(ii) The second line of discussion concerns the problem of what might commonly be called 'method'. Of course, critical social theory has no method if by the term we mean a theory of object relations from which one may derive a series of algorithms to guide research and experiment about the empirical world. Hence, its characteristic discourse is reflexive and hermeneutic rather than scientific in the 18th century meaning of the term. For above all, critical theory is a discourse about the relation of subject and object exemplified in the texts of philosophy, literature, and social and cultural theory and criticism (Aronowitz, 1992: 292). In this sense, it approximates, however, unwittingly, collective biography of intellectuals situated in a concrete historical moment—the period between the two world wars when nearly all the old assumptions about the equilibrium conditions appeared to have collapsed or were in the process of disintegration. Following Lukacs' revision of Marx, the Frankfurt School insisted upon the relevance of subjectively meaningful action to the constitution of social relations. Lukacs, influenced by Simmel's theory of reification, situated the reversal of capitalism's collapse in the power of the commodity from over human consciousness and restricted his inquiry to the level of philosophic and literary discourse. The Frankfurt School, however, having rejected metaphysical speculation as a vestige of bourgeoise ideology, turned to performing relentless criticism of contemporary fashions in German philosophy, and in addition to the practice of sociology (Aronowitz, 1992: 293). In the 1930s, its studies of the institutional frameworks of advanced capitalist social life, particularly the family and mass culture; the historical legacy of science and technology, and finally its studies of that great absence in historical materialism, the state, were in their totality efforts to break from the economistic bias of Marxist social theory and methodology.

In effect, the first major contribution of critical social theory was to explain the failure of the western working class in the inter-war period to reverse the rise of totalitarian and authoritarian states in advanced capitalist societies. They sought answer in the psychological deformations of mass consciousness. Thus, the central category of explanation for the rise of fascism was not, at the root, the laws of economic life; it was the transformation of mass psychology on the one hand and on the other hand, the transformation of science and technology from forms of subordinate knowledge—tools of human purposes to a new normative order. Of course, Aronowitz refers here to 'really existing' Marxism of the socialist and communist (internationals), which heavily emphasized the study of political economy as the preeminent paradigm for understanding politics, culture and ideology.

Besides Marx and Freud, each of whom influenced the scaffolding of critical theory providing the key orientations, we must add that of German phenomenology, particularly Heidegger and Spengler, whose different though closely linked critiques of the scientific Enlightenment and its philosophical underpinnings stunned the post-war intellectual communities, including scientists themselves (Marcuse, 1973, 1987; Forman, 1971; Friedman, 1981). Aronowitz, like Foucault (1972), suggests also for the inclusion of the name of Hegel, who prowls through the 20th century reminding us of the price we have paid for our anti-foundationalism especially our refusal of the totality. By this Foucault means the possibility of a historical process of emerging self-consciousness whose outcome is the identical subject/object. With Hegel, the critical theory insists that the subject/object dialectic constitutes the structuration of society, the starting point of which is the part played by labour in the formation of humans and whose key category is that of domination. In contrast to the Marxist concept of labour exploitation as the foundation of social structure, critical theory borrows from both the early Marx and from Weber the more general term 'domination' because it encompasses a wider sphere of social relations, it thereby refuses to locate the determination of social divisions in economic life (Marcuse, 1964). Consequently, the subject is not identical with itself. It is fractured not only by class relations (the unequal division of the product of labour) but also by civilization's greatest achievements, science and technology. In effect, Horkheimer and Adorno argue, we have subordinated ends to means: the powers of our tools of dominion over nature have penetrated our social unconscious, so that the self in both individual and collective terms has become little more than an instrument of its own domination by technology and technology's most egregious form, administration (Horkheimer and Adorno, 1972; Horkheimer, 1947). In modern industrial societies executive authorities rule persons in the model of the administration of things since the reflexive self is inimical to the achievement of a conformist social order which requires an other-directed character structure

(Horkheimer, 1947). And, because the rewards of the awesome industrial machine mankind has constructed on its knowledge achievements are so seductive, we can no longer critically reflect on domination as a generalized social form because we have lost the capacity to distance ourselves from the world we have constructed on the basis of science. The subject is object dominated even as it, in turn, dominates its natural environment (Aronowitz, 1992: 294).

These constructed objects now constitute our second nature. Reason, which became the religion of the bourgeoise Enlightenment, had through its permutations within science become thoroughly instrumentalized and could no longer provide the way to any truth beyond the propositions of science and their technological application in the work of dominating nature and humans. In effect, ethical and philosophical inquiry, now subordinated to science, had lost their critical character (critical in the sense of transcending the conditions of given, empirical world). Having completely subordinated to the external environment to fulfil human needs as configured by capitalist social relations, humans were themselves in danger of extinction.

Taking nature as pure, instrumentally mediated object was itself the product of our blind evolutionary ideology. According to this, all lower organic and inorganic forms are subordinate to our will and inorganic nature is taken as inert matter, a passive receptacle of human intervention. Precisely, what Parsons posits, the control by the cultural system over all human relations, produces not equilibrium but crisis. Although the crisis has not fulfilled the letter of Marx's fateful prediction of proletarian revolution, but has been displayed into what C. Wright Mills (1951) calls 'private troubles', ecological disasters and permanent wars, for the Frankfurt School there is no question of characterizing our social world by terms such as intertia (Aronowitz, 1992: 295).

Thus, the historical sociology of the Frankfurt School conducted its research on the basis of a philosophical anthropology that became the surrogate for method. Accordingly, the starting point of critical theory was to define the problematic of human *sociation* in terms of the need to secure human existence against a vicious and recalcitrant nature (Horkheimer and Adorno, 1972; Marcuse, 1978). This ontological need is mediated by historical needs which are ever changing according to the development of our collective powers over nature, but remained the irreversible element, both the boundary condition of the social order and the content of its social unconscious. Where Parsons holds time constant to enable sociology to predict human action, critical theory problematizes the goals of prediction and control, since these are the stuff of domination. While Parsons posits adaptation of actors and the integration of the action situation into the large system of control as a natural event subject only to exigencies; critical theory views the project of system maintenance as a system of domination, as inimical to freedom. Freedom consists in the capacity of actors to make themselves subjects, i.e., being capable of reflexivity and consequently self-management. Thus, the critical theory, Aronowitz says, must negate science as conventionally understood as unimpeachable knowledge. Its negative philosophy is premised on the requirement that we need to be jolted from the ideology of inertia and equilibrium. The categories of general social theory cannot be taken at face value, but must be subjected in the interest of emancipation from positive science to critical reflection (Aronowitz, 1992: 296).

From the perspective of the contemporary worship of natural techno-sciences as the model for knowledge, critical theory appears, on the one hand, a legatee to the Romantic movement in German philosophy for which science had become one of the obstacles to freedom, and, on the other, a throwback to metaphysics, which science supposedly consigns to the past (Schelling, 1988; Aronowitz, 1992). Critical theory refuses the radical distinction between science and ideology but claims, to the contrary, that the goals of science-prediction and control—are forms of interest (Habermas, 1976; Aronowitz, 1988). To this, Aronowitz adds that—the claims of science to value neutrality, by means of the scientific method, presuppose the efficacy of the laboratory situation, that is, abstraction of the object or processes from the natural context (1992: 296).

To the reductionism characteristic of idealist dialectics, in which the object is reduced to form which permits contradiction, Adorno counterposes the notion that "dialectics is the consistent sense of nonidentity" (1973: 5). This view contrasts with that of Hegel and Marx, for whom contradiction and totality are inextricably linked by the requirement that difference be resolved by a synthesis in which the elements of opposition are simultaneously preserved and transformed on a higher level. The negative dialectic asserts only the ineluctability of difference, and in Gaston Bachelard's (1984) somewhat differently rooted version argues that new knowledge can be generated only by an epistemological break between past and future. In Bachelard's *The Philosophy of No* (1968) critical exploration of the foundations of knowledge replaces method. Bachelard distinguishes his conception of the dialectic from an effort to follow in Hegel's footsteps. "What Bachelard calls dialectic is the inductive movement which recognizes knowledge and enlarges its base, where the negation of concepts and of axioms is only an aspect of their generalization" (Canguillhem, 1983: 196). By dialectic Bachelard means difference— not difference as pure negation but as a determinate complementarity. His major concern is to oppose monologism as an impediment to the further development and enrichment of science. Nor does the notion of a synthetic dialectic appear in Bachelard, for synthesis implies reconciliation of opposites on a higher level of identical being. Bachelard's theory of the development of scientific knowledge as a series of epistemological 'breaks' prefigures by a quarter-century the perspectives of Thomas Kuhn (if not Paul Feyerabend), which have become virtually canonical for the philosophy of science since the 1960s. Bachelard's work best known works, *The New Scientific Spirit* and *The Philosophy of No* were really readings of the philosophical implications of developments in modern physics which may be taken as an unintended effort to bring the 'subject' back into considerations of scientific knowledge. "As a consequence of the crisis of representation, Aronowitz says, the reflection theory of knowledge and the correspondence theory of truth have been overthrown; because acts of measurement are part of the field of inquiry, all knowledge is relative to its frame of reference and its truth value is at best probabilistic. These changes have only begun to call into question social scientific knowledge which appears firmly ensconced in 18th century assumptions" (1992: 297).

Thus, in place of determinate categories of which positive science is so fond, negative theory in its quest for the sources of transformation is caught between a critique of categories as fulfilling an ontological need, and its own will to explanation, a programme which requires positive, unhistorically mediated categories (Aronowitz, 1992; Adorno, 1973). Bachelard (1968) addresses this difficulty by relying on categories of physical sciences to trace the transformations in their meaning. By rigorously adhering to the actual movement of science, he is able to show the remarkable degree to which this so-called empirical category is suffused with philosophical, metatheoretical presuppositions. From this style of theorizing, Bachelard powerfully influenced social theory and method. A similar strategy is adopted by critical theory with the important difference that the death of the subject is not made axiomatic at the theoretical level but is traced as the outcome of distinctive historical developments. At the most philosophical level, Adorno's work is an extensive meta-critique of the Hegelian categories, showing that, intentions notwithstanding, they remain profoundly anti-dialectical by affirming the positive as the outcome of negation and synthesis. But its concrete critical objects are the categories of sociology. As a consequence of its disdain for system building, critical sociology becomes a critique of sociology's own categories—society, group, social agents, culture, science, and technology, politics, and the state, considered as forms of social knowledge and social practices.

In its short volume *Aspects of Sociology* (1972), the Frankfurt School announced its critical intention from the outset:

> "Sociology is a child of positivism, which although commendably founded to free knowledge from religious beliefs and metaphysical speculation, surrenders, in its quest for scientific accuracy, the sense of the totality and condemns itself to partial knowledge. Sociology is charged with having sought not the specifically social or human relations but the 'natural laws' governing human action in order to modify or control them. The facet claim in this critique of sociology is that it is concerned not merely with discerning the 'facts', however, they are construed, but with modifying and otherwise controlling human action. In effect, social science can study humans with the methods of natural science because it takes social relations as objective relations and at a distance. That is, the process of investigation is abstracted from the object of knowledge. Further, by slicing up society into a series of domains, the investigator is able to better grasp the data and make partial generalizations. But these domains are conventionally defined and do not possess the status of 'natural fact'. After the critique of the epistemology of sociology, it is to the sources of conventional categorical construction that critical theory devotes its attention, except where in the case of prejudice, a

solution serves the interest of general emancipation. The critique of categories becomes, for critical theory, an alternative to the artificial positivities of mainstream sociology". (1972, quoted in Aronowitz, 1992: 298–99)

Yet, the Frankfurt School recognizes the legitimacy of the specific domain of sociology—to discern "the laws of sociation; that is, of social formation and integration" (Aronowitz, 1992). If this is the case, then the sociological investigation of the individual, given an understanding of society as a mere aggregation of individuals, is faced with severe epistemological and historical difficulties. Here, Aronowitz poses the following questions: Should sociology accept the liberal evocation of the autonomous thinking individual as the foundation for social investigation? If as critical theory claims, the basis of the satisfactory relation of individual to society is a healthy, humane social order, it follows that the individual fate is linked to that of society and the liberal assumption of individual autonomy (whether as an ontological or a methodological concept) is put into question. Further, is the individual an irreducible unit or is the individual nothing other than an ensemble of social relations, as Marx claims? The presumption of methodological individualism which forms the basis of much contemporary sociological research becomes untenable if either of these preposition is accepted. *Aspects of Sociology* (1972) argues that the individual is itself a historically constituted category and presupposes the emergence of civil society in the late medieval period when market relations with their concomitant characteristics—competition between independent procedures and other owners of property—dominated economic, social and ideological relations and, as Habermas argues, the separation of the public from the private spheres constructs new conditions for human interaction. By denaturalizing the individual and other categories of sociology, critical theory tries to show that, abstracted from its frame of reference, sociological knowledge becomes ideological in the sense of interested inquiry. In its characteristic American form (against which Parsons was the most outstanding exception), sociology puts the idea of society itself as a social fact in question and with it structuring concepts such as system and classes as historical actors (Aronowitz, 1992: 299).

Thus, the critical theory joins sociology's critics such as Robert Lynde, C. Wright Mills and Alvin Gouldner in asking fundamental question: Knowledge for what? (Mills, 1964; Merton, 1951). Their reading of pragmatism as well as the history of the physical and biological sciences warned both Mills and Merton against large generalizations, even general theory. Merton's famous argument that science develops by empirically verifiable hypothesis, which inevitably can only be of the middle range, became the basis for Mills' celebrated but misunderstood works *Sociological Imagination* (1959). In this essay, Mills takes both Parsons and his antimonies—the empiricists of dominant American sociology—to task for failing to observe both the critical and the middle range routes to knowledge. However, science is not irrevocably debunked and philosophy installed as the arbiter of all knowledge-claims, in which the criterion of the historical frame of reference mediates truth claims. Instead, this historical frame of reference constitutes a series of categories which, taken together, may be construed as a general social theory. It is to this social theory; Aronowitz is concerned with.

Contemporary social theory is deeply enmeshed in a debate about the relation between social structure and social agency. All of the canonical figures of social theory—Marx, Weber, Durkheim, Simmel and their later 20th century successors—have puzzled over the question because of its saliency to the problem of historical determination. None of the major theorists can avoid dealing with structure and agency but their emphasis usually focuses on one or another side. For example, Marx is alternately labelled an economic or historical determinist or a voluntarist. But it is clear that as a thinker influenced by 19th century science as well as by its economics and philosophy, he was obliged to name historical subjects—classes—but placed strong emphasis on naturalized social forces which propelled classes, groups and individuals to engage in action of historical consequence. Conversely, Weber's strong sense of the influence of economic structure on the course of ancient history was tempered by his investigation of the transition from feudalism to capitalism where the role of subjectively meaningful ideas (in the Kantian, not the Hegelian sense) in producing social change is accorded primacy. Similarly, at the pinnacle of Parsons' structured social totality stand values which powerfully influence action; the cultural system, really the internalized values of any society, controls relatively variable sub-systems. Indeterminancy is produced by external and internal variability, but Parsons is constrained to insist upon the objectivity of belief systems and their controlling power.

Critical theory, which itself rejects the artificial totalizations of classical Marxism, criticizes sociology's rejection of the totality but refuses, equally, a conception in which society is conceived as sum of its parts, whether constituted by differentiated systems, by Durkheimian categories of solidarity and other equilibria, or by a single hypostasized structure such as Simmel's money economy. Even more, does critical theory attack the positivistic penchant, following writers such as Robert Merton, to divide the field of investigation into a series of social problems. The only unity of these problems is provided by methodological inscriptions the dominant values of which are observation and quantification.

The empirical referent of critical sociology is the history of societies. Its crucial 'method' is immanent critique, if that phrase is connoted a close analysis of texts—historical, literacy, philosophical—even, as in the atypical case of Adorno's magisterial study *The Authoritarian Personality* survey forms. For each of the examined texts, the object of reading is to disassemble, and otherwise disrupt apparently seamless narratives to show the hidden text, particularly its linkages with knowledge, power and action. This investigation takes the form of ideology—critique, showing that knowledges that purport to be neutral observation—value-free theory, empirically verified fact—are a veiled discourse of domination. Beneath this mode of inquiry is the assumption that narratives, scientific texts, information typically conceal their content, which can only be revealed by interrogation as to underlying motives and values—regardless of whether they are consciously held. This procedure presupposes a sociological community which has freed itself of scientism—the doctrine according to which scientific facts can be established by rigorous methods of empirical research whose fundamental feature is the apodictic status of knowledge gained through the senses supplemented by rational calculation (Aronowitz, 1992: 301).

Horkheimer and Adorno's *Dialectic of the Enlightenment* (1972) and Marcuse's *One Dimensional Man* (1964) exemplify best how critical sociology generates new, we may say positive, categories—not in the course of constructing analytic categories such as system and structure, but as a concomitant of historically and hermeneutically based inquiry. *Dialectic of the Enlightenment* problematizes the rupture between myth and science and thereby begins an investigation of the Enlightenment by subverting one of its underlying claims—to have freed knowledge and therefore humanity of the thrall of superstition. This is accomplished by choosing, as a starting point, the viewpoint of its most articulate tribune, Francis Bacon. In Bacon's words,

> "the acquisition of knowledge is not undertaken for the purposes of 'satisfaction', but to achieve the better endowment and help of man's life. The old mysteries are to be laid aside, the old rituals abandoned, and our relation to nature is conceived as purely instrumental. In the process by which knowledge is subordinated to the specific ends, all social relations are instrumentalized, is made subordinate to the imperatives of production. In turn, the development of science and technology becomes the key to such commercial activities as navigation, mining and trading. While the aim of Enlightenment thought and practice is to facilitate the return of the subject to the social process in which 'men' make their own history against a feudal order which subordinated individuals to the dictates of ecclesiastical law (identical with civil law in many instances), its long term effects have been to raise technology to the level of social principle. In the service of endowing human life, nature has been subdued, but, so has mankind itself. Scientific evidence becomes the arbiter of human affairs". (quoted in Aronowitz, 1992: 304)

Finally, Stanley Aronowitz argues:

> "no critical theory, including that of the Frankfurt School, can dispense with either categories or meta categories from which to make historical and empirical judgements. Surely, ideas such as the totally administered society, domination of nature, and one-dimensionality are 'synthetic' categories upon which critical social theory depends. In turn, these are really constellations constructed from such abstractions as domination, bureaucracy, reason, ideology, nature and in a different register, class, labour, the state and so on. Similarly, when, Adorno writes on the 'Culture Industry' or, the Enlightenment, he is invoking capitalism, culture, science, and technology as basic categories from which the concatenation is made. In short, just as doing science entails making judgements in the sense that its axiomatic structures may be interrogated, so those who would interrogate social life cannot avoid 'science', if by this

> constellation we mean positing a hierarchy of existents without which empirical judgement is arbitrary". (1992: 314)

When we seek to explain social relations, we must go beyond negative dialectics. From critical theory's own perspective, what lies beyond must necessarily be historically and practically situated. Aronowitz believes that just as Foucault is right to point out that intellectuals no longer work in categories of the 'universal' truths but theorize and do practical research in situated locations either professional or within their conditions of life so the categories of social knowledge must also be specific. We can no longer characterize entire societies by division into sectors, orders, or invariant relations of determination such as economic infrastructure or great ideas. One possible explanation, Aronowitz gives, for this perspective is the historically conditioned disaggregation of social totalities such as 'organized' capitalism, socialism, the third world, and other constellations from which these universals were crafted. On the other hand, post-structuralist historiography has maintained that the past was never constituted as more than unstable totalities of incommensurable discourses, the most powerful of which are undermined by the economic infrastructure. Rather, they may be considered the resultant of a conjuncture particularly of power/knowledge constellation.

Nevertheless, the intention to be specific, to avoid large abstractions, has not spared even the most meticulous of local histories from being generalized. Foucault's work has been shamelessly appropriated by his universalizing disciples, who, nudged by academic environments, are prone to overtheorization. Foucault's fecund use of categories such as discourse, discursive formation, power/knowledge, produced the rudiments of an alternative social-theoretical paradigm from which history has been rewritten. As Derrida once readily acknowledged, we are not able to avoid logocentric Western culture among whose leading themes is the high value placed upon intellectual knowledge and its core of abstract universals. It was, after all, in consideration of the dangers entailed by such a use of science that schools of social inquiry, including Marxism as well as positivist social science, bid us return to concrete. Although we need not return to what C. Wright Mills once called 'abstracted empiricism' to grasp the concrete, nor can we avoid general theory (Aronowitz, 1992: 315).

Conclusively, Aronowitz (1992) argues that critical theory is today in need of reconstruction. Its social analysis has rendered social change virtually impossible. Its standpoint has become one dimensionally negative and rhetorical. Aronowitz calls for a reconstruction of critical theory that evolves general categories which both articulate social conflicts and assume a critical stance towards them.

Other intermediate positions are somewhat more electic in their choice of material to draw upon in building a more flexible notion of general theory. Craig Calhoun sees general theory as traditionally reflecting both a concern for breadth of application (universality) and for the formulation of law like statements. In *Culture, History and the Problem of Specificity in Social Theory* (1992: 244–79), he suggests that there is an alternative to both traditional concerns. He argues for a general theory that is culturally sensitive (both to the problem of difference in values and to the value of differences) and historically specific. In his view, the production of theories is a historical phenomenon that yields categories adequately only in a specific epochs and theories that are alternatives in a discursive field. Nevertheless, such work can be theoretically grounded more generally through continuous effort at cross-cultural and historical description.

This processual approach generates for Calhoun a 'polyphonic discourse,' not a single right answer to sociological questions. Local, mid-range and general claims must always remain separate; there can be no strong deduction, reduction or aggregation. Postmodernism, in Calhoun's understanding, is actually an internal product of modernity. Its challenge to this more general approach is flawed in two ways. First, it is unable to provide grounds for the normative judgements made in the postmodern critique. Second, its elevation of difference to absolute importance does violence to the notion of inter-subjectivity. Consequently, while the postmodern critique has had much to contribute, it is ultimately only one contributor to sociological understanding.

At this juncture, it is imperative to refer to Jeffrey Alexander who challenged the dichotomization of scientific theory and relativism as false and dangerous.

> "Either knowledge of the world is unrelated to the social position and intellectual interests of the knower, in which case, general theory and universal knowledge are viable, or knowledge is affected

> by its relation to the knower, in which case relativistic and particularistic knowledge can be the only result. This is a true dilemma because it presents a choice between two equally unpalatable alternatives. I argue that neither pole of the dilemma should be accepted. The alternative to positivist theory is not resigned positivism; the alternative to relativism is not positivist theory. Theoretical knowledge can never be anything other than the socially rooted efforts of historical agents. But this social character does not negate the possibility for developing either generalized categories or increasingly disciplined, impersonal, and critical modes of evaluation". (1992: 323)

To Alexander, to acknowledge relativism is not necessarily to imply that actors impose on knowledge personal and idiosyncratic imprints. Actors can be bound—by their societies and themselves—to standards that are rooted within, and after a manner are reflections of, broader and more inclusive social institutions and groups. They may also be bound by traditions that have a distinctively rational, impersonal bent. One must differentiate, then, within the category, 'relativist'. Evaluative criteria, while contextually relative, can be both more universalistic and less so. The search for truth can be fused with the search for other kinds of knowledge—with the search for beauty and moral purity—or it can be separated from them and controlled in specialized and more impersonal ways. In other words, Alexander says, it is possible to defend the search for universal truth, and the possibility of gaining valuable approximations to it in a manner that does not reflect positivist credulity.

Alexander seeks to overcome the epistemological dilemma regarding the presentation of alternatives in a variety of ways. He presents the arguments that universalistic standards of evaluation, and impersonal conceptual constructs, are products of millennia-long development in human civilization. Because the effort to gain distance from objects outside of the self—to separate the knower from the known—did not begin with the positivism of the 17th century scientific revolution, the quest for universalism cannot be evaluated on the grounds of a simple objection to philosophical positivism as such. He introduced the counterpoint to universalization that, in different guises, is the critical object throughout much of his analysis. The demand for a turning away from universalism has been intrinsic to cultural history.

> "To advocate the necessity for general theory is to uphold the possibility of universal thought. Universalism rests upon the capacity for actors to decentre themselves, to understand that the world does not revolve around them, that they are not its creators, that they can study it in a relatively impersonal way". (Alexander, 1992: 325)

As Nagel writes in his important arguments about the paradoxical pursuit of objective knowledge:

> "The aim of such understanding is to go beyond the distinction between appearance and reality by including the existence of appearances in an elaborated reality. But this expanded reality, like physical reality, is centerless. Though the subjective features of our own minds are at the centre of our world, we must try to conceive of them as just one manifestation of the mental in a world that is not given especially to the human point of view". (1986: 18)

Alexander adds:

> "Yet paradoxically, this decentered world is at the same time a world view, and the human view of it a human creation. When this agency is forgotten, universalism becomes an objectification that seems not just to decenter human beings but to deny them. Objectivity is viewed not as world mastery but as alienation. The consequence is the return to the concrete". (1992: 325)

The process of decentering actors from their world is the process upon which the claims of civilization rest. The earlier the human society, the more its members experience centredness. The world is whole, it is experienced in its subjective immediacy. Actors live in the dreaming, in circular narrative time, in myths, conventions, parables, stories. As societies become larger and more complex, experience becomes more fragmented. Reality is posited more as something that exists outside the actors that is removed from immediate experience and the concrete. As it becomes more universal, time flattens out; reflection and self-consciously constructed recipes, maps, and hypotheses take their place alongside myths as organized orientations for social action.

With the great monotheistic religions, particularly with Judaism and Christianity but also with Buddhism, Hinduism and Confucianism, this reality is expressed as a higher truth that not only stands completely outside of subjectively experienced time and place but actually creates them. The interplay between expanding religious abstraction and secular universalism continued to develop in the modern world. Depersonalization brings individuation, not simply domination. It was the great world religions that gave birth to the very conception of autobiography (Misch, 1973). Cosmic abstraction brings metaphysical dualism; such dualism is the key to the experience of the separated 'self'. Thus, even while the world is increasingly experienced as objective and impersonal—as rational and rationalized—actors can experience an intimate connection to the objective forces from which they have become estranged. Insofar as this experience can be sustained, there exists what Alexander calls 'present reason' (1992: 326).

Alexander adds,

> "The experience of present reason is difficult to maintain. In the course of its progress, impersonal reason is continually negated by the demand for the concrete. As soon as the existence of the universal is posited, it is denied. This negation is generated because depersonalization is experienced as having caused reason to be absent. Actors experience the fear of obliteration from the forces that they have themselves created, from the isolated and demanding self, from the impersonally organized society, from an omnipresent God, from the rationally reorganized forces of nature". (ibid.: 327)

This is not a deception, but rather another form of truth. The dialectic of present and absent reason forms the main topic of Hegel's phenomenology. In so far human beings posit reason as outside of themselves, they create conditions for the alienation of reason from its human origins. Religion becomes an orthodoxy in which the faithful lose touch with their own spiritual life. Philosophy becomes a dogma that is casuistic, obfuscatory, elitist, and merely abstract. When decentred reason becomes objectified in colossal weapons of death that obliterate human beings, the alienation of reason assumes more than a metaphysical form (Alexander, 1990). Because reason appears to be absent from the objects created by rational human beings, people deny its very existence. In response to this alienation of reason, truth is sought within, not without, in the concrete rather than the abstract. Reason is abandoned for experience, rationality for the irrational. This counter-movement is expressed by sophistry, skepticism and idealism in philosophy.

This dialectic of universal and concrete, in the realm of thought, has been conceptualized as the relation of the knower to the known. Alexander wishes to maintain that in important respects the world outside of the self can in fact be comprehended. The human beings create the world view that allows them to conceive of this world as such. Nor do they invent the society whose regularities this decentering allows them to see; regularities, which if not lawful in the same sense as physical laws, exhibit powerful and consistent patterning. The counter-movement against impersonal rationality allows us not to forget that it is we who are seeing this society and world; it is not seeing itself through us. This is the achievement of romantic social thought in its modern guise. Yet we can decentre ourselves from this personal process of objective knowing in turn. In so far as we do so, we can understand and explain what this process of constructing rational perceptions involves. This understanding, however, does not threaten the universality of perception. To the contrary, it can become another equally universalistic theory—a theory of knowledge and perception—in its own right (Alexander, 1992: 329).

These broad considerations are central to the problem of general theory and method, and its critics. One can argue that what exactly theory is, whether it is a model, a set of interlinked propositions that produces testable hypothesis, a frame of reference, a set of classifications, a conceptual scheme. However, one cannot argue, with the notion that, no matter how defined, theory implies abstraction from the concrete. The more general the theory—the greater its interpretative and explanatory reach—the more general the abstraction. Theory is the quintessence of the decentering process that distinguishes the modern world.

> "The universalism of general theory cannot be justified if this universalism is understood, and experienced, as a decentering that demands the alienation of reason. General theory is not something that simply reflects the objective out there. Positivism and empiricism reduce theory in just this way, viewing it merely as the studied reflection of the natural world. For this reason, their justifications for theory have been particularly vulnerable in the contemporary period, for in this recent period the agentic contribution to our perception of the objective world has become increasingly well

understood. In the present context, general theory can be justified only in a post positivist way as the case of present reason." (Alexander, 1992: 329)

Alexander comments on the limitations of positivism and empiricism:

> "Positivism and Empiricism take their warrant for universal theorizing from the role it seems to play in the sciences of nature. In its natural science form, the practice of general theory has become at least in its normal science mode, a process of absent reason. Scientists experience themselves as mirroring nature (Alexander, here, uses Rorty's (1979) phrase ironically to emphasize that it is the practioners, not the philosophers of science, who are compelled to understand objectivity in a mirroring, subject-less stance). Their own exercise in rationality—the manner in which it is this rationality itself which has allowed perceptual access to a world which mathematics and scientific methods can model—is forgotten. For many decades absent reason also characterized the philosophy of natural science. Effacement, abnegation, objectivity, transparency—when these terms describe the relation of scientists to nature their agentic construction of the natural world is ignored. Theories are held to be proved or falsified by exposing their human-made tenets to the force of non-human empirical facts. With natural science methods, social scientists would not have to construct generalizations on the basis of their interpretive insights, intellectual power, and wit; on the basis simply of their commitment to the ironclad experimental codes of science, generalizations would emerge out of the data themselves". (1992: 331)

This vision of absent reason can be found in the work of sophisticated theorists like Talcott Parsons. Parsons, while conceiving his own theorizing on the model of Newtonian mechanics, was not troubled by the possibility that general theory placed the construction of the knower onto the very perception of the known (Parsons, 1937: 579–639). To the contrary, Parsons confidently presented his action theory as a powerful reflection of the 'real', even if a reflection that had been mediated in an analytic, a *priori* way (Parsons, 1954; Parsons and Shils, 1951).

This utopian rationalism was not the product of Parsons' functionalism. Louis Althusser (1969) confidently separated his own version of Marxist social theory from mere bourgeois ideology.

Post-war semiotics agreed to the idea that truth was accessible without the intervention of subjective frames. Roland Barthes (1959) illustrated how social structural pressures distorted merely denotative analogies into redolent myths, without giving any thought to the question of how his own thought could have escaped the same mythic fate.

Contextualism as the Neo-Romantic Alternative

In 1960s, there emerged in reaction against such absent reason an extraordinary neo-romantic critique. Optimism about the objectively progressive course of the post war had begun to fade; renewed racial, ethnic and class conflicts, and the emergence of newly strengthened primordial attachments, made the unthinking commitment to universal and social and intellectual structures more difficult. When they protested against the meaningless abstraction in their newly expanded universities, college students were experiencing the absence of reason in the very heart of intellectual life; they viewed the university not as the expression of human creativity and imagination but as an objectified machine. They indicted science for its reification in weapons of war. The classical embodiments of rational theory and methods also were challenged in an antinomian way.

Against the reconstruction of Weber by Parsons and Bendix as the embodiment of rational sobriety, Mitzman's (1970) claimed that charisma, pathos and eros formed the revealing underside to Weber's rationalizing theme. Against Rieff's (1961) moralist Freud and Jones' (1963) scientific one, Norman O. Brown's (1966) created a Freud of play and joy, while Russel Jacobys' (1975) indicated American revisionists for ignoring the critical and erotic Freud that Marcuse (1964) had earlier unearthed. Garfinkel (1967) became dissatisfied with Husserl's epistemological stance, fearing that it too easily endorsed the existence of impersonal forms; inspired by Heidegger and Wittgenstein, he pushed ethnomethodolgy into a more radically anti-normative mode, away from the belief in, and the hope for, consensual normative constraints as they were embodied in theorizing of a Parsonian form (Alexander, 1987: 257-80; 1992: 332).

By the end of the 1960s, an antitheoretical orientation had begun to emerge throughout Western intellectual life. It was not visible at that time, however, because of the continuing influence of critical theory, which insisted on the reality of the external world. Alexander calls this broad movement 'contextualism' (1987: 257–80). Thus, in what became an extraordinarily influential quarrel with functionalist theory, Clifford Geertz (1973a, 1973b) attacked the notion that cognitive truth was relevant to the study of ideology, arguing against Parsons for an interpretive and relativist approach that emphasized the close link between political action and the rhetorical creation of meaning. Thomas Kuhn (1970) rebelled against reason in natural science in an equally constructivist and contextualist way. While not denying the possibility of doing natural science, he identified the decentred scientist as a kind of 'normal science' idiot while describing creative and revolutionary science in a subjective and recentred way. Also beginning to get serious attention was the work of Peter Winch (1958), which in questioning the very possibility of a social science went further than either Geertz or Kuhn. Following Wittgenstein, Winch argued that social scientists were imprisoned by linguistic-conceptual worlds that made it impossible to create even relatively independent knowledge about the actions and intentions of those outside one's cultural group.

In the 1970s and 1980s, the neo-romantic reaction deepened. What are taken to be the epistemological implications of contextualism—conventionalism and skepticism—have been explicitly formulated; in many quarters, theory has given way to the investigation of the concrete. Arguing from the mere existence of context, social scientists and philosophers have concluded that universalistic modes of argument are impossible. The facile and ultimately false dichotomy between positivism and relativism has thus inserted itself as a principal rubric in contemporary debate. The possibility that the context within which we operate is itself the very tradition of objective reason has been ignored. This movement from the acknowledgement of context to the embrace of relativism and the abandonment of theory is no where more clear than in the intellectual odyssey of Geertz. In his 1970s essay on ideology and religion, Geertz had emphasized interpretative over scientific reason in order to avoid the sociological reductionism so prevalent in the social sciences of that day. Ideology and religion could be viewed as cultural systems only if their relation to social actors was evaluated by some criterion other than scientific truth. In other words, ideological and religious actors should not be mistaken for scientific ones. Geertz argued that scientific theorizing should not be goal of analysisists themselves. Not universalistic theory but 'thick description' of concrete behaviour should be the goal of the human studies (Geertz, 1973c).

Once positivist and theoretical social science have been rejected, the only alternative Geertz can foresee is a return to the concrete. Social analysis must "turn from trying to explain social phenomena by weaving them into grand textures of cause and effect to trying to explain them by placing them in local frames of awareness". Ethnography, not generalizing social science, is the discipline best suited to this particularist task. "To an ethnographer, sorting through the machinery of distant ideas, the shapes of knowledge are always ineluctably local, indivisible from their instruments and their encasements. One may veil this fact with ecumenical rhetoric or blur it with strenuous theory, but one cannot really make it go away" (Alexander, 1992: 335). Geertz concludes that while his approach is a hermeneutic one, "one will not find very much in the way of 'the theory and methodology of interpretation ... in what follows". Not surprisingly, Geertz believes that there are enough general principles in the world already. He does not wish to see hermeneutics, 'reified into a parascience.' What the essays in *Local Knowledge* (Geertz, 1983) offer instead of theorizing are 'actual interpretations of something'. In his relativising task, Geertz aligns himself with the views of such philosophers as Heidegger, Wittgenstein, Gadamer on Ricoeur, such critics as Burke, Frye, Jameson or Fish, and such all-purpose subversives as Foucault, Habermas, Barthes or Kuhn (Geertz, 1983). These are the scholars who have been central to the contextual reaction against universalistic thought (Friedman, 1987).

It is important to mention here that later development in Thomas Kuhn's intellectual career manifest the epistemological dilemma in similar ways as those in Geertz's. Despite his quite legitimate protests that he had not intended to produce an irrationalist theory, Kuhn's revision of his paradigm concept (1970) made it impossible to identify it with theoretical presuppositions of a universal bent (Alexander, 1982b). Neophytes learn to exercise their scientific skills not by understanding intellectual frameworks but by mimicking the plots of specific problem solutions which Kuhn calls 'exemplars'. Scientific results are controlled not in the first instance, by universalistic theories or impersonal methods but by a 'disciplinary matrix', which Kuhn is careful to define not as a set of ideas but as a social network of situated human relations. In one of his monographs, (Kuhn, 1978) seems to have given up on efforts at theoretical clarification altogether. Eschewing even the claim to exemplify his theory of scientific revolution, he has returned to detailed historical description of a specific scientific case (Alexander, 1992: 336).

Post-structural Movement

Equally revealing of the increasingly radical implications of contextualism is the poststructural movement beyond semiotics and structuralism. Since Saussure set forth semiotic philosophy in his general theory of linguistics, its key stipulation has been the arbitrary relation of sign and referent: there can be found no 'rational reason', no force of correspondence in the outside world, for the particular signs that actors have chosen to represent the world. Alexander has indicated that early elaborations of the semiotic position exempted from the critique of objective reference semioticians themselves. He adds that perhaps, it should not be surprising that the founder of the American pragmatic tradition of semiotics, Charles Pierce was confident that practical experience eventually aligned scientific symbols with objective truth. What is striking, however, is that the same assurance of universalism marked the French semiotic school. Saussure showed no anxiety about his ability to perceive linguistic systems in a realistic way. Levi-Strauss triumphantly described his structuralist interpretations as exemplifying the science of myth (Alexander, 1992: 336). Inheritors of the semiotic and structuralist tradition were disappointed with the fate of what they conceived to be truth and reason in the 1960s. In addition to their experience of absent reason, they had well justified concerns with the epistemological naivety of their theoretical predecessors. In accord with the logic of the epistemological dilemma, poststructuralists moved to extend the arbitrary relativism of the semiotic field to the semioticians themselves. Acknowledging the arbitrary reference of reality, Alexander says, "they felt compelled to reject out of hand the very concept of an objectively differentiated world exercising an independent influence on the knower. Experience replaces reason, relativism and the embrace of hyper contextualism displace the search for universalistic truth.

Emancipation is a logical impossibility, domination a condition that cannot logically be overcome" (1992: 336–37).

Baudrillard's (1983) concept of the simulacrum represents the *reductio ad absurdum* of the poststructuralist positions, the inevitable conclusion of an insistence not only on the referential arbitrariness but the particularism of symbolic codes. Where the early Barthes saw myth as the corruption of realistic reference at the hands of objective social power, Baudrillard sees the play of signifier and signified as a closed circuit into which the reality of social needs can never intrude. The contrast between Levis-Strauss and Bourdieu can be seen in much the same way. Levi-Strauss' overwhelming rationalism led him to cut symbolic thought short before the entry of the modern world. The *bricoleur* was replaced by the scientist. With Bourdieu, we can see, once again, how a latter-day follower of structuralism responds to the earlier faith in objectivity with cynical disappointment. Denying the very possibility of reference to critical universalism, the perceptual structures of bourgeoise and proletarian actors alike are for Bourdieu (1983) mere particularistic reflections, primitive codes from which there is no escape (Alexander, 1992: 337).

Derrida and Foucault supply the deep justification for such poststructural argument. Whereas Bourdieu seems blithely to exempt himself from his own relativizing structures, Derrida (1981) has insisted that the knower is simply a literate *bricoleur*. Reality, in turn, can be nothing other than a text, a symbolic construction that is itself related to other texts-not to history or social structure-in arbitrary ways. Indeed, texts cannot themselves be accepted as representations, even of arbitrarily signified referents. Composed not just of presences but of absences, texts do not exist as complete wholes.

To this reconstruction of the epistemological dilemma in its most nihilistic form, Foucault adds a history and sociology. Against the possibility of contemporary universalism, he makes a double critique. First, there is his substantive historical demonstration of absent reason. The rationalization of modern society, as manifest particularly in the thought and activity of the scientifically trained professions, is a fraud (Foucault, 1977, 1978). Professionals actually engage in the manipulation of reason, their ministrations are forms of surveillance, their goal is technical control. Enlightenment universalism amounts to the particularism of power; it results in the suppression of subjectivity, not in the exercise of present reason.

Foucault's second critique is an analytical one. In his later work, he insists on the virtually complete identity of knowledge, or discourse, with power. In doing so, the very possibility of decentred experience is denied. The subject, Foucault is fond of repeating, is completely constituted by discourse. In this way, discourse becomes both the basis for power and merely its manifestation in another form. Because truth is relative to discourse, it is impossible to appeal to universalizing standards against worldly power: "Truth is not outside power or lacking in power … . Each society has its regime of truth, its 'general politics' of truth: that is the types of discourse which it accepts and makes function as true" (Foucault, 1986: 131). To set about rationally to evaluate the logical consistency, theoretical implications or explanatory value of a given discourse is obliviously a waste of time (Alexander, 1992: 338).

The simple and dangerous dichotomy is firmly set. The only alternative to the fallacy of absent reason, to positivism, is a thoroughly relativist sociology of knowledge, an archeology of the historical conditions of discourse (Taylor, 1986; Alexander, 1992).

At this stage of argument, it is important for us to introduce the philosophy of Richard Rorty and its postmodern reprise. Rorty, while on his own account a good "postmodern bourgeoise liberal" (1985), reluctantly embraces the Nietzschean frame. He does so because, like Nietzschean, he experiences the history of Western ratiocination not as the radically imperfect expression of present reason but as the alienation of subjectivity from itself. When Rorty describes the scientific revolution, it is the pathology of absent reason of which he writes:

> "This is reality conceived as somehow represented by representations which are not merely ours but its own, as it looks to itself, as it would describe itself if it could … . This fantasy of discovering, and somehow knowing that one has discovered, Nature's Own Vocabulary seemed to become more concrete when Galileo and Newton formulated a comprehensive set of predictively useful universal generalizations, written in suitably 'cold' 'inhuman' mathematical terms". (1982a: 174)

This perception of absent reason leads Rorty to embrace the dichotomy between scientism and relativism. He writes, "the urge to tell stories of progress, maturation and synthesis might be overcome, if we once took seriously the notion that we only know the world and ourselves under a description" (1986: 48). Rorty is caught on the horns of the epistemological dilemma. He believes that if we acknowledge context, there is no possibility of evaluating the worth of various perspectives in a universalistic way. He writes:

> "If we once could feel the full force of the claim that our present discursive practices were given neither by God, nor by intuition of essence nor by the cunning of reason, but only by chance, then we would have a culture which lacked not only a theory of knowledge, not only a sense of progress, but any source of what Neitzche called metaphysical comfort". (ibid.)

To embrace fully such relativism, indeed, one must avoid not only progressive theories but theorizing as such Rorty explains, "a Nietzschean must not want any substitute for theories" (ibid.). To theorize is to imply the possibility of at least partly circumventing the particularism of context. This is impossible, for a Nietzschean "views the very idea of theory as tainted with the notion that there is something there to be contemplated, to be accurately represented in thought". The possibility of accurate representation is what Rorty wants to avoid. He sees the history of philosophy as directed to the relation between universals and particulars (1979: 149). Because Rorty's 'Philosophy and the Mirror of Nature' is an argument against the possible existence of the concrete. It is necessarily an argument against the history of philosophy as well. Rorty suggests "the metaphor of knowing general truths by internalizing universals became the intellectual's substitute for the peasant's belief in life among the shades" (1979: 42).

As a matter of fact, Rorty did not succeed in justifying his own assumption that universals do not exist. This, perhaps, places the intellectual edifice he is constructing on rather flimsy foundations. Because universals, do not exist, an effort to construct intellectual foundations is a hopeless enterprise from the start. At any rate, it is the implication that Rorty draws from this assumption against universals that makes his work interesting (Alexander, 1992: 341). "Because there are no universals we can talk in good faith only about experience, not abstract norms; we can refer only to common sense and common practice for details about what counts as justification" (Rorty, 1979: 151). As Rorty sees it, the real problem is not to abjure such hypostatized universals but to explain why anyone had taken them seriously. He laments the passing of the traditional world: "there would not have been thought to be a problem about the nature of reason had our race confined itself to pointing out particular states of affairs-warning of cliffs and rain, celebrating individual births and deaths" (ibid.: 38). Unfortunately, for no particular reason, some philosophers got it into their heads that 'knowledge of universals' held the key to personhood and freedom. With the entrance of the Greeks, the slide down slippery slope began. Among philosophers at least, it has come to the point that 'to suggest that there are no universals ... is to endanger our uniqueness' (ibid.: 43).

Philosophers who espouse universals, have justified their importance by describing them as objectives entities. Against this, Rorty insists over and over again that it is impossible to have 'pre-linguistic awareness' (1979: 181). His epistemological point is that there is no transcendental standpoint of our present set of representations from which we can inspect the relation between these representations and their object (ibid.: 293). He concludes, "the epistemological quest for a way of refuting the skeptic and underwriting our claim to be talking about notification is hopeless" (ibid.). The epistemological claim is hopeless because it is empiricist. It reflects the absence of reason. Rorty points to the coercive implications that flow from this loss. He writes, such philosophers believes that knowing a proposition to be true is to be identified with being caused to do something by an object (ibid.: 157). According to this view, the object which the proposition is about imposes the proposition's truth.

Rorty's claim is that philosophers seeking objectivity see themselves as reflectors, or mirrors of reality; hence, they set out to establish the 'foundations of knowledge'. Foundational arguments are universals that establish the grounds for truth in what are conceived of as objectively rational ways, "truths which are certain because of their causes rather than because of the arguments given for them" (ibid.: 159). Because they move "beyond argument to compulsion from the object known", foundational arguments are inhuman; they claim that "anyone gripped by the object in the required way will be unable to doubt or to see an alternative". Rorty insists that "foundationalism is the end product of an original wish to substitute confrontation for conversation as the determinant of our belief" (ibid.: 163).

In this context, Alexander comments, "Rorty is right to demand that reason be present, and he is also right that this can be achieved only if a hermeneutic rather than mechanistic stance is achieved" (1992: 342).

> "If the study of science's search for truth about the physical universe is viewed hermeneutically it will be viewed as the activity of spirit-the faculty which makes—rather than as the application of the mirroring faculties, those which find what nature has already made". (Rorty, 1978: 344)

Alexander adds, Rorty is wrong, however, to think that this can be accomplished only by abandoning the search for universals as such. The problem lies with his conviction that every argument against skepticism and for universalism is an epistemological quest, that it is based upon reflection theory and the absence of reason. Philosophers who seek truthful foundations may perceive themselves as mirroring reality, but the interest and power of their arguments do not stand or fall on whether this claim can itself be true. These philosophers can be seen, rather, as rational agents who create frameworks within which to interpret a world whose objectivity and impersonality they take on faith. To the degree that they succeed, they falsify Rorty's epistemological syllogism, his claim that the proposition, "there is no neutral ground on which to stand" (Rorty, 1978: 181), follows logically from the notion "there is no such thing as prelinguistic awareness".

Rorty says that when foundationalists make their arguments, they are playing the language game of philosophy as epistemology. Alexander comments that but surely he is himself playing the same game from the other side of the net. Rorty characterizes foundationalism as the demand for some transcendental standpoint outside our present set of representations from which we can inspect the relations between those representations and their objects (Rorty, 1978: 293). He believes that to deny the transparency of reality is to deny the interest and importance of universalistic ambition. Because he is caught within the epistemological dilemma, he cannot differentiate the levels and complexity of present reason in an appropriate way. Acknowledging representational subjectivity does not mean abandoning the possibility of differentiating our representations from objects in the outside world. The possibility for so comparing "objective and 'subjective' is produced by the development of human culture itself, which can be seen as progress because it has allowed an increasingly decentered construction of nature and social life. Reason can be exercised in a present way" (Alexander, 1992: 343).

Thus, Alexander outlines several reasons for the false antagonism between scientific theory and relativism. For example, relativistic analysis traditionally focuses an individual perception, interpretations and beliefs. But actors can be and are bound to collective standards and traditions of rationality. Theoretical analysis is relative to those collective standards, not unique and individual. Similarly, relativistic analysis treats theoretical claims as incommensurable. But incommensurability is not the same as incompatibility, which more accurately characterizes the relation between theoretical arguments.

Furthermore, there is some correspondence between our reason—created conceptual structures and reasonable observation statements. We can reach agreement about the value of at least some of our theories, even without assuming that observations exist entirely independently from them. Perhaps most important, the act of seeking consensus is the central goal. Even hermeneutical philosophy, Alexander argues, is based on the notion that life worlds are impersonal and assume a universal consensual form. Thus, the seeking of foundations, the attempt to create shared and binding norms of sociological activity is central to the theoretical enterprise. Alexander concludes that if social theorizing had secure foundations, they could be put in the background and ignored. Ironically, then, it is the very absence of foundations that necessitates our pursuit of them.

The debate between postmodern theorists and methodologists and their critics is part of a broader public discussion in academic world over the meaning, method and social role of science today. The optimism of the philosophies and their heirs that science would produce truths that promote a good society has come under attack. The connection of science to warfare and Nazism, public discontent over scientific medicine and psychiatry, the assault on science by the black, women's, and gay movements, has rendered an unequivocal Enlightenment faith naïve. Yet, science continues to have an aura and a cultural currency that is frequently appealed to by entrepreneurs, politicians and scholars. Undoubtedly, it is science's social entanglement and its politicization initially by the left and more recently by the right that promotes much of the current debate over the meaning, method and social role of science.

Within the disciplines, this discussion typically takes the form of an epistemological questioning. Is science a unique privileged form of knowledge? What kind of mode of knowing is science? How should we understand the scientific method and the way science is social? This questioning of science within the disciplines has been intensified by two developments: (a) the institutional elaboration of science and its increasingly visible links to social institutions and the state have rendered it a powerful social force; and (b) from a different vantage point, as universities have opened up to hitherto excluded populations—feminists, lesbians, gay men, the differently-abled, the elderly minorities, scheduled castes and tribes—questions have been raised about the new method in social science and also the social role of science. The exclusions, and absences of science have suggested to some that the disciplines are tied to social projects. The meaning of the social entanglement of science, the question of how science can be both a discourse claiming objective knowledge and a social force shaping social identities and normative and institutional order, we believe, lies at the root of the debates between postmodernists their critics, particularly in the context of method in social sciences. These are ultimately debates about the meaning and method of science and to recall Weber, our vocation as scholars.

References

Adorno, Theodor W., 1973, *Negative Dialectics*, New York: Seabury Press.

Alexander, Jeffrey and Colomy, Paul, 1991, "Neofunctionalism Today: Reconstructing a Theoretical Tradition", in George Ritzer (ed.), *Frontiers of Social Theory*, New York: Columbia University Press.

——, 1992, "Traditions and Competition: Preface to a Post-Positivist Approach to Knowledge Accumulation", in George Ritzer (ed.), *Methodology in Sociology*, Newbury Park: Sage.

Alexander, Jeffrey, 1982b, Kuhn's Unsuccessful Revisionism: A Rejoinder to Selby, *Canadian Journal of Sociology*, 7/2.

——, 1987, "On the Centrality of the Classics", in A. Giddens and J. Turner (eds.), *Social Theory Today*, Cambridge: Polity Press, pp. 11–57.

——, 1990, "Between Progress and Apocalypse: Social Theory and the Dream of Reason in the 20th Century", in J.C. Alexander and Piotr Sztompka (eds.), *Progress and Social Theory: Movement, Forces and Ideas at the End of the 20th Century*, London: Unwin and Hyman, pp. 5–38.

——, 1992, "General Theory in the Post-Positivist Mode: The Epistemological Dilemma and the Search for Present Reason", in Steven Seidman and D.G. Wagner (eds.), *Postmodernism and Social Theory*, Oxford: Blackwell.

——, 1992, "Post Positivist Epistemological Dilemma" in Steven Seidman and David G. Wagner (eds.), op. cit.

Althusser, Louis, 1969, *For Marx*, Harmondsworth: Penguin.

Arendt, H., 1956, *The Origins of Totalitarianism*, Glencoe, Ill: The Free Press.

Aronowitz, S., 1992, "The Tension of Critical Theory: Is Negative Dialectical All there is?" in S. Seidman and D.G. Wagner, 1992, op. cit., pp. 289–322.

Bachelard, Gaston, 1968, *The Philosophy of No*, New York: Orion Press.

——, 1984, *The New Scientific Spirit*, Boston: Beacon Press.

Bacon, Francis, 1972, Basil Montague, ed. and trans. *The Works*, 3 Vols. (Philadelphia: Parry & Macmillan, 1854).

Barthes, Roland, 1959, *Myth Today in Mythologies*, New York: Hild and Wang, pp. 109–59.

Baudrillard, Jean, 1975, *The Mirror of Production*, St. Louis: Telos Press.

——, 1981, *For a Critique of the Political Economy of the Sign*, St. Louis: Telos Press.

Bernstein, Basil, 1971, *Class, Codes and Control*, 3 Vols., London: Routledge.

Bodner, Judith, 1987, "Another Approach to Semiotics", unpublished manuscript, Department of Sociology, Johns Hopkins University.

Bourdieu, Pierre, 1977, *Outline for the Theory of Practice*, New York: Cambridge University Press.

——, 1984, *Distinction: A Social Critique of the Judgement Taste*, London: Routledge.

Brown, Richard Harvey, 1987, *Society as Text: Essays on Rhetoric, Reason and Reality*, Chicago: University of Chicago Press.

——, 1992, *Social Science and Society as Discourse: Towards a Sociology for Civic Competence*, New York: McGraw-Hill, pp. 223–44.

Calhoun, Craig, 1992, "Culture History and the Problem of Specificity in Social Theory", in S. Seidman and D.G. Wagner, 1992, op. cit., pp. 244–79.

Canguillhem, G., 1983, *Etudes d`histoire et de philosophie des sciences*, Paris: Vrin.

Carnap, Rudolf, 1956, "Empiricism, Semantics and Ontology", *Meaning and Necessity*, Chicago: University of Chicago Press.

——, 1963, *Philosophy of Rudolf Carnap*, ed. by Paul Arthur Schilpp, La Salle, Ill: Open Court.

Collins, Randall, 1992, "The Confusion of the Modes of Sociology", in Steven Seidman and D.G. Wagner (eds.), op. cit., pp. 179–99.

D'Amico, Robert, 1988, *Historicism and Knowledge*, New York: Routledge.

——, 1992, "Defending Social Science against the Postmodernist Doubt", in Steven Seidman and D.G. Wagner (eds.), op. cit., pp. 137–56.

Denzin, Norman K., 1987, On Semiotics and Symbolic Interactionism, *Symbolic Interactionism*, 10/1: 1–19.

Derrida, Jacques, 1981, *Positions,* Chicago: University of Chicago Press.

Douglas, Mary and Isherwood, Baron, 1978, *The World of Goods*, New York: Basic Books.

Douglas, Mary and Wilolavsky, Aaron, 1982, *Risk and Culture: An Essay on the Selection of Technological and Environmental Dangers*, Berkeley: University of California Press.

Douglas, Mary, 1972, "Deciphering a Meal", in *Implicit Meaning; Essays in Anthropology*, London: Routledge and Kegan Paul, 10/1: 1–19.

Durkheim, Emile, 1966, *Rules of Sociological Method*, Glencoe, Ill: Free Press.

Ford, James E. and Klumpp, James F. 1985, Systematic Pluralism: An Inquiry into the Bases of Communication Research, *Critical Studies in Mass Communication*, 2 (December): 407–34.

Forman, Paul, 1971, *Weimar Culture, Causality and Quantum Theory in Historical Studies in the Physical Sciences*, Philadelphia: University of Pennsylvania Press.

Foster, Hal, 1983, *The Anti-aesthetic: Essays in Post Modern Culture*, Port Townsend, Wash: Bay Press.

Foucault, Michael, 1972, *Discourse on Language, The Archaeology of Knowledge*, tr. by A.M. Sheridan Smith, New York: Pantheon.

Freely-Harnik, Gillian, 1978, "Divine Kingship and the Meaning of History among the Sakalava of Madagascar", *Man*, n.s. 13/2, 402-17.

Friedman, George, 1981, *The Political Philosophy of the Frankfurt School*, Ithaca, NY: Cornell University Press.

Garfinkel, Harold, 1967, *Studies in Ethnomethodology*, Englewood Cliffs, NJ: Prentice-Hall.

Gasset, Ortega Y., 1932, *The Revolt of the Masses*, New York: Norton.

Geertz, Clifford, 1973 (a), "Ideology as a Cultural System" in Greetz, *The Interpretation of Cultures*, New York: Basic Books, pp. 193-233.

——, 1973 (b), "Religion as Cultural System" in Greetz, *The Interpretation of Cultures*, New York: Basic Books, pp. 87-125.

——, 1973 (c), "Thick Description: Towards an Interpretive Theory of Culture", in *Interpretation of Cultures*, New York: Basic Books, pp. 3-32.

——, 1983 "Introduction" in Geertz, *Local Knowledge*, New York: Basic Books, pp. 3-16.

Giddens, A., 1977, *New Rules of Sociological Method*, New York: Basic Books.

Goffman, Ervin, 1974, *Frame Analysis*, New York: Harper and Row.

Habermas, Jurgen, 1971, *Knowledge and Human Interests*, tr. by Jeremy Shapiro, Boston: Beacon Press.

——, 1974, "Rationalism Divided in Two", in Anthony Giddens (ed.), 1974, *Positivism and Sociology*, pp. 195–225.

Harre, Rom, 1979, "Architectonic Man: On the Structuring of Lived Experience", in Richard Harvey Brown and Stanford M. Lyman (eds.), *Structure, Consciousness and History*, New York and London: Cambridge University Press, pp. 139–72.

Hempel, Carl G. 1965, *Aspects of Scientific Explanation*, New York: The Free Press.

——, 1980, "Science and Human Values", in E.D. Klemke, Robert Hollinger and A. David Kline (eds.), *Readings in Philosophy of Science*, Buffalo, NY: Prometheus Books.

Herzfeld, Michael, 1985, Converging Paths in Semiotics and Anthropology, *Semiotica*, 56/1 and 2: 153–77.

Horkheimer, Marx and Adorno, Theodor, 1972, *Dialectic of the Enlightenment*, tr. by Cumming John, New York: Seabury Press.

Jacoby, Russel. 1975, *Social Amnesia,* Boston: Beacon Press.

Jones, E., 1963, *The Life and Work of Sigmund Freud*, New York: Doubleday.

Kafka, Franz, 1956, *The Trial*, New York: Modern Library.

Kelemen, Janes, 1982, "Lucaks's Ideas on Language", in Ferenc Kiefer (ed.), *Hungarian Linguistics*, The Hague: Mouton, pp. 245–68.

Kellner, Douglas, 1988, *Jean Baudrillard: From Marxism to Post Modernism and Beyond*, Cambridge: Polity Press.

Kuhn, T.S., 1970, *The Structure of Scientific Revolutions*, Chicago: University of Chicago Press.

Lash, Scott, 1985, Post Modernity and Desire, *Theory and Society*, 14:1-33.

Lemert, Charles, 1979, "Sociology and the Twilight of Man: Homocertrism and Discourse", in *Sociological Theory*, Carbondale: Southern Illinois University Press.

——, 1992, "General Social Theory and Irony Postmodernism", in Steven Seidman and D.G. Wagner (eds.), op. cit., pp. 17–47.

Lukacs, Gyorg, 1971, *History and Class Consciousness*, Cambridge: MIT Press.

Marcuse, H., 1964, *One Dimensional Man*, Boston: Beacon Press.

——, 1973, "Foundations of Historical Materialism", in *Studies in Critical Philosophy*, Boston: Beacon Press.

——, 1978, "Some Implications of Modern Technology", in A. Arato and Eike (eds.), *The Essential Frankfurt School Leader*, New York: Urizen Books.

——, 1987, *Ontology and the Theory of Historicity*, tr. by Seyla Benhabib, Cambridge, Mass: MIT Press.

Marx, Karl, 1946, *Capital*, New York: Everyman's Library.

——, 1971, *Marx's Grundrisse*, (ed.) David McLellan, London: Macmillan.

Mehan, Hugh and Wood, Houston, 1975, *The Reality of Ethnomethodology*, New York: John Wiley.

Mills, C. Wright, 1951, *White Collar: The American Middle Classes*, New York: Oxford University Press.

——, 1959, *Sociological Imagination*, New York: Oxford University Press.

——, 1964, *Sociology and Pragmatism*, New York: Oxford University Press.

Misch, Georg, 1973, *The History of Autobiography in Antiquity*, London: Routledge.

Mitzman, Arthur, 1970, *The Iron Cage,* New York: Knopf.

Mulkay, Michael, 1985, *The Word and the World: Explanations in the Form of Sociological Analysis*, London: Allen and Unwin.

Nagel, T., 1986, *The View from Nowhere*, New York: Oxford University Press.

Nicholson, Linda, 1992, "On the Postmodern Barricades", in Steven Seidman and D.G. Wagner (eds.), op. cit., pp. 82–101.

Norman O. Brown, 1966, *Love's Body,* New York: Vintage.

Parsons, Talcott, 1937, *The Structure of Social Action*, New York: The Free Press.

——, 1951, *The Social System*, Glencoe, Ill: The Free Press.

——, 1954, "The Present Position and Prospects of Systematic Theory in Sociology" in Parsons, *Essays in Sociological Theory*, New York: Free Press, pp. 212-37.

——, 1955, "An Approach to Psychology Theory of Action", in Simon Koch (ed.), *Psychology: A Study of Science*, Vol. 3, New York: Mc-Graw Hill.

Parsons, Talcott and Edward Shils (eds), 1951, *Towards a General Theory of Action*, Cambridge, Mass: Harward University Press.

Pertti, Ahonen, 1989, "The Meaning of Money: Comparing a Piercean and de Saussurean Perspective", unpublished manuscript, University of Tampere, Finland.

Ricoeur, Paul, 1980, "Existence and Hermeneutics", in Joseft Bleicher (ed.), *Contemporary Hermeneutics: Hermeneutics as Method, Philosophy and Critique*, London: Routledge.

Rieff, Philip, 1961, *Freud: The Mind of the Moralist*, New York: Doubleday.

Roche, Maurice, 1973, "Class Analysis and the Showing of Dichotomy", in Paul Filmer, Phillipson Michael, Maurice Roche, Barry Sandy Well and David Silverman, *Stratifying Practices*, unpublished manuscript, Goldsmiths' College, London.

Rorty, Richard, 1979, *Philosophy and the Mirror of Nature*, Princeton NJ: Princeton University Press.

——, 1982(a), "Method, Social Science and Social Hope", in *Consequences of Pragmatism*, Minneapolis: University of Minneapolis Press, pp. 191–210.

——, 1982(b), "The World Will Lost", in *Consequences of Pragmatism*, Minneapolis: University of Minneapolis Press, pp. 3–18.

——, 1985(a), "Postmodernism Bourgeois Liberalism", in Robert Hollinger (ed.), *Hermeneutics and Praxis*, Notre Dame: Notre Dame University Press, pp. 214–21.

——, 1985(b), "Habermas and Lyotard on Postmodernism", in Richard J. Bernstein (ed.), *Habermas and Modernity*, Cambridge, Mass: MIT Press, pp. 161–75.

——, 1986, "Foucault and Epistemology", in David Couzens Hoy (ed.), *Foucault: A Critical Reader*, Oxford and New York: Basil Blackwell.

Rossi-Landi, F., 1975, *Linguistics and Economics*, The Hague: Mouton.

——, 1983, "Language as Work and Trade: A Semiotic Homology of Linguistics and Economics", in Martha Adams et al., South Hadley, Mass: Bergin and Garvey.

Sahlins, Marshall, 1985, *Island of History*, Chicago: University Chicago Press.

Saussure, Ferdinand de, 1966, *Course in General Linguistics*, tr. by Wade Baskin, New York: McGraw-Hill.

Schelling, F., 1988, *Ideas for a Philosophy of Nature*, Cambridge and New York: Cambridge University Press.

Seidman, Steven and Wagner, David G. 1992, *Postmodernism and Social Theory*, Blackwell: Cambridge, MA and Oxford, UK.

Seidman, Steven, 1992, "Postmodern Social Theory as Narrative with a Moral Intent", in S. Seidman and D.G. Wagner (eds.), op. cit., pp. 47–48.

Simmel, George, 1978, *The Philosophy of Money*, tr. by Tom Bottomore and David Frisby, London: Routledge.

Taylor, Charles, 1986, "Foucault on Freedom and Truth" in David Couzens Hoy (ed), *Foucault: A Critical Reader*, Oxford: Basil Blackwell, pp. 69-102.

The Frankfurt Institute, 1972, *Aspects of Sociology*, Boston: Beacon Press.

Thomson, Grahame, 1989, "Homo Rhetoricus: Economics and the Social Sciences Discover the Linguistic Model and Postmodernism, or Do They?" Unpublished Manuscript, Faculty of Social Sciences, The Open University, Milton Keynes, England.

Turner, Jonathan H., 1984, *Societal Stratification: A Theoretical Analysis*, New York: Columbia University Press.

——, 1986, *The Structure of Sociological Theory*, Chicago: Dorsey Press.

——, 1987, 'Analytical Theorizing', in A. Giddens and J.H. Turner (eds.) *Social Theory Today*, Cambridge University Press.

——, 1988, *A Theory of Social Interaction*, Palo Alto, CA: Stanford University Press.

——, 1992, "The Promise of Positivism", in Steven Seidman and D.G. Wagner (eds.), op. cit., pp. 156–79.

Turner, Stephen, 1986, *The Search for a Methodology of Social Sciences: Durkheim, Weber and the 19th Century Problem of Cause, Probability and Action*, Boston Studies in the Philosophy of Science, 92, Dordrecht: Reidel.

Wagner, David G., 1992, "Daring Modesty: On Meta-theory, Observation and Theory Growth", in Steven Seidman and D.G. Wagner (eds.), op. cit., pp. 199–223.

Willer, David and Webster, Murray Jr., 1970, Theoretical Concepts and Observables, *American Sociological Review*, 25th August, pp. 748–57.

7

Towards a New Direction

Methodology and Research

The purpose of this book is to explore some of the new directions that sociology is currently taking. The emphasis is upon the methodology used in contemporary research and how this reflects within the subject itself. The first task is to look at some of the main elements in sociological method, how they have arisen and how they have been put into operation in the research process.

There have always been various types of sociology within the broad confines of the subject, which has no unifying paradigm as may be found in a developed science (Dawe, 1970). There has been constant controversy about both the nature of the subject and its legitimate fields and methods of enquiry. Sociological theory cannot be seen as a set of interrelated schemes merging to form one theoretical structure but rather as a series of perspectives that reflect the ideological components of both the society of their origin and individuals who develop them. These perspectives have tended to follow cyclical paths, being alternatively in ascendancy and decline. Within this broad picture a growing distinction between academic or traditional sociology and radical and critical sociology has developed (Thorns, 1976: 161). Some writers (e.g., Gouldner, 1971) have seen this growing distinctiveness as the herald of a crisis in Western sociology regarding the nature and purpose of the subject and the research procedures it currently employs.

Academic sociology is the heir of the positivist tradition, which became dominant from the 1920s onwards in America and elsewhere powered by the desire to emulate the procedures of the natural sciences (Lundberg, 1929). This drive was motivated by a number of factors, notably the desire to gain academic respectability and acceptance within the universities. This concern led to the emphasis being placed upon empirical research, which was seen to have an important relationship to the development and refinement of theory. With this came the development of the notion of the neutrality of the role of sociologist who could speak as a sociologist devoid of value commitment, representing the facts in a positive way. This would be achieved through the utilization of the apparatus of his science such as survey methods. A new group of experts, able to provide a set of answers to the kinds of problem afflicting Western society, emerged. The desire for and affectiveness of this kind of a sociology has been related to a number of factors (ibid.: 162):

(i) Firstly, there was the enormous prestige of the physical sciences at the time, which gave rise to a desire to imitate them and by so doing acquire the same kind of prestigious position both within the academic world and society as a whole.

(ii) Another factor has been the influence of systematic empiricism, beginning in the writings of J.S. Mill (1862) and continued through the work of British statisticians, particularly Fisher (1956, 1960) and Pearson (1948) in 1930s. This factor was aided by the growth of the sophisticated means of processing data via computer programmes and the enormous growth in statistical techniques, both parametric and non-parametric, which grew up primarily as aids to empirical induction (Blalock, 1961). This emphasis arises from the concern among sociologists to trace causal regularities to be observed in human societies.

However, this has caused controversy between those favouring the role of understanding as seen in Weber's concept of 'Verstehen' and those favouring more formally obtained knowledge via standardized procedures (as discussed in Chapter 3). This controversy has been glossed over by traditionalists within methods' texts by the device of describing the first as a 'hypothesis seeking' technique and the second as a 'hypothesis confirming' technique. The increasing discomfort with such a simplification is one of the reasons for the increase in criticism of traditional sociological research. The criticism comprises, firstly an attack upon the scientific method utilized in sociological research as not a method of science but rather one of systematic empiricism; secondly, the continuing controversy regarding the role of values, and the advocacy of a more reflexive sociology (discussed in the chapter on postmodernism); and finally, what might be termed as the revolt from below—the increasing influence of the respondents upon the nature of the research process, in particular their emphatic raising of the question: knowledge for whom and for what purpose?

The first strand of criticism is that sociology has utilized the methods of systematic empiricism rather than science (Thorns, 1976). Empiricism is the systematic observation of facts to form general statements of relation and correlation. The projection from such statements into the future assumes that what has occurred or is occurring will continue to occur in the same way or fairly similar ways. Science, however, possesses theoretical schemes from which concepts are derived, and these form the basis of observations. This means that the theories are not as time-and-situation bound as are those of the empiricist but allow the integration of new knowledge into the existing explanatory system (Thorns, 1976: 163). Sociology's use of systematic empiricism, rather than science, has led to the impoverishment of theory and to its overconcern with observed facts, which are always in the past, even if in the immediate past. Initially the search for causation was based upon J.S. Mill's rules of inductive logic, but these have now been replaced by the methods of correlation and contingency, through the work of social statisticians. Therefore, the criticism of sociology as systematic empiricism strikes at the heart of the dominant rationale of much of sociological activity by indicating that this activity is pseudo-scientific.

The second strand of criticism of the dominant systematic empiricism of sociology, represented by survey methods, large-scale projects and formal concepts, are the desire for a more reflexive sociology. Gouldner's (1971) answer to the coming crisis in the Western sociology was to advocate the constant awareness of the investigator's own value commitments, so that sociologists might become self-consciously aware of their own activities and their own influences upon the research process. This view highlights the continuing controversy surrounding the role of values and ideology in social research. It is probably both impossible and undesirable to conceive of a sociology without values or ideological input. These inputs are reflected in every aspect of the subject choice of investigation—choice of a given range of concepts with which to investigate the chosen topic, and methods of data collection, analysis and interpretation. In all these various choices, the researcher is required to make assumptions about the nature of society, and about what is theoretically important and what is insignificant. The way these choices are made is a reflection of the researcher's own ideological predisposition. What is being increasingly debated is the way to deal with this problem. Is it, as Myrdal (1970) has suggested, to present the readers of the research, as clearly as the investigator is able, with his value preconceptions and to aim within the work for an 'objectively neutral position', or is to work within the framework of a particular ideology for explicit ends. In this latter case, sociology ceases to have any pretensions to objectivity and becomes a form of social criticism allied to and inspired by particular political and social theories (Thorns, 1976: 164).

The final aspect of this criticism of academic or traditional sociology is the 'movement from below' (Thorns, 1976). The manipulation of the various groups of people for the purpose of social and psychological research is usually justified by reference to norms of science and to the quest for knowledge to which the subjects through their cooperation with the researcher are able to contribute. But, the question that has now been raised by some researched groups is 'knowledge for whom'? Growth of the survey industry within universities, research institutes, schools, and private and governmental agencies has led to the quest for information becoming an aspect of the power struggle within society, in that it is the elite groups or those connected with them who commission and conduct research into the problems and lack of conformity to the established structure of society of the other groups within the population. Does this therefore not provide these elite groups with additional abilities to preserve or further entrench their own position? Major projects in developed countries, for example, project Camelot in America (Horowitz, 1967), which was a large-scale interdisciplinary study of conditions conducive to internal conflict and insurgency in developing countries and the ways in which such conditions might be coped with and thereby prevented, and funded by the United States Army Research and Development Office, would give credence in many ways to such criticisms. In this case, the project became a political embarrassment, being seen as a form of espionage, and was dropped virtually before it really began to develop.

The desire of the subject groups to receive some benefit in the form of usable information is now more prominent and indeed advocated by one group of researchers as an integral part of the research process, in the sense that the observer should seek to check his observations and interpretations against those of the people he is studying. This is seen as a means of validating his work and is of course also a means of helping the people to classify their own conceptions, thereby possibly modifying them and influencing the subsequent course of activities. The growing militancy of American respondent, in particular, is allied to the growth of protest and action groups within American society (Thorns, 1976: 165). This growth is seen in all areas of American society where the public comes into contact with officials of public agencies (Goodman, 1972). If this kind of militant participatory involvement was to spread to sociological research, then research of a traditional type would no longer be possible and entirely new forms would have to be organized.

The emerging consciousness of the limitations of some of the approaches employed within sociology and the failure of researchers to come to terms with sensitive areas such as social change, conflict and power distribution have led to the rise of alternative sociologies. In one of the discussions, Birnbaum (1971) points to the limitations of sociology as it has been practised. He sees the increasing range and intensity of social conflict as discouraging scholars from anything but superficial and conventional political options, and rendering them increasingly remote from the inner, and therefore, real, conflicts of their society. The other factor is the detachment of the techniques of empirical research from their original theoretical and political uses and their wholesale usage by a wide variety of agencies. He concludes that this has resulted in sociology being emptied of critical ideas and its identification with techniques of data gathering, to the impoverishment of sociological theory. It is as a response to such faults in academic sociology that the rise of the radical sociology in the latter half of the 1960s and in the 1970s can be attributed.

The radical movement has the same concern about the nature of society, social structure, order and change as traditional sociology, but it differs in the interpretations it places upon these features and in those parts of past tradition they have inspired it. Prominent here are the work of Marx, particularly as this has been interpreted by Marcuse (1964), the work of the humanistic schools of psychoanalysis, particularly the work of Fromm (1941) and finally the Frankfurt School, particularly the work of Jurgen Habermas (1974). Also central to its writing and work are other important distinguishing features. There is a recognition of the importance of a political theory, and in this way the value freedom question is solved by replacing neutrality by an express political position, in response to the acceptance of the integral place of ideology in social research. The ideological position of radicals is anti-capitalist, and one that leads to the criticism of the existing structures of Western society. The problem of knowledge for what purpose has been solved by stating that it is for involvement in direct social action (Thorns, 1976: 166-167)..

The attack upon the subject for its conservatism expressed in such models as structural functionalism has also led to an attack upon American sociologists. Nicolaus (1972), for example, described prominent American sociologists "as the direct financial creatures, the functional house-servants of the civil, military and economic sections of American society". This is coupled with an attack upto 'entrepreneurial sociologists' who build up large research programmes for the sake of career enhancements thus reducing the value of the research to a secondary level of importance.

The radical position, however, with its rejection of the traditional research methods of social enquiry and the extreme relativism of much of its writing, means that it is a position in which no kind of objective truth can be entertained, for there is no reality outside the particular context of the writer and his case. The radicals, according to Willer and Willer (1973), made the mistake of rejecting science when what they should really have rejected, was systematic empiricism masquerading as science. In doing this, they have cut themselves off from the opportunity of involvement in the quest for a true science of society, which would transcend empiricism.

In many ways it related to the radical critique, but yet distinct in the critical school of sociology which is associated with Frankfurt

School of German Sociology, and has been primarily concerned with an attack with positivism. The central concern of this group has been about the role of the dialectical connection between facts and values rather than with the independence of facts, as is asserted in the positivist approach. Habermas (1974), one of the central figures in this school, has been concerned with the differences between analytical and dialectical theories of knowledge, the relation between theory, facts and history, and that between the philosophy of social science and sociological practice. The claimed value neutrality of positivism and its lack of analysis of its value presuppositions are seen to be a profound weakness. The need for a critical examination of these aspects of the search for knowledge through the development of a sociology that would heighten sociologists' critical self-awareness is seen as the task of critical theorists.

The discussion in the present work begins from the examination of some of the controversies at the level of the subject and its approach in terms of positivist or alternative perspectives. These criticisms have been concerned with the total nature of the subject rather than the particular problems faced in research operations. The concern with particular problems, whether the practioners have come from positivist or non-positivist traditions, has led to the growth of a second level of criticism promoted by research workers who have been faced with problems for which the existing methods have been unsatisfactory or only of limited usefulness.

In the criticism of methodology, there are four important areas around which the discussion has been centred. These are the validity of data, the role of independent and dependent variables, the role of statistical procedures and finally, the problems of relativity and bias. The present work has not focussed much on the role of statistical procedures mainly because of its emphasis on the philosophical discourses in research methodology and theory in social sciences. We have in short discussed this issue in Chapter 1.

The problem of the validity of data: The problem of the validity of data has been a significant issue in social science research, partly as a result of the growth of the phenomenological critique of sociological theory and research, which raises the question of the meanings people themselves place upon their own world and their activities (discussed in detail in the chapter on phenomenology). Survey techniques may provide consistent responses with similar socio-economic status groups giving a highly correlated set of answers, but these could simply be a stereotype set of answers which the group felt were the expected ones for their socio-economic groups. Therefore, the results may have very little relation to the actual behaviour exhibited by the studied population. This problem of the relation between sentiments and actions has been examined in a famous study by La-Pierre (1970). This study is mainly concerned with the attitudes of hotel proprietors towards Chinese. These hotel proprietors were subsequently visited by two Chinese people seeking accommodation to test the verbal attitudes in a concrete situation. La-Pierre concludes that there was very little relation between what proprietors said they would do and what they did in practice. As much sociological enquiry is conducted in interview and questionnaire form, where the data are dependent upon verbal or written response of the respondents, the continuing evidence of discrepancies between words and actions raises question over the validity of data derived from these sources. The concern about improving the validity of data led to the advocacy of convergent validity where data becomes acceptable when there is confirmation from more than one independent source—from both questioning and from the observation of behaviour or the analysis of recorded data in the form of reports, statistical documents, letters, diaries, etc. (Denzin, 1970, quoted in Thorns, 1976: 169).

The role of independent and dependent variable: The argument regarding the validity and the appropriate place of observation of behaviour vis-à-vis questioning led in the 1930s and 1940s to a split into quantitative and qualitative researches. The former proceeded on the basis of defined variables, some of which were seen as dependent and others independent. The emphasis on variable analysis was the dominant mode, which linked the desire to create a science of society through the adoption of the method of natural sciences. The opposition to the use of variables has centred in the phenomenological perspective. Sociologists within this perspective have argued that the social world is not one of the discrete variables that can be isolated by the researcher and examined separately. The independence of variables in the social world is rare and difficult to demonstrate. The use, for example, of such variables as social class, education, family status and ethnicity as independent variables in research operations, is of dubious validity, as all these are in fact the product not of one variable but a composition of separate factors that vary in their intensity according to the situation in which they are being investigated. The conclusion of Deutscher (1973) and Philips (1971, 1973), in their analysis of the problem of validity, is that the social situation in which the data is collected is one of the prime influences upon the response. The denial of the possibility of isolating variables into independent and dependent categories and the total relevance upon the subjective analysis of the social situation of the actor and his consequent behaviour, lead very quickly to the complete rejection of all forms of rational proof, which is the position currently held by ethnomethodologists (Cicourel, 1964; Douglas, 1971).

The role of statistical procedures: The third area of discussion surrounds the role of statistical techniques within the research process (not discussed much in the present work). The work of Pearson (1948) on associational measures, and Fisher (1960) on significance tests, laid the foundations of contemporary social statistics. The results of development from this base have been the use of contingency testing and correlational analysis as approximation to causal analysis. The limitations of this approach arise both from the problem of the existence of different orders of variables and their independence or not, and the relative arbitrariness of the levels of significance accepted. The unease at these procedures felt by many, including social statisticians, has resulted in a re-examination of the reliance upon statistical significance and a desire to explore alternative strategies—those that rely less on the isolation of independent and dependent variables, but treat all variables as of importance and through multivariate techniques attempt to isolate a set of variables that may provide an explanation for a high proportion of the total observed variation. However, these strategies are still subject to the earlier consideration of whether or not it is practical or legitimate to isolate particular variables that are sufficiently discrete to be treated by many of these statistical techniques—for example, factor analysis, which makes the assumption that a number of discrete factors can be defined and accurately measured.

The study of status crystallization by Lenski (1956) illustrates some of these problems. In this Lenski computes such attributes as education, occupation, income level and ethnicity to produce a measure of status crystallization (i.e., extent of convergence of an individual's ranking on these four dimensions). This method seems, however, to be suspect, as these are not four independent variables, each to be given an equal weight, as Lenski appears to treat them, but are all closely interrelated. Scales of occupational prestige, for example, are based upon income, education and ethnicity in American society, where the study was conducted. The basic questioning of statistical methods, therefore, arises from the concern with the problem of the validity of the data used by social researchers and the appropriate role of variables. If the collected data itself does not represent accurately the area of investigation, even the most sophisticated of the contemporary social science computer packages is unlikely to produce a result that illuminates the social process under study (Thorns, 1976: 170–71).

The problems of reactivity and bias: The final aspects are reactivity between observer and observed and bias. The participant observer based study is perhaps the most susceptible to this kind of reactivity, as the investigator is consciously trying to enter into the world of meanings of the subjects under study. The result of this has, sometimes, been the almost complete loss of the observer's neutral role and his complete identification with his subject group, for example, in Gan's study (1964) of the west end of Boston, where he became identified with the flight against urban renewal. However, in all forms of data collection there is some form of interaction between the observers and observed. The phenomenological critique has stressed very strongly the fact that data gathering is a social process and needs to be understood as such. This again reflects the calls for sociologists to heighten their own self-consciousness of the process that they themselves are engaged in. The modification of results produced by the reactivity of researcher and subject has led to an increased interest in measures that remove the observer form the scene and collect information unobtrusively (Webb et al., 1966; Thorns, 1976). This places great reliance upon available data in the form of documentary records of various sorts.

Having examined some the controversies about research methods and about the broader scope of the subject, we have considered what are the possible future paths of progress for sociological activity. The continuing debate about whether sociology should proceed via the induction or deduction method is the starting point largely because it points to some of the misconceptions and failures that have limited the development of a genuine science of sociology. The separation of the two methods during research is, in fact, generally neither possible nor even desirable, and stems from a consideration of the actual practice of research but from the philosophical or logical analysis of the research procedure (Thorns, 1976: 1972). The nature of sociological discovery requires that both activities are performed concurrently, for within the human mind the inception of research is not fitted into neat boxes, but is in fact a dialectic process constantly moving from imagination to evidence and back to imagination again. This is well put by Sir Peter Medawar, when he writes: "In real life, the imaginative and critical acts that unite to form the hypothetic-deductive method alternate so rapidly, at least at the earlier stages of constructing a theory that they are not spelled out in thought. The 'process of invention', trial and acceptance or rejection of the hypothesis goes no rapidly that we cannot trace it in its successive steps" (1967: 171, quoted in Thorns, 1976: 172).

This means that our methodology is to be seen as a process of discovery that has elements of both imaginative creations linked to the continuing body of knowledge and elements of exposure to the ideas of the real world via the assessment of data. The reassertion of these qualities within methodology should raise it above the level of preoccupation with the improvements of the technology of social inquiry, i.e., the refinement of data collection and processing and lead to a genuinely innovative process of discovery.

The next question this re-examination of methodology raises is the origin of sociological research (discussed in Chapter 1). The link has already been indicated between the imaginative role of the researcher and the continuing corpus of knowledge. This means that the concern should be with the substantive problems of the society within which the activity is taking place. This would lead to the reuniting of the research process and the real world politics, which Birnbaum (1971) identifies as being separated in much conventional sociological activity. This reintegration will also provide movements forward in the theoretical apparatus of the subject. The concern with substantive problems means that sociology has to be concerned with both structures and individuals. Undoubtedly, individual conceptions and worlds of meaning are vital components and without re-emphasizing of this perspective, the weaknesses of much of contemporary sociology would be all the more. Nevertheless, the structures of society, such as its power distribution or its system of housing opportunities, however, people regard them or their place within them, are important elements in contemporary society that require analysis. Further, the parameters of people's lives are largely determined by agencies or governments whom they never see or with whom they have very limited contact. The decision, for example, regarding the nature of housing provisions within a country with a market economy is the decision primarily on such groups as governments, private land and building developers, local planning authorities, and finance and mortgage companies, rather than that of the prospective house owners or dwellers (Thorns, 1976). Consequently, to understand the nature and distribution of this commodity, it is necessary to examine the market operation and the relative influence of these different interest groups, rather than the feelings or constructions of the house dwellers themselves (Thorns, 1976: 174).

The concentration upon the substantive areas, and the development from this concern to the empirical level of demonstration of the analysis, which is the product of the prior theoretical consideration, dictate that the investigational procedures adopted are integrally connected with the problem area. The techniques, for example, adopted to study the attitudes of groups towards racial or other minorities, are dependent upon whether the concern is with the investigation of the verbal expressions of the groups of people or with the way they behave to particular minority groups. Further, it would be necessary to consider not merely this behaviour but the situation under which it was to be studied, for example, in a public place, such as a public house or in the more private situation of the person's own house. Some sociologists (e.g., Deutscher, 1973) suggest, with something of an oversimplification, that phenomenological methods emphasize social processes and the constantly changing nature of social relationships, whereas positivist methods emphasize stability and balance as normal conditions. Deutscher concludes by suggesting that the best way is to use whatever methods are required to meet the research goals. Clearly, the techniques of data collection themselves are not an end, and the data itself does not possess intrinsic meaning.

The meaning it has, derives from the particular context in which it is interpreted. This is shown by Hindess (1973) where he examines the Indian census of 1951 both from the Indian government point of view and from the Marxist point of view. The different results obtained show the importance of the system of categories used to both record and present the data.

The alternative to the concern with the substantive problems and the development from this point to the empirical level is a perpetuation of systematic empiricism and the continued reliance upon the facts themselves providing some kind of explanation. This way also leads to a greater concern for the elegance of the data analysis rather than for the substance of the research. One of the examples of this is shown in Sonquist's paper (1969) *on finding variables that work*.

The tension between universality and difference has, of late, come to the fore as perhaps the central issue informing contemporary debates in the social and cultural theory. We do not come to the issue of difference in a world that encourages simple, unconditional endorsement. 'Difference' appears as importantly in the forms of violent ethnic, nationalism, racism and religious fundamentalism as in movements and personal choices about gender, sexual orientation and ethnic pluralism. Some lines of difference, like national boundaries, are used not only to distinguish one human group from others but to demand internal conformity. The very rhetoric of difference, in other words, can be turned to the repression of differences. Recognition of differences can be the basis for mutual engagement, or for failure to appreciate and respect common humanity, and not all differences are equally valuable. Social theorists are challenged by issue of difference precisely because they do not admit of easy answers. It is not so hard to suggest that there must be some 'both/and' approach to human difference and commonality; it is very hard to make consistent sense of the approaches that have been offered. The problem is an eminently theoretical ad methodological one, for it calls for going beyond the surface appeals of various immediate agendas of affirming difference (appeals from ethnic or lifestyle minorities in the US and some developing countries) and recognizing common humanity (acting responsibly amid the tragedies in Rwanda and Bosnia) to grasping how different ways of invoking difference and identity affect our understanding of the world and shape the categories through which we make sense of it. This is above all an issue for 'Critical Social Theory and Method' (to quote Calhoun, 1995), since it exists largely to facilitate a constructive engagement with the social world that starts from the presumption that existing arrangements—including currently affirmed identities and differences—do not exhaust the range of possibilities. It seeks to explore the ways in which our categories of thought reduce our freedom by occluding recognition of what could be.

Critical theory and method have come under widespread criticism, however, for its universalist tendencies and its failures to consider the full impact of the cultural diversity of human existence. In order to establish a ground for critical engagement, critical theorists have commonly claimed the basis of a more or less undifferentiated human condition. Their view of this human condition has been deeply shaped by the specifics of the Western intellectual tradition.

Even where the critical theory has been radical, its tacit universalism has often allied it to aspects of the liberal political tradition. It has been disposed to speak of humanity in ways that obscured in the multiplicity of actual human beings and human possibilities. Marxists, for example, found it hard to make adequate sense of the commitment of members of the international working class to specific national cultures. Marxist critiques of bourgeois liberalism focused on incomplete universalism, the ways in which putatively illegitimate differences among human beings were maintained despite allegedly universal political freedom. Yet this is not the whole story. The founders of the Frankfurt School, who made critical theory a catchword in the mid-20th century, were passionate critics of administrative normalization and alienation, admirers of artistic individuality and resistance to convention. Adorno sought to develop a many-sided theory of non-identity, or rather of the forms in which non-identical could, paradoxically, be given consideration (Wiggershaus, 1994). Even Habermas' more straightforwardly universalistic theories and methods owe a great deal to Adorno, especially in their persistent pursuit of a move beyond the philosophy of the subject (Chapter 4).

Part of the problem is that a great deal of modern social science has tacitly assumed that human beings normally live in one social world at a time. Modern social science has produced a notion of bounded and internally integrated societies and has treated both cross-border relations and sub-cultures as problematic. It has presumed that the individual consciousness is itself integral and that requires a stable and consistent social environment. Monolinguality and religious orthodoxy has been taken as normal and multilinguality and religious syncretism or variation as deviant cases to be explained. Yet, in these and a range of other ways, it does not seem obvious that people usually live in one social world at a time, but rather that it is now, and throughout human history often has been, common to inhabit multiple worlds simultaneously and to grow as a person by the ability to maintain oneself in connection to all of them. This means that anyone's horizon of experience, to borrow the phenomenological term, is unlikely to be fixed by a single collectivity or categorical framework (Anselm, 1978).

Even where the change of universalistic inattention to the politics of difference is justified, it does not seem a reason to abandon the venture of critical theory. It does seem a reason to change it. One of the concerns of the present book is to explore the challenge of taking seriously the difference among human beings—a challenge not only to critical theories but to more conventional social science theories. This challenge has powerful implication for shaping the new research methodology. We do not think that the challenge admits of an easy answer. Too often, self-proclaimed multiculturalists offer a sort of cheap celebration of the existence of difference without a serious grappling with the challenges posed both by difference in general and by specific differences.

In this book, no sustained exploration of particular cultures or the differences among them, has been attempted. Rather, we have tried to focus on something of what challenge posed by difference is, why it is basic and how it might be confronted without sacrificing commitment to theory and method or critique. The challenge is one that runs through many sorts of theory and methods as well as many sorts of differences. Gender, race and nationality figure prominently, for example. But, the problem is apparent in class differences, differences among regions within countries, and cultural differences that should demarcate nation.

We have introduced in some of the chapters of the book (mainly Chapter 4 and 6) the powerful but sometimes problematic contributions of the Frankfurt theorists—both the first generation of Theodor Adorno, Max Horkheimer, and their colleagues, and the second generation of Habermas. Their work shapes the nature of research methodology in social sciences. A critical theory of exceptional scope and many advantages, Habermas' work brings together themes, which are crucial from the methodological point of view. Though our arguments implicitly engage and attempt to advance the lines of work initiated by the Frankfurt theorists, we have focused also on suggesting some of the ways in which other lines of theory (as Calhoun has propounded) might inform the project of critical theory.

In particular, we have explored feminist and post-structuralist theory because these two discourses (they are not really the unified theoretical positions sometimes implied) have done a great deal to open up the issue of differences as a basic categorical problem rather than a merely contingent empirical issue in research methodology. We have discussed the work of Pierre Bourdieu and especially his idea of habitus and field. Bourdieu's approach to knowledge was found in the structuralist crucible of the 1950s and early 1960s France, and remains deeply shaped by it. Yet, like his contemporary, Derrida, he moved beyond structuralist orthodoxy partly by recovering elements of a phenomenology that had been suppressed and by resisting the complete enclosure of system. Like Foucault, he sought to recover the significance of human embodiment. But, unlike Derrida and Foucault, Bourdieu has remained consistently sociological. Though trained initially as a philosopher, he has neither stayed within an almost entirely cognitive argument, like Derrida, nor attempted to claim the body as an extra-social standpoint for critique like Foucault. Although Bourdieu's work is ambiguous about its cultural and historical specificities, it offers important possibilities for developing an approach to the concretely social and embodied dimensions of human life that are frequently slighted by those post-structuralists, who are taken as intellectual sources for postmodernism. This approach certainly provides a sociological insight for the research methodology in social sciences.

Finding a variety of problems with modernity, many feminists and other attentive to the politics of difference have been drawn to postmodernist ideas. This move raises problems, however, for a critical method in social sciences: First, as we have shown in Chapter

6, the idea of postmodernism commonly involves a pseudo-historical claim to an epochal transition that in fact theorists cut off from the necessary analysis of the conditions and possibilities for truly transformative changes in modern society. Second, postmodernists too often write as though all knowledge is discursive and therefore cut themselves off from understanding much of culture and practice. Too often they focus on certain sorts of culture, especially those that seem most like language, without attending to the construction and organization of social relations. Feminists are generally more attentive to embeddedness in social relations and to embodiment, but even within feminist theory, there is an unfortunate split between thinkers who focus overwhelmingly 'on ideas, symbol and forms of consciousness' as Iris Marion Young (1987, 1990), Flax (1990: 180-1) describes the significance of the category of gender, and those who undertake the analysis of concrete social relations, whether within families or on large scales of societal organization. Third, in many of its versions, postmodernist theory encourages a relativism that makes it hard to explain why feminist theories should be more persuasive than others or on what basis feminists and other critical theorists can defend strongly normative conclusions.

It has also been shown that we can draw on many of the positive achievements of post-structuralist thought without buying the problematic package sold as postmodernism. Likewise, then, we can avoid the notion of a forced choice between this postmodernism and a so-called modernism which turns out to be usually rigid whether in outright universalism or in defence of certain essentialized differences. The problems of postmodernism have encouraged many feminists to stick to problematically fixed notions of standpoint inherited from androcentric Enlightenment thought as the basis for critique. For some, following Foucault and/or Lacanian psychoanalysis, this standpoint is an essentialized extra-social and extra-linguistic notion of the body. It is very hard for such theory, as for conservative counterparts that rely on conventional biological determinism, to be opened to genuinely social and cultural argumentation. Feminist standpoints modelled on ideas of class standpoints are more radical sociological but are not without serious drawbacks.

These different theoretical strategies have longstanding precursors. We have also shown (in Chapter 4) something of the older roots of critical theory before the Frankfurt School, including in the ways in which problems of cultural diversity and historical specificity have shaped social theory and method throughout the modern era.

Outside the realms of art, literature and philosophy, the Frankfurt School's appropriation of history was largely (though not exclusively) a matter of knowing canonical European history—the product of good gymnasium education, rather than a matter of involvement in actual historical research. Breaking with the giveness and immediate facticity of the social world, however, calls not only for historical knowledge as a precondition of theory but also for a continual engagement with history and rethinking of historical assumptions. To take a simple example, thus, it is remarkable to what extent the understanding contemporary sociologists have of the individual revolution is based on the syntheses incorporated into theoretical discourses by Max Weber, Emile Durkheim and Karl Marx—and how little need most sociologists feel to allow their inherited ideas to be challenged by the enormous more recent production of historical research and analysis that puts the so-called industrial revolution in new light. Much the same could be said with regard to sociological neglect of anthropology and cross-cultural knowledge.

The lead of the classical social theorists has also been followed in the area of gender, though here the lead was more to ignore the significance of the matter than to appropriate any particular historical account. Developing ways to take seriously such fundamental categorical differences as gender is a basic and urgent project for Calhoun's critical social theory (Chapter IV). There is no aspect of social life on which the contributions of Marx, Weber and Durkheim are more strikingly unable to speak to current concerns. None of the most important sociological theorists at work today has written more than glacingly of gender—not Habermas, not Bourdieu, not Giddens, not Luhmann (though each has opened the door to serious gender concerns farther than most of their predecessors). Giddens in his *Transformation of Intimacy* (1922) and Luhmann in *Love as Passion* (1986) have written on love and sexuality—topics that bring sexual difference to their attention—but neither makes the category of gender basic to his more general social theory. The issue is not just that these theorists have ignored women, but that they have ignored the extent to which the category of gender exerts a basic and pervasive in its structuring of a most of forms and dimensions of social understanding. In realms that seem quite separate from biological differences between sexes (let alone from sexual relation) the category of gender helps to give meaning to the world, even encouraging cultures in their common proliferation of binary oppositions (male sun to female moon).

Feminist theory, in turn, remains remarkably disconnected from this disciplinary mainstream of sociological theory. This less true in the broader, interdisciplinary discourses of social, cultural and political theory, where feminist theory is itself an important organizing theme and where it is in close relationship to other thematic clusters such as post-structuralism and postmodernism. Sociologists are, however, remarkably underrepresented in both feminist theory and these cognate discourses. Post-structuralists and postmodernists have played a crucial role in bringing themes of differences to the forefront, and this combined with the failure of mainstream sociological theory to take gender seriously perhaps accounts for some of the affinity many feminists feel for the post-structuralist and postmodernist currents. Unfortunately, however, these currents are in many cases refractory to sociology; they encourage analysis of culture and power shorn of serious attention to the constitution of social relationships and especially to problems of societal integration.

Taking the constitutive centrality of categorical differences seriously within a genuinely social theory offers the possibility of a kind of bridge across discourses in research methodology in which not only does sociological method stand to gain from taking gender seriously, but there is potential for a stronger notion of the social to be developed in feminist theory and method. This is why opening up the possibility of sociological method from a feminist standpoint is more than strategic interest, why it is not just a way of remedying an absence in conventional sociological theory and method but an attempt to remake uncritical method as critical method. Dorothy Smith rightly puts it:

> "it is not enough to supplement an established sociology by addressing ourselves to what has been left out or overlooked, or b y making women's issues into sociological issue. That does not change the standpoint built into existing sociological procedures, but merely makes the sociology of women an addendum to the body of objectified knowledge". (1990: 13)

Smith's points, rather, is to use the standpoint of women to reconstitute sociological inquiry as "a critique of socially organized practices of knowing" (ibid: 12). Such a critique is deeply needed if sociology is to become truly adequate to the project of feminist theory. But there is some question about whether "the standpoint of women" is an adequate account of what makes feminist insights so pivotal, and about whether the experience of women can readily be claimed as a basis for knowledge without brooking a troubling essentialism. Whether the standpoint theory is an unduly essentializing move or a way to recognize plurality and difference remains, in Charles Lemert's (1992) phrase "the unsolved riddle of the standpoint".

From Kant on, most critical theory has claimed, or at least aimed at, a standpoint of universal validity. This remains true of Habermas' theory of communicative action, but too often, the seemingly universal is the presentation of a partial view as though it were all encompassing. Marx spoke in the *Thesis of Feuerbach*, for example, of the 'this sidedness' of all thought. He sought elsewhere to show how the seemingly universal categories of early liberal political thought in fact reflected bourgeois interests. The emancipation of man as citizen could never be more partial, therefore, while man as labourer remained in chains. And, if the term 'citizen' implicitly meant property owner even while it claimed a sort of universality, so did it also implicitly mean men. In many countries, only men of European ancestory were included in the seemingly universal category. And, though Enlightenment thought about citizenship treated nationality in universal terms, as something that everyone might have, this internationlism which was present at the birth of nationalism all too rapidly faded after Napoleon into a much more persistent invocation of the priority of certain identities at the expense of others. Socialism seemed at times the answer, but workers shooting each other from the trenches of World War I suggested that in and of itself, this answer was inadequate.

Ironically, it may even be the case that this very rhetoric of universality predisposed thinkers to use categorical terms—man, citizen, worker—in ways that obscured their own partiality and prejudice. The logic of market equivalents also encouraged a semblance of identity that made it hard and even made it seem dangerous to recognize difference. So difference became constituted as 'other' to universality. The logic of 'both/and', the possibility of recognizing simultaneously connection and distinction, was submerged. Advocates of difference became too often advocates of radical particularity, even while invoking universalistic rhetorics like the rights of national self-determination in support of their anti-universalistic positions. The sharp opposition represented only a seeming clarity.

We should be equally cautious about treating the Enlightenment without complication as the era of universalism, succeeded then by a Romantic epoch of particularism. Neither era was so simple. Indeed, the Enlightenment and early modern social thought generally were shaped extraordinarily deeply by the confrontation with difference. The attempts to construct universal truths or norms followed from the rupture in unquestioned 'doxic' acceptance of traditions that constituted not multiple truths and value (Arendt, 1977). This rupture was one made not merely by science or capitalism or industrialization, but by a whole categories of factors that brought Europeans into new relationships across lines of difference. The reformation and the later rise of desism and unbelief were crucial. Confrontations with difference were basic to the voyages of discovery and colonization, to the institution of slavery, to the expansion of interregional trade within what were to become nations, to the mobilization of citizen armies, and to the spread of printing and literacy. Ruptures in doxic assumptions and engagements across distances and differences brought the corresponding challenge of building relations recognizing both distinction and connection.

Today, the sharp opposition of universalism and particularism has returned to the fore. Some writers, indeed, see the very possibility of critical theory as impunged by the impossibility of benign universalism. This issue is not of purely academic interest. The challenges posed by the 'politics of identity' involve the creation of collective movements that aim to reconcile personal positions in cultural and historical space with broader patterns of social organization. Feminism, the gay movement, and a range of racial, ethnic and sub-cultural movements, all figure prominently. Less commonly seen in the light, but as important as any, is nationalism. All these movements and discourses reflect the extent to which the problem of myriad theoretical constructs, particularly critical theory and cultural differences, extend beyond the abstract and academic to shape the immediate and practical issues which are significant academically for the research methodology in social sciences.

Can such theorization reach beyond the purely practical, yet remain sensitive to culture and difference—one of the significant ingredients for methodology in social sciences? The present book is an attempt to think through this issue, and to think the possibility of a theory and methodology imprisoned by neither universalism nor particularism, speaking with some general moment and yet attending to difference. This is not a compressive review of all available theoretical perspectives and discourses in research methodology nor a book about all the many and inherently specific forms of cultural diversity having implication for research methodology in social sciences. It is about the challenge such diversity poses to the task of sociological theories and research methodology.

In our analysis we have referred to Philips' (1973) advocacy of abandoning methods where he adopts a point of view that is neither the empirical orientation of the traditionalist nor the ideological position of the radicals, but, it is theoretical advocating the substitution of 'human curiosity' as the basic approach. This would lead to the continued failure of sociology to generate cumulative knowledge around the central problems of society. Hindess (1973: 40) points to the results of such an approach when he writes that if we send into the field a team of ideal observers, stripped of all concepts (to avoid the possible influences of alien categories), they would return with nothing to report and no vocabulary with which to report it. Rather than moving in this direct sociology should be attempting to reintegrate sociological concepts and research with the problems, crises and conflicts of contemporary society, which would provide the springboard for new theoretical insights. An attempt to show both the need for this and manner in which it can be attempted is provided by William Catton's idea regarding the role of sociology within a world faced by growing environmental crisis. These points have also been raised by Bourdieu and Alexander, of course, in different fashion. The final area of concern is the nature of validity. The issue of validity is at centre of much of the contemporary concern of the nature of the subject. The type of validity most likely to be helpful to the development of the subject is 'convergent validity' where the subject under consideration is investigated by a number of different means, using a whole range of techniques of both data collection and analysis. The overemphasis upon the survey has been a major weakness of much research of the 1960s and earlier decades. The extension of alternative research strategies is of extreme importance. The renewed interest in participant observation and the development of unobtrusive measures are two areas of particular note. Other new directions have already been examined in different chapters of the book. The criticism noted earlier of the systematic empiricism highlighted the failure of research to comprehend adequately the historical dimension of social situations. This is particularly important where the stress is to be placed upon substantive areas and the structures of the society rather than upon interpersonal behaviour, although even in this has antecedents that cannot be ignored.

The development of sociological methodology has therefore been charted along a path that, firstly, rejects the artificial and at times overwhelming argument about the relative significance of deduction and induction within the research process. In the second place, it emphasizes both the role of imagination and the importance of research into areas of substantive concern within our society. Thirdly, it identifies as the correct locus of enquiry the problem area itself, out of which are produced the theoretical notions that are then examined by empirical research. The development of the research is dictated by the considerations of convergent validity and the utilization of procedures appropriate to the questions being asked, rather than ones thought to have universal applicability. The extremes of systematic empiricism, with the denial of theoretical construction and of 'abandonment' of method in favour of individual, often, idiosyncratic research, are both to be rejected. Sociology's direction must therefore be directed by an awareness of both the limits of its theories and of its techniques, and the vital interconnections of one with the other, and not with the rejection of one or the other by 'theoreticians' and 'empiricists', both of whom operate within a restricted and restricting view of science and of sociology.

References

Anselm, Strauss. 1978, "A Social World Perspective" in *Studies in Symbolic Interaction: A Research Annual*, Volume 1, pp. 119-128, edited by N. Denzin, Greenwich, CT: JAI Press.

Arendt, H., 1977, *Between Past and Future*, New York: Penguin.

Birnbaum, I., 1971, *Towards a Critical Sociology*, New York: Oxford University Press.

Blalock, H.M. , 1971, *Causal Models in the Social Sciences*, Chapel Hill, NC: University of North Carolina Press.

Cicourel, A.V., 1964, *Methods and Measurement in Sociology*, New York: The Free Press.

Dawe, A., 1970, The Two Sociologies, *British Journal of Sociology*, 21, 2.

Denzin, N.K., 1970, *Sociological Methods: A Sourcebook, The Research Act in Sociology*, Chicago: Aldine.

Deutscher, I., 1973, *What We Say, What We Do*, New York: Elsevier.

Douglas, J.D., 1971, *American Social Order: Social Rules in a Pluralistic Society*, New York: The Free Press.

Fisher, R., 1956, *Statistical Methods and Scientific Inference*, Edinburgh: Oliver and Boyd.

——, 1960, *The Design of Experiments*, Edinburgh: Oliver and Boyd.

Flax, Jane 1990, "Thinking Fragments: Psychoanalysis, Feminism and Post Modernism" in *The Contemporary West*. Berkeley: University of California Press, pp. 180-1.

Fromm, E., 1941, *Escape from Freedom*, New York: Owl Books.

Gans, H.J., 1964, *The Urban Villagers*, New York.

Giddens, A., 1992, *The Transformation of Intimacy*, Cambridge: Polity Press.

Goodman, R,. 1972, *After the Planners*, Harmondsworth: Penguin.

Gouldner, A.W., 1971, *The Coming Crisis in the Western Sociology*, London: Heinemann.

Habermas, J. 1974, "Rationalism Divided into Two", in A. Giddens (ed.), *A Positivism and Sociology*, London: Heinemann Educational Books.

——, 1989, Morality and Ethical Life: Does Hegel's critique of Kant apply to discourse Ethics? *Northwestern University Law Review*, 83, pp. 38–53.

Hindess, B., 1973, *The Use of Official Statistics in Sociology*, London: Macmillan.

Horowitz, I.L., 1967, *The Rise and Fall of Project Camelot*, Cambridge, Mass: MIT Press.

La-Pierre, R.J., 1970, "Attitudes v/s Action", in D.P. Forcese and S. Richtor (eds.), *Stages in Social Research*, New Jersey: Prentice-Hall.

Lemert, Charles, 1992, Subjectivity's Limit: The Unsolved Riddle of the Standpoint, *Sociological Theory*, 10(1), pp. 63–72.

Luhmann, Niklas, 1986, *Love as Passion: The Codification of Intimacy*, Cambridge, Mass: Harvard University Press.

Lundberg, G.A., 1929, *The Foundations of Social Research*, New York: Russell Sage Foundation.

Marcuse, H., 1964, *One Dimensional Man*, Boston: Beacon Press.

Medawar, P., 1967, *The Art of Soluble*, Harmondsworth: Penguin.

Megill, Allan, 1985, *Prophets of Extremity: Nietzsche. Heidegger, Foucault, Derrida*, Berkeley: University of California Press.

Mill, J.S., 1862, *A System of Logic*, Honolulu: University Press of the Pacific.

Myrdal, G., 1970, *Objectivity in Social Research*, London: Duckworth.

Nicolaus, M., 1971, "The Professional Organization of Sociology: A View form Blow", in R. Blackburn (ed.), *Ideology and Social Sciences*, Great Britain: Fontana.

Pearson, K., 1948, *Karl Pearson's Early Statistical Papers*, Cambridge: Cambridge University Press.

Philips, D.L., 1971, *Knowledge from What*, Chicago: Rand McNally.

——, 1973, *Abandoning Method*, Chicago: University of Chicago Press.

Smith, Dorothy, 1990, *Conceptual Practices of Power*, Boston: Northeastern University Press, p. 13.

Songuist, J., 1969, 'Finding Variables that Work', *Public Opinion Quarterly*.

Thorns, D., 1976, *New Directions in Sociology*, New Jersey: Prentice-Hall.

Webb, E. et al., 1966, *Unobtrusive Measures*, New York: Rand McNally.

Wiggershaus, Rolf, 1954, *The Frankfurt School: Its History, Theories and Political Significance*, Cambridge, Mass: MIT Press.

Willer, J. and Willer, D., 1973, *Systematic Empiricism*, New Jersey: Prentice-Hall.

Young, Iris Marion, 1987, "Impartiality and Civic Virtue" in S. Benhabib and D. Cornell (eds), *Feminism as Critique*, Minneapolis: University of Minnesota Press.

——, 1990, *Justice and the Politics of Difference,* Princeton: Princeton University Press.

Index

Abercrombie, N., 116
academic sociology, 247
  criticism of, 247-50
Adorno, Theodor W., 28, 135, 136, 138, 139, 143, 145, 146, 147, 148, 149, 216, 217, 221
Agassi, J., 54
Albert, H., 30, 31, 137, 143
Alexander, Jeffrey, 224, 225, 226, 227, 228, 229, 230. 231, 232, 233, 234, 235, 236, 238, 239
Althusser, L. and E. Balibar, 130, 166, 167, 168, 169
Althusser, Louis, 165, 166, 168, 169, 171, 229
Althusserian historical materialism, 168
Althusserian Marxism, 169
Anselm, Strauss, 260
APC, 122-23
Arendt, Hannah, 212, 266
Aronowitz, Stanley, 210, 211, 212, 213, 214, 215, 216, 217, 219, 222, 223, 224
Austin, J.L., 120

Bachelard, Gaston, 217
Bacon, Francis, 222
Bair, 134
Bargstrom, G.,
Bar-Hillel, Y., 116
Barnes, B., 89
Barthes, Roland, 159, 230
Baudrillard, Jean, 207, 234
Bauman, Z., 110, 116
Becker, H., 114
Berger, P. and T. Luckman, 110
Bernstein, Basil, 200
Birnbaum, I., 250, 256
Blalock. H.M., 247
Bodner, Judith, 205
Bohm, D., 63, 71
Booth, Charles, 4, 12

Bourdieu, Pierre, 196, 200, 201, 202
bourgeoise, 41, 48
Bowley, A.L., 7, 8
Brown, Richard Harvey, 196, 197, 200, 201, 202, 205, 206, 207, 208, 209, 210
Bruner, J.S., 71, 74
Bruyn, S., 12, 14
bureaucratic socialism, 153
Burgess, E.W. and D.J. Bogue, 4
Burtt, E.A., 69

Calhoun, Craig, 224, 259
Canguillhem, Georges, 217
capitalism, 41
Carnap, Rudolf, 59
caste society, 164
Cicourel, A.V., 112, 113, 119, 127, 130, 254
Collins, Randall, 186, 187
commonsense thinking/knowledge, 99, 100
  socialization of, 105-7
commonsense world, 123
Comte, Auguste, 1, 136
contemporary society, 147
contexualism, 230
conventional sociology, 111
  ethnomethodological critique of, 112-17
Coulter, J., 122

D'Amico, Robert, 152, 188
Dawe, A., 246
decisionism, 138
democratic cosmopolitanism, 48
Denzin, Norman K., 110, 207, 253
Derrida, Jacques, 234
determinance
  and dominance, distinction between, 168
Deutscher, I., 254, 257
deviant, 114
  types of, 114-15
Dewey, John, 99
Douglas, J.D., 110, 113, 115, 125, 254
Douglas, Mary, 196, 200
Duhem, P., 73, 74
Durkheim, Emile, 4, 36, 37, 38, 180, 211

economy of signs, 203
Edge, D.O. and M.J. Mulkay, 67, 69, 82
Emmett, Dorothy and A. MacIntyre, 118
empirical knowledge, 97
empirical sciences
  theory in, 97
empiricism
  limitations of, 229
epistemology, 49
  in sociology of knowledge, 49-52
ethnomedological research, 111
  trends in, 111
ethnomethodology, 109
  and Schutz, 117-19
  and Wittgenstenians, 120
  foundation of, 110
  philosophical roots of, 110

fact, 55
  and theory, 56, relationship between, 56-69
Flax, Jane, 262
Frake, C.O., 63

Festinger, L., 13
Feyeraband, P.F. 62, 131
Filmer, P. et al., 123
Fisher, R.A., 7, 8, 64, 274, 254
Ford, James E. and James F. Klumpp, 196
Foster, H., 184
Forman, Paul, 214
Foucault, Michael, 159, 214, 234
Frank, G.P., 77, 78, 79
Freely-Harnick, G., 206
Friedman, George, 214, 232
Frisby, David, 28, 131, 132, 135, 136, 137, 139, 140, 141, 142, 144, 145, 146, 148, 149, 150
Fromm, E., 251

Gans, H.J., 255
Garfinkel, Harold, 22, 110, 111, 112, 116, 118, 210, 230
Gasset, Ortega Y., 212
Geertz, Clifford, 231, 232
Geiger, Theodore, 148
Gellner, Ernest, 24, 25, 118, 121, 122, 123
genealogical charts, 201
Gibson, Q., 6
Giddens, Anthony, 1, 2, 3, 4, 17, 18, 19, 20, 21, 22, 23, 24, 25, 26, 29, 30, 31, 32, 263
Gidlow, B., 110
Gilbert, G.N., 66
Glass, B., 64
Glucksmann, Miriam, 158, 160, 162, 163, 164, 167, 169, 170, 171, 175
Godelier, M. 159
Goffman, Ervin, 110
Goldthorpe, J.H., 110
Goodman, R., 250
Gouldner, A.W., 110, 246, 248
Grandy, R.E., 58, 68

Habermas, Jurgen, 29, 32, 39, 133, 134, 135, 136, 137, 141, 142, 147, 149, 152, 189, 216, 219, 251, 252
Hagstrom, W.O., 59
Hall, E.T., 15
Hanson, N.R., 54, 62, 63, 64, 76
Harre, Rom, 200
Harris, E.E., 73
Hempel, Carl G., 60
Herzfeld, Michael, 207
Hesse, M., 61, 62
Hessen, Boris, 41, 42, 45
Hindess, B., 110, 113, 123, 258, 267
Hofmann, W., 144
Hoijer, H., 63
Horkheimer, M., 133, 134, 140, 149, 154, 214, 215
Horkheimer, Marx and Theodor, Adorno, 210, 211, 214, 221
Horowitz, I.L., 249
human sociation, 197

ideology, 148
- and sociology of knowledge, 148-55
- critique of, 148

indexical expression, 116
indexicality, 116

Jacoby, Russel, 230
Jakobson, R. and M. Halle, 159
Jakobson, R., 159
Jones, Ernest, 230

Kafka, Franz, 201
Kelemen, Janes, 207
Kellner, D., 184
Kish, L., 11
Kituse, J. and A.V. Cicourel, 113
knowledge-claims, 43, 48, 87
  assessment of, 77-86
Kolakowski, L., 3
Kruger, M., 150
Kuhn, T.S., 65, 66, 74, 75, 126, 191, 216, 217, 231, 232, 233
Lacan, Jacques, 159
Lakatos, I. and A. Musgrave, 68
Lakatos, I., 65, 75, 80
Lane, M., 159
La-Pierre, R.J., 253
Lash, S., 184
Lassman, Peter, 118
Lavine, Thelma Z., 108
law of nature, 55
Leach, Edmund R., 159
Lemert, Charles, 184, 208, 265
Lenski, Gerhard, 5, 254
Levi-Strauss, C., 160, 161, 163, 173, 174
Lewis, C.I., 76
linguistic philosophy, 121
  pillars of, 121
logical empiricism, 140
Louch, A.R., 120
Luhmann, Niklas, 263
Lukacs, Gyorg, 133, 207
Lundberg, G.A., 247
Lundz, C., 140

Madge, J. and T. Harrisson, 13
Malinowski, B., 12
Mannheim, Karl, 45, 46, 47, 48, 49, 50, 51, 52, 87
Marcuse, Herbert, 31, 39, 133, 210, 214, 221, 251
Marx, Karl, 36, 38, 41, 130, 204, 205, 207, 265
Marx, Karl and F. Engel, 40, 42
McGinnes, R., 11
McHugh, P., 117, 119, 130
McHugh, P. et al., 120
Medawar, Peter Sir, 256
Mehan, Hugh and Houston Wood, 204
Menger, Carl, 132
Mennell, S.J., 109, 112, 119, 122, 123, 124
Merton, R.K., 41, 42, 43, 75, 124, 141, 220
Misch, G., 227
Mill, J.S., 8, 248
Mills, C. Wright, 215, 220
Mitzman, Arthur, 230
Morrison, D.E. and R.E. Henkel, 10
Mulkay, M.J. and A.T. Williams, 84
Mulkay, Michael, 36, 39, 40, 41, 43, 47, 49, 51, 52, 53, 57, 58, 60, 62, 64, 65, 66, 67, 68, 70, 72, 75, 76, 77, 79, 81, 82, 83, 84, 87, 88, 136, 141, 186
Myrdal, G., 249

Nadel, S.F., 6
Nagel, E., S. Bromberger and A. Grunbaum, 67
Nagel, Ernest, 56, 96, 97
Nagel, Thomas, 226
natural sciences, 94-95
  and social sciences, difference between, 98, 124
  methodology of, 95

neo-positivism, 130-32
Nicholson, Linda, 182, 185
Nicolaus, M., 251
Norman O. Brown, 230

Outhwaite, W., 46

Parsons, Talcott, 21, 26, 211, 212, 229
Parsons, T. and E. Shils, 229
participant observation method, 12-14
  in science, 69-86
  observation, 69
  positivists, 2
Pearson, K., 7, 8, 9, 247, 254
phenomenology
  and positivist method, 96-109
Philips, D.L., 254, 267
Plato, 151
Pollner, M., 114
polymorphism, 121-22
Popper, Karl R., 28, 29, 77, 80, 87, 123, 135, 137, 138, 144, 146
positivism, 1, 3, 28
  in Frankfurt School, 151-55
  in social sciences, 134-37
  limitations of, 229
  methods in, 6, 137-45, case approach, 6; scientific method, 6-7; critical tradition, 138-41
  phenomenology and, 96-109
  philosophy of, 2, elements of, 2-3, 5-6
positivist sociology, 153
positivistic attitude
  in sociology, 4
postmodernism, 182
  critique of, 182-85
post-structural movement, 233
Propp, V., 159

Radcliff-Brown, A.R., 160, 161
Ravetz, J.R., 66, 72, 79, 80, 81, 84, 85, 86
Ricoeur, Paul, 210
Rieff, Philip, 230
Ritzel, G., 132
Roche, Maurice, 204
Rodnitsky, G., 137
Rorty, Richard, 181, 229, 235, 236, 237, 238
Rose, H. and Rose, S., 43
Rossi-Landi, F., 196, 205, 206
Ryle, G., 61

Sacks, Hervey, 124
Sahlins, Marshall, 206
sampling, 7-8
Saussure, Ferdinand de, 159, 203, 204, 208, 233
scandal of philosophy, 101
Scheffler, I., 62, 63, 66, 74
Schegloff, E. and Sacks, H., 124
Schelling, F., 216
Schroyer, T., 153
Schutz, Alfred, 19, 20, 21, 27, 31, 95, 96, 98, 100, 101, 102, 103, 104, 105, 106, 107, 109, 117, 118, 119
science, 38, 74
  fact-theory relationship in, 55
  observation in, 69-77
  sociological analysis of, 38, 87, by Durkheim, 38; by Marx, 38-45; by Mannheim, 46-48

scientific discipline, 135
scientific education, 131-32
scientific knowledge, 39, 53, 56, 77, 87, 88, 137
  emergence and growth of, 39
  form and content of, 41-42
  modernist quest for, 178-80
scientific method
  in positivistic tradition, 6, components of, 6-7
scientific observations, 69, 72, 75
  criteria for judging, replicability, 77-79; consonance, 79; theoretical adequacy, 80-81
scientific theory
  and postmodernism, 185-95
Seidman, Steven and David G. Wagner, 177, 182, 195
Seidman, Steven, 183, 185
Selvin, H.C., 10, 11
Shepherd, J. and R. Johnson, 79
Simmel, George, 180, 207
Skinner, B.F., 120-21
Smart, J.C., 57
Smith, Dorothy, 264
social formation
  concept of, 168
social processes, 41
social reality, 98, 125
  concept of, 234
  simulacrum
social sciences, 94, 177
  and natural sciences, difference between, 98, 124
  schools of thought, 94-95
social scientist, 107
  functionality of, 107-8
social signs, 202, 205
social structure, 41
  conception of, 160-62
social theory
  modes of appraisal, 212-13
  traditions in, 16, 209
social thought, 47
  and scientific thought, distinction between, 88-89
society
  concept of, 145-46
  discursive analysis of, 199-207
sociological insinuations, 86-90
sociological research
  cause-effect relationship in, methods of, 9
  criticism of, 252-56
  ethnographic, 12, methods in, 12-15
  significance testing in, 10
  steps in, 7-8
  traditions in, positivistic, 1 methods in, 6-7, 9
sociology of knowledge, 36, 148
  perspectives on, 36, Durkheimiam, 36-38; Marxian, 39-45; Mannheim's, 45-52; Stark's, 52-55
  ideology and, 148-55
sociology, 1, 4, 247
  criticism of, 247-50
  origins of, 1
  perspectives on, 32, 183
Stark, Werner, 45, 52, 53
statistical hypothesis
  types of, 11
Strawson, P.F., 62
structuralism, 158, 200
  as an analytical approach, 159-60

structuralist anthropology, 160
Levi-Straus's approach to, 161-65
structuralist Marxism, 165
Althusser's approach to, 165-72
structure, 160, 208
characteristics of, 161-62
system
concept of, 146, weakness of, 146-47
and totality, distinction between, 146

Taylor, Charles, 235
Thomas, W.I., 106, 124
Thomson, Grahame, 202, 203
Thorns, David C., 6, 8, 9, 11, 12, 13, 14, 15, 246, 248, 249, 250, 251, 253, 255, 256, 257
totality
concept of, 146
totemism, 163
Toulmin, N.J., 85
Touraine, Alain, 26, 27
Turner, Jonathan H., 191, 192, 193, 194, 195
Turner, Stephen, 181, 192, 193

uniformity of nature
principle of, 54
Unity of Science movement, 109

Veblen, T., 141
Verstehen concept of, 100, 117, 121, 247
as a method, 102-5
as an epistemological problem, 101-2
features of, 106

Wagner, David G., 190, 191
Wagner, Helmut R., 119
Webb, E. et al., 255
Webb, E., 14
Weber, Max, 18, 19, 21, 180
Wellmer, A., 144, 153
Whyte, W.H., 13, 21
Wiggershaus, R., 259
Willer, J. and D. Willer, 270
Wilson, T.P., 115, 116
Winch, Peter, 22, 23, 24, 120, 231
Wirth, L., 6
Wittgenstein, L., 23, 24, 78

Young, I.M., 262

Zimmerman, D.H. and D.L. Wieder, 110
Zimmerman, D.H. and M. Pollner, 113, 116, 124